DEMOCRATIC CITIZENSHIP AND THE EUROPEAN UNION

MANCHESTER
1824

Manchester University Press

SERIES EDITORS: THOMAS CHRISTIANSEN AND EMIL KIRCHNER

Albert Weale

DEMOCRATIC CITIZENSHIP AND THE EUROPEAN UNION

MANCHESTER UNIVERSITY PRESS
Manchester and New York

distributed exclusively in the USA by Palgrave

Published by Manchester University Press
Oxford Road, Manchester M13 9NR, UK
and Room 400, 175 Fifth Avenue, New York, NY 10010, USA
www.manchesteruniversitypress.co.uk

Distributed exclusively in the USA by
Palgrave, 175 Fifth Avenue, New York,
NY 10010, USA

Distributed exclusively in Canada by
UBC Press, University of British Columbia, 2029 West Mall,
Vancouver, BC, Canada V6T 1Z2

British Library Cataloguing-in-Publication Data
A catalogue record for this book is available from the British Library

Library of Congress Cataloging-in-Publication Data applied for

ISBN   0 7190 4425 1   *hardback*
EAN   978 0 7190 4425 0

First published 2005

14 13 12 11 10 09 08 07 06 05   10 9 8 7 6 5 4 3 2 1

Edited and typeset in Minion with Lithos
by Frances Hackeson Freelance Publishing Services, Brinscall, Lancs
Printed in Great Britain
by Biddles Ltd, King's Lynn

CONTENTS

A NOTE ON TERMINOLOGY

How does one refer to a political entity which in less than fifty years has moved from an original trio of bodies through the European Communities to the European Community, which in conjunction with its intergovernmental arrangements is known as the European Union? I have chosen the path of simplicity and referred to the 'European Union' (or EU) throughout. This is liable either to offend or provoke feelings of superiority in historians and lawyers. So much the worse. For those interested in reading and writing about the politics of this strange beast, the single designation seems the best and most straightforward. At least, that is my choice in this volume.

PREFACE AND ACKNOWLEDGEMENTS

There are a number of reasons why citizens of the European Union should be interested in the principles of democratic association. They are being increasingly asked in referendums in many countries to ratify treaty changes and in that case the concern is a political one. For them, the concern is a practical and imminent one. But it is also a concern that brings into focus more general lines of political interpretation. For some the growth of the Union is a challenge to the democratic achievements of post-war welfare states; for others it offers the only economic conditions in which those achievements can be maintained. For some, the European Union departs too far from the democratic norms of political responsibility and accountability to be legitimate; for others it is a system of governance that is flexible enough to deal with the complex inter-relationships that the politics of integration throws up. For some, transboundary issues like pollution require the European Union to act more decisively; for others, only high environmental standards mandated through national democratic processes are acceptable. No one with any sense of European history can ignore the profound change in the structure of European relations brought about by the collapse of the Iron Curtain and the expansion of the European Union eastwards. Whether Europe's citizens ever can occupy a common European home is a matter for debate and conjecture. That the question is important is surely obvious.

However, interest in democratic citizenship and the European Union should not be limited only to those who are touched as citizens materially and politically by the decision. Theorists of politics in general, and theorists of democracy in particular, should take an interest in the future of the European Union. By common consent the EU is a unique system of political authority. Seeking to understand its workings and outcomes takes us to the heart of what is involved in political cooperation and construction. What is a political association? What are the terms and limits of its legitimate political authority? How might the development of the EU be justified to its citizens? What reasons can be advanced when making choices over the future of Europe and the European Union? Seeking to answer these questions involves conceptual and theoretical concerns that are deep and difficult. The very rationality of democratic citizenship is necessarily involved.

In this book I have tried to address this demand for reasoning about the European Union. My motives are in part personal and in part professional. At the personal level I have always enjoyed living and working in Europe. There is no place in which I would rather have my home. I love Europe's diversity, its many languages, its rich historical legacies in architecture and cities, its scenery, its food, its music, its art and its manners. I also try to take seriously the responsibility to vote intelligently in elections and referendums, and all elections now have some implications for the future of the EU. Yet, I recognise that when thinking about these matters it is not easy to take up a well-reasoned position. One of the privileges of being a political scientist is that you have the time to read and reflect on the research that is relevant to such choices. This book is the outcome of that reading and reflection.

Normative political theory is at once the most abstract and the most applied of all the sub-disciplines of political science. As I have tried to explain in the text, normative questions are the staple diet of everyday political arguments, and they have immediate bearing on the political choices that any community needs to make. On the other hand, political theorists accept constraints on what is allowed to count as an acceptable argument and this can often give their work an obscure or laboured appearance. It is all too easy to engage in a detailed demonstration of what everyone knows to be the case. It is equally easy to wander off into what most people, perhaps rightly, might regard as an irrelevance.

I have tried to deal with some of these problems by addressing what seem to me to be the central political issues using the apparatus of practical rationality, an apparatus that I have sought to explain in the text. I have tried to test this approach by discussing particular issues where the development of European integration is a challenge to democratic citizenship. I have done this as a way of seeking to test the implications of the theoretical position I have adopted, rather as empirical political scientists test their theories by making predictions. I do not pretend, however, that I have provided definitive answers to difficult policy problems, even in outline. At one time I used to think that policy issues could be settled by rigorous argument from well-articulated premises. I no longer think that. This is not because I have given up on the idea of rational argument, but because I recognise that in matters of practical politics there are too many unknowns and conjectures for demonstration of the unique rationality of a course of action ever to be a plausible goal. The reader will find my own conclusions stated as clearly as I can. I hope that, for those who disagree, the logic of the argument is clear enough in each case to show where reasonable differences of opinion might exist.

A paradox of authorship is that it is a lonely occupation in which you come to rely upon a great many other people. In some ways the project started many years ago, when I was being driven very fast down the motorway between Amsterdam and The Hague by Percy Lehning, and we concocted the plan of convening a group of people to discuss what normative political theorists might have to say in response to the call from the Research Committee of the European Consortium of Political Research for research workshops on the 'New Europe'. Through the support of ECPR and Erasmus University that conversation led to the edited volume that Percy and I published in 1997, *Citizenship, Democracy and the New Europe*. In 1996 Michael Nentwich and I convened an ECPR workshop session in Oslo on normative political theory and European union, and papers from that meeting were published in a volume in 1998, *Political Theory and the European Union*. I am grateful not only to Percy and Michael but to all the contributors and authors involved in those meetings. A few will even find some of their ideas used or discussed in this book.

When I embarked on writing this book, I thought that I could take my earlier work on the topic, some of which had been presented at those meetings, and simply bring it up to date. Alas, on rereading, I found that I did not agree with what I had written, or at least I disagreed with enough of it that I had to go back and rethink the project afresh. It was this rethink that took me deeper into questions of political association than I had originally thought I needed to go. In this context, a chance meeting with Robbie Wokler in the Cambridge University Library tea-room (often for me a place of interesting intellectual encounters) and a subsequent kind gift of one of his book, *Rousseau: A Very Short Introduction* revived an old interest of mine. One of the pleasures of writing this book has been to savour the scholarship on Rousseau, as a way of thinking about the rationality of political association. I am sure I have not done that scholarship justice. But the enjoyment of reading it has been great and I thank Robbie for being such a good guide.

I have tried out the ideas contained in this book at various seminars at the universities of Bergen, Exeter and Hull. I am grateful to all participants for comments and suggestions on these occasions. I am also grateful to colleagues at the University of Essex, which has provided me with such a supportive and constructive environment in which to work. As well as presenting the argument in the Department of Government seminar, I have also been able to present written versions of the argument to members of the Essex Political Theory Workshop. For their comments, my thanks go to Jason Glynos, David Howarth, Sheldon Leader, Aletta Norval, Ian O'Flynn and Lasse Thomassen. Richard Bellamy kindly provided me with detailed and helpful comments, as well as participating in the discussions. I also presented some of the material at my own PhD seminar and I am grateful to Deborah Savage and Judy Robertson for their comments and I take this opportunity to thank the latter for some timely and valuable research assistance.

Lynn Dobson and Myrto Tsakatika, both of whom have thought deeply about these issues themselves, gave me written comments on an early draft. Both managed to be kind and insightfully critical at the same time, and I am extremely grateful to them for the trouble they took. I should also like to thank Derek Matravers and Susan Mendus for tracking down the source of my misremembered account of Bernard Williams on constitutive rationality.

I owe a large and very special debt to my colleague Emil Kirchner. It was he who first commissioned this project. When I undertook it, I did so in the naive belief that all I had to do was bring up to date some thoughts that I had previously published in article form. I did not realise how much time would go into the rethink. Even with the delay, Emil has not only been patient but generous with his time and knowledge. At various times I have tried out thoughts and lines of argument with him, and he has provided evidence, made counter-suggestions or pointed out complexities where I saw only simplicities.

One should try to avoid clichés where possible, but sometimes they say something that is true, so let me use the conventional cliché at this point: with all this help I have avoided many mistakes, but the remaining ones are all mine.

1

The European transformation

Consider the following schematic account of European integration. At the end of the third war fought between France and Germany in less than eighty years, a small but influential group within the European political class determined that a new structure of political cooperation was needed among European nations. Realising that previous federalist ambitions had failed because they presented too direct a challenge to the powers and interests of the nation-state, the architects of the new Europe (inspired by the ideas and activities of Jean Monnet) devised a process of functional integration, which began with common institutions and policies in the field of coal and steel production and were then progressively extended through the 1960s to the construction of a common market. Even in the 1970s, the period in which the political impetus for integration stalled, there was a significant growth in the powers of the European Court of Justice with its assertion of the principles of direct effect, the supremacy of European law and the doctrine of mutual recognition. The single market programme of the 1980s took the original functional logic further, removing non-tariff barriers to trade and entrenching freedom of movement in the areas of goods, services, capital and workers. The same programme also provided the first formal recognition of environmental policy competence for the EU. The 1992 Maastricht Treaty committed member states to the single currency and a common monetary policy for eurozone states. In the first decade of the twenty-first century, the peoples of Europe will decide the question of a European Constitution, and increasingly policy makers, even in traditionally Eurosceptic countries, see the logic of common policies to deal with migration and cross-border security. Beyond these developments lies the ultimate prize for those who favour the erosion of the nation-state and the European intergovernmentalism that goes with it, namely an effective common defence and security policy.

Together with this deepening of integration, there has been a widening of the European Union with an increase in the number of member states. The original six were turned into nine when Denmark, Ireland and the UK joined in 1973. In the 1980s the Mediterranean accessions added Greece in 1981 and Spain and Portugal in 1986. In 1995, Austria, Finland and Sweden joined. In 2004, the accession of ten countries, with eight of them from the former communist bloc, marked a further decisive expansion, though not the end of the process. Romania and Bulgaria are waiting in the wings, together with Croatia and others in the Balkans, possibly to be followed by Turkey. An original compact across the Rhine has become the blueprint for a continent.

European integration in this mode has been favoured by national political elites for a number of reasons. Initially, the scars of war were so deep and painful that leading politicians thought they should never be reopened. The emphasis upon functional integration through low politics meant that there was no political challenge to the core activities of the nation-state, at a time when democratic legitimacy at the national level was high. In any case, it was possible to construct the European order, particularly in respect of agriculture, such that policies could both build integration and help rescue the nation-state. Later, when techniques of Keynesian growth and demand management appeared to fail, market integration and the single currency offered a policy regime that would provide an economic space large enough to withstand the shocks of an increasingly globalised economic order and the EU became the representative of member states in international trade negotiations. Pooling sovereignty in these circumstances could still be construed as compatible with maintaining the powers of the nation-state. It is not difficult to see how this logic could be increasingly transferred from the realm of economic policy to foreign and security policy, particularly in an era when some European elites felt that there should be an alternative voice to that of the USA as the global hegemon.[1]

What has been the role of European citizens in the process of integration? The answer can be summarised in the conventional phrase from political science (Lindberg and Scheingold, 1970): permissive consensus. Over the vast bulk of the post-war period, for most of the countries involved, European integration was neither a subject of political contest nor a topic of political salience. Until 1979 the citizens of member states were not called upon to elect members to the European Parliament, and when they eventually did so, they used the occasion to treat European elections as second-order events, passing judgement on the performance of their national governments rather than addressing a European political agenda. No subsequent election has been fought on a European agenda. With some notable exceptions, Denmark and Ireland in 1972 and the UK in 1975 being obvious examples, citizens were not involved in the ratification or confirmation of the international treaty agreements that progressively enhanced the powers of the EU's supranational political institutions. Moreover, they neither carried passports as citizens of Europe nor developed affective attachments to common European political symbols. For most citizens, for most of the time while integration was occurring, Europe was merely a geographical expression.

This is to speak politically. In other senses of course citizens were involved in the construction of the new Europe, of which the most obvious was in terms of increased trade and travel. By the 1960s democratic affluence enabled many who in previous generations would have holidayed in their own country to enjoy the Rhine and the Mediterranean. Cities like Paris or Florence, which had been part of the Grand Tour for the aristocracy in the eighteenth century and the professional middle classes in the nineteenth became destinations for the many rather than the few. The French Riviera, the playground of the rich and famous – as well as the literary aspirant – in the 1920s and 1930s, was transformed by the advent of the package tour and the family summer holiday. There is much more in detail to be said of this. But what we can say is that though European citizens were involved in increasing integration in Europe, it was not as citizens that they were involved.

At least until 1992 that is. The original Danish 'no' to the Maastricht Treaty and the French 'petit oui' in that year produced the first shock to the European political class. The fall of the Berlin wall in 1989 and the subsequent reunification of Germany, as well as the collapse of communism in central and eastern Europe, provided new challenges to the construction of a Europe that could no longer rely upon an image of 'the other' to help constitute its own identity. Euroscepticism spread in party systems, including in those party systems where a commitment to the European project was conventionally taken for granted among the political class and where a commitment to the European ideal was common ground among political parties who might be opposed on many other issues. Preparations under the Stability Pact, in the run-up to the introduction of the single currency, meant that public budgets had to be trimmed, heightening widespread anxiety about the effects of European integration on the economic and social security provided by European welfare states. When confronted in national referendums with a decision to ratify the European Constitution, a significant body of citizens might say no. The permissive consensus can no longer be assumed to hold. In their political choices and behaviour, European citizens might neither consent nor permit.

Citizenship and the nation-state

The era of the permissive consensus was also one in which it was possible to identify a dominant and influential conception of democratic citizenship. In saying this, I do not mean that there was universal agreement on what citizenship involved. Indeed, the dominant account was one that provoked reaction and critique. Even so, because in the second half of the twentieth century European states converged towards a form of liberal, welfare state democracy, a certain set of assumptions became entrenched in their political cultures about what it meant to be a citizen. This convergence was compatible with considerable variation in institutional arrangements (Esping-Andersen, 1990; Lijphart, 1984), but there were enough elements in common for us to identify a specific state form together with a conception of citizenship that was associated with that form.

The first point in common is that they were all mass democracies in which, in Schumpeter's (1954: 269) famous phrase, the principal mechanism of leadership selection was 'a competitive struggle for the people's vote'. The contrast here was with pre-war authoritarian and totalitarian systems, as well as with one-party states in communist Europe. There were of course significant variations in the form that the electoral connection took – particularly between those systems which practised proportional representation and those which did not – with consequent differences in the way that governments were or were not based on coalition bargaining. Yet, even with these differences, important in so many ways, there was the massive common fact of the centrality of the electoral connection in linking the people with those who governed them.

In this context, the principal political role of citizens was as voters, since voting was the method that enabled citizens to exercise some control over their governments. To say that the principal role was that of voters is not of course to say that citizenship rights pertained exclusively and specifically only to the act of voting. In order to engage sensibly and intelligently in the act of voting, citizens need to enjoy other rights, in particular freedom of association and freedom of communication. Indeed, the contrast case of the communist states highlights the importance of these elements. Citizens did vote in those states, although the voting system was rigged and biased in various ways. But, just as importantly, their rights to associate freely and to communicate with whomever they wished were severely circumscribed and in consequence their political powers were virtually nugatory.

There is one important aspect in which turning to Schumpeter to understand post-war European democratic welfare states is misleading, namely in respect of practices of public consultation in the making of policy. Schumpeter (1954: 295) notoriously argued that the public in a democracy should refrain from back-seat driving, by which he meant seeking to influence political decision makers between elections. However, in their workings, governments did not simply use the device of elections in order to secure legitimacy for policy choices. Practices of regular or intermittent consultation were institutionalised, by which policy makers could sound out and assess the opinions of citizens and social groups about particular policy proposals. The most extensive of these mechanisms were developed in corporatist policy-making systems, in which, in the limit, governments shared their policy-making privileges in the economic realm with associations representative of workers and owners (see, *inter alia*, Berger, 1981; Katzenstein, 1985; and Lehmbruch and Schmitter, 1982). Hence, if we are to catalogue the political rights of citizens in late twentieth-century states, we have at least to include the rights to consultation in the making of policy and in some cases for some social groups an even more extensive right to participate in the making of decisions.

The traditional civil rights, including freedom of movement and occupation, freedom of religion, and the rights to family life and privacy were continued in those societies that had remained democracies during the war and re-established in those societies that had fallen to fascism and totalitarianism. An important right in this context was the right to own property, in particular the right to own productive property. It is difficult to recapture the scepticism about the function and role of private productive property that prevailed in the wake of the Great

Crash of 1929 and the subsequent depression. However, some sense of the scale of doubt is revealed by reading Harold Macmillan's *The Middle Way* written in 1938, and which from a Conservative perspective proposed widespread socialisation of the means of production. As Greenleaf's (1983: 78–194) survey makes clear, Macmillan's advocacy of planning was part of the temper of the times. By contrast, it took only a few years after the ending of the war before commentators like Strachey (1952), formerly on the far left, began to assert that there was no longer any problem of production, merely a problem of distribution.

What was established, in fact, in the post-war period was not by and large the socialisation of the means of production, but the socialisation of the means of consumption, in the form of social rights to health care, education, housing and income support when sick, old or injured (Heidenheimer *et al.*, 1990: 218). To be sure, the developments that took place in the post-war period were often extensions of schemes that had been available at local level before. And, at least in the case of Germany a catalogue social rights had been developed through the occupationally based social insurance scheme in the 1880s before the mass extension of democratic rights. However, the post-war period saw such schemes extended in all west European societies and supplied on an increasingly universal, rather than occupational basis. Perhaps as important was the assumption that the public provision could be stated in the language of rights. Marshall set out a clear description of what this involved:

> By the social element I mean the whole range from the right to a modicum of economic welfare and security to the right to a share to the full social heritage and to live the life of a civilised being according to the standards prevalent in society. The institutions most closely connected with it are the educational system and the social services. (Marshall, 1950: 11)

What this quotation highlights is the universalisation of expectations to social and economic welfare solely on the basis of citizenship and not, for example, on the basis of occupation or ability to pay.

There are a number of points to make about the conception of citizens' rights as they were institutionalised in European liberal democratic welfare states. First, there is a good case for saying that the commitment to social rights rested on a view that the value of citizenship was enhanced not simply by extending rights, but by extending those rights that could be seen as part of a mutually reinforcing system. Social rights can be seen as giving substance to political and civil rights. For example, freedom of movement is a hollow right for those who cannot afford housing costs in the place to which they would wish to move. Freedom of expression and communication is equally hollow to those who cannot afford even the price of a newspaper. One way of putting this is in terms of the familiar distinction between freedom that is formal and freedom that is real. In this sense the development of social rights could be seen not simply as an extension of some already existing rights, but as a way of enhancing civil and political rights.

Secondly, there was a specific account of equality presupposed in this conception of rights. Marshall noted that the continued private ownership of the means

of production produced a system of economic inequality, so that the development of the welfare state could not be seen as a simple egalitarian set of measures.
This was one of the reasons why in discussing the value problems of welfare capitalism, he spoke of the 'hyphenated society', that is a 'democratic-welfare-capitalist
society' (Marshall, 1972). However, in relation to social rights, there was a form of
equality, involving the gaining of access to certain important goods solely on the
test of citizenship. The economist James Tobin (1970) coined the phrase 'specific
egalitarianism', which he defined as the view that certain goods and services should
be more equally distributed than the ability to pay for them. It was equality in this
form that the system of rights produced. As Marshall (1950: 56) stressed, what
mattered in this conception was 'a general enrichment of the concrete substance
of civilised life, a general reduction of risk and insecurity, an equalisation between
the more and less fortunate at all levels ...'

Thirdly, the system of rights rested upon a set of conditions that cannot themselves be understood in terms of rights, most importantly economic growth. Without rising incomes it would not have been possible to finance the growth of public
expenditure – or publicly mandated expenditure in social insurance funds – on
which the provision of rights depended. Moreover, as Lipset (1963) pointed out
in a justly famous analysis, economic growth was also a precondition for the secure enjoyment of the political rights, for it was economic growth that moderated
the intensity of the pre-war class struggle and facilitated the expression of cross-
cutting political cleavages. The collective identity of citizenship could become a
meaningful category of political analysis to the extent to which class identities
ceased to hegemonise the consciousness of the electorate.

Yet there is another aspect to economic growth. One of the consequences of
economic growth was the risk of combining – in Galbraith's (1970) famous phrase
– 'private affluence and public squalor', particularly environmental squalor. Without the development of environmental protection policies, the quality of life that
citizens experienced would deteriorate, eroding the value of social and political
rights. As with policies of social protection, policies for environmental protection
date back to the nineteenth century, with the emergence of public health measures. However, in the late 1960s and early 1970s a wave of environmental protection measures spread across many developed countries, with new pieces of
substantive legislation and reorganisations in administration. More often than
not these policies did not establish measures from scratch but rather nationalised
and strengthened powers many of which already existed at the sub-national level
(Weale, 1992: 10–23). In many ways, these developments were simply the logical
extension of welfare-enhancing measures that had been present in earlier policies
of social protection in the post-war establishment of the welfare state, yet taking the
form of policies for public goods rather than redistribution through social rights.

If we put these ideas together, we have something like the following account
of citizenship as it developed in west European democracies. Citizens within a
constitutional, democratic welfare state have the traditional liberal rights, together
with the power to participate in the selection of political representatives who make

the choices on public policy. These rights and powers are supplemented by the benefits of public goods and social rights, secured through governmental action. A political system of this type is well run when the citizens accept the constraints of democratic governance and when governments adopt policy measures to ensure that all citizens are advantaged by public action. Political differences are expressed through the process of party competition, the competitive struggle for the people's vote, but the political struggle is conducted in a framework in which all are guaranteed inclusion. Solidarity and difference are balanced against one another in a way that produces political legitimacy.

Implicit in this account is the location of the rights and powers of citizenship within the nation-state. Marshall (1950: 40–1) stressed that citizenship requires a 'sense of community membership based on loyalty to a civilisation which is a common possession'. The democratic-welfare-capitalist state conception of citizenship thus rested on a sharp demarcation between insiders and outsiders. Where rights were tied to citizenship, it followed that those who were non-citizens would not have the same rights. This is most obviously true in the case of political rights (leaving aside anomalies like the reciprocal rights of Irish and UK citizens to vote in the elections of the other when resident), but it was also true in the case of social rights, especially in those social security systems that rested upon beneficiaries themselves having contributed to a scheme of social insurance. Welfare state social rights cannot be rationalised solely in terms of a theory of needs, because the needs of the developing world are considerably greater than the needs of most of those in the developed world. Indeed, it was central to the conception of the welfare state that the national community would provide the framework for entitlement, since citizens exercising their political rights would be doing so as members of such a community, with social rights providing for the needs of its members.

Behind these post-war developments, there is a long history of state building in Europe. The salient features of this process were well brought out in Rokkan's model of the political development of European national states (see Flora, Kuhnle and Urwin, 1999: 131–4 and Flora and Alber, 1981: 45–6.) Rokkan distinguished four stages in the political development of European states. The first was that of state formation, which in different countries lasted from the sixteenth to the nineteenth centuries. In this phase there was administrative, military and cultural unification at the elite level, accompanied by territorial consolidation and the establishment of the elementary infrastructure of the economy. The second stage was that of nation building, in which there were more and more direct contacts between elites and the mass of the people, and in which there was widespread socialisation into national consciousness by means of education, linguistic standardisation, conscript armies and the growth of transport and newspapers. The third stage involved an extension of the franchise and the creation of competitive political parties. The fourth stage was that of redistribution achieved through the growth of welfare states and the establishment of social citizenship.

As Peter Flora stressed in his introduction to Rokkan's edited writings, these four variables should probably be regarded in theoretical terms as sets of relations rather than a general pattern shaping the stages of historical development, since placing the elements in a four-stage sequence fits only the older nation-states of western Europe (Flora, Kuhnle and Urwin, 1999: 84). But insofar as these elements can be seen as stages, the Schumpeter–Marshall–Galbraith theory of citizenship is an attempt to state explicitly the norms and values that are implicit in the third and fourth stages of nation-state development. In saying this I am not asserting that the welfare state should be seen historically as a means by which governments consciously pursued the principle of welfare for democratic citizenship. It is clear that in many cases the origins of social policy programmes are to be found in the attempts by conservative ruling classes to forestall mass democratic pressure for the extensive redistribution of property. Rather what I am saying is that when theorists came to reflect upon the development of the democratic welfare state, one way in which it could be rationalised was in terms of ideas of democratic citizenship.

The other respect in which Rokkan's account is important is that it underlines the extent to which democratic citizenship and welfare state development were historically linked to the practices and ideology of the nation-state. In part this is because political elites saw the necessity for welfare policies in order to ensure that citizens could cooperate in national projects, of which preparation for war on the part of large land-based armies was the most important and pressing. But conceptually there is a close connection between nationhood and democratic citizenship in the following sense. One way of thinking about democracy is to see it as the political means by which a body of citizens can together determine the conditions of their collective life. Such a conception presupposes a distinction between those who are part of the body politic and those who are outside the scope of collective self-determination. Ancient independent city-states might be said to satisfy such conditions by contrast with cities and towns that were part of an imperial system of rule. Similarly, independent, territorially bounded nation-states can also be thought of as satisfying the conditions under which the principle of collective self-government can be realised. (In this connection, it is not irrelevant that Rokkan himself stressed that the independent city-states of Mesopotamia, Greece, the Hanseatic League and Renaissance Italy were political formations in which habitat, not kinship, determined one's affinities (see Flora, Kuhnle and Urwin, 1999: 99)). From this point of view, whatever the intentions of political elites at Rokkan's different stages of political development, the effect of their actions over time was to create the institutions within which citizens could democratically determine the conditions of their collective life. Popular government leads to welfare policies and welfare policies reinforce the ability of citizens to participate as equals in the political process through which collective self-determination is achieved.

Although the system of liberal democratic welfare rights was widely and extensively institutionalised, it was not uncontroversial. Liberals of a firmly individualist persuasion were critical of the development of social rights and of the increasing share of national income that was required to finance the entitlements they represented. Socialists and radicals were often critical of the limited extent of democratisation that the welfare state seemed to provide, and became particularly interested in workplace and community democratic initiatives. Yet, despite the considerable rhetoric that has accompanied these critiques, they have had little effect on the concrete substance of the system of rights itself. Thus, the 'dismantling' of the welfare state under right-of-centre liberal governments in the 1980s and 1990s showed an inability to move public provision to a residual set of arrangements (Pierson, 1994). From a more left-wing position, initiatives in workplace and community democracy, often advocated as ways of dealing with the bureaucratic features of the welfare state, pale into insignificance beside the continual centrality of the competitive party system.

There is one further implication that we can derive from the Rokkan model, and this concerns issues of international security. The dominant military alliance in the post-war period in Europe has been the transatlantic NATO one. Its success contrasts with the failure to produce a system built upon European integration after the collapse of the proposals for the European Defence Community in 1954. NATO of course rested on the traditional principles of the independence and sovereignty of states in the international system (admittedly under the leadership of and dependent upon the finances of the United States). In this respect it was entirely consistent with an account of European political development that stressed strong states in the realm of social and political rights. The mutual obligations that were part of citizenship in the national-democratic-welfare-capitalist state bound individuals to a community of common fate – literally so in an era of nuclear weapons of mass destruction. While it made sense for such communities to enter into military alliances to increase their mutual protection within an insecure world, it would also only make sense to do this on the assumption that the decision was a national one. It is one thing for a national community to commit itself to an alliance in which the members agree of their own accord that an attack on one is an attack upon all. It is an entirely different matter to cede authority to a supranational entity that would commit one's fate to a course of action of which one's own community disapproved. In the historical circumstances of post-war Europe, NATO not the EU was the guarantee of national democracy in the international order.

The problem of democratic legitimacy

So far I have reconstructed two narratives of European political development. The first is a narrative in which the EU develops through a dialectic of the functionalism of Monnet and the coincidence of the ambitions and interests of national political elites. The second is a narrative in which the principles of democracy, welfare and security are embedded in the institutions and cultures of the national-democratic-welfare-state. As narratives, they involve different characters, develop different plots and offer competing accounts of what constitutes a happy ending. In one, multi-level governance supersedes the structures and achievements of the nation-state; in the other, it is a threat to those structures and achievements. In one, political interests and values can depend upon a variety of attachments on the part of individuals; in the other, the national identity of citizens is presupposed as the basis for their collective life. In one, nationalism is the foe that needs to be overcome; in the other, national solidarity is the basis upon which citizens will live as political equals with one another. In one, European peace and prosperity depend upon supranational cooperation and development; in the other, political legitimacy resides in the institutions of the nation-state. In one, nation-states are allied with one another militarily but maintain their own political identity; in the other, ancient national rivalries can only be overcome when the separation of political authority among potentially warring states is trumped by a supranational system of governance.

We can highlight these issues if we focus on the problem of democratic legitimacy from the viewpoint of the Rokkan narrative. From that viewpoint, a political association is legitimate to the extent to which it is the agent and servant of the will and interests of its members. Of course, among citizens there will be different and competing accounts of what this will and these interests require, but political contestation within a democratic polity only makes sense on the assumption that the purpose of the political association is to serve citizens' interests and enact their collective will. Against this background, why and how do European integration and the accompanying growth of supranational political authority pose a problem of political legitimacy? What features of the European project make it seem problematic from the point of view of the principles of democratic citizenship? After all, the EU in many ways enjoys as high a level of legitimacy as many nation-states in the world and possibly a higher level than some of its own member states – at least if we judge the issue by its ability to secure effective compliance with its rules and procedures. How, then, can the development of European integration pose a problem of legitimacy when contrasted with that of west European states?

We begin to gain an answer to this question when we see that within the Rokkan narrative European nation-states exemplified institutional forms of political association that could plausibly be interpreted as embodying the values of democracy. Competitive party elections, institutionalised parliamentary opposition, the free association of interest groups, freedom of expression and the other elements of democratic institutions have all contributed to the values of representation and accountability. By contrast, the development of the European Union, involving a form of political association in which the political powers of the member states have been pooled, can also be said to have shifted accountability for the exercise of these powers away from the scrutiny of citizens and their representatives. As a form of political authority, the governance structures of the EU do not resemble the pattern of European parliamentary systems in which the executive emerges from the parliament and in which it is dependent on a majority in that parliament for its continued existence. Nor does it resemble the semi-presidential system of France, in which the chief executive is directly elected and has to govern – or cohabit – with the majority from the National Assembly. Instead, there is a complex pattern of multi-level and horizontally complex governance, which incorporates a strong version of the separation of powers, and in which different institutions are involved in the passing of legislation.

One consequence of this structure of governance is that the practice of party government is lost, and with it the main institutional devices linking government to the mass of citizens. The process of party competition in national parliamentary systems means that parties have to formulate programmes of action and offer principles of political choice in terms of which they propose to enter into government. Party competition also means that competing party programmes are subjected to public criticism and the performance of governing parties is evaluated in the light of possible alternatives. Although in coalition systems the electorate cannot be said to choose the government directly, it has been shown that in such systems governing coalitions typically include parties representing the preferences of the median voter in a left–right policy space (McDonald, Mendes and Budge, 2004). In other words, the electoral connection provides a genuine link between voter preferences and the policy orientation of the government. By contrast, in the EU system of government this link between key decision makers and the electorate is lost. Important institutional decision makers, like the Commission and the Council of Ministers, are not linked to a European public through processes of party competition. Insofar as European elections are second-order events in which turn-out is often low, the problem is, if anything, made worse by the increasing powers of the European Parliament.

This shift of power upwards to institutions not linked to the mass electorate by party competition might not matter if the powers involved were technical, trivial or of low political salience. For those who categorise the EU as an extended type of international organisation, this is the way out of the dilemma in theoretical terms (Moravcsik, 2003). International organisations do not require direct accountability between rule makers and the citizens affected by their rules in order to secure political legitimacy. To suppose otherwise is to suppose that nation-states lack the authority to enter into international agreements with one another, and this would be an absurd supposition. In many of the traditional areas of policy of the EU, perhaps even including fisheries and agriculture, it might be argued that the issues involved, though important to those working in the sector, were of low general political salience, and were often dealt with on a technocratic or specialist basis anyway within the nation-state. For example, before the UK joined the European Union in 1973, it is difficult to think of an election campaign in which agriculture and fisheries were important issues. When one turns to the more arcane details of, say, phytosanitary regulations, it is impossible to maintain the view that issues of high democratic politics are involved.

Yet, in a number of ways, this summary judgement needs to be qualified. One of the key findings of studies of the policy-making process in many states is that detailed rule-making is subject to capture by those who are supposed to be regulated, and any such process of capture has implications for how well a democratic political system performs. Although the policy issues in which the EU has been involved for some time are typically ones in which the controversial elements are technical, it is equally true that apparently technical details can have large and important effects on policy outcomes. For example, the details of car emission standards or wastewater quality standards are technical issues, but depending upon the precise standards that are adopted there can be large differences of environmental effect or cost implications (see Wurzel, 2002: 98–9). Moreover, many issues that at one time might have seemed primarily technical, for example food safety, have become of increasing political salience. Finally, it is difficult to argue that the EU is merely dealing in technical and marginal issues once economic and monetary union is in place. Interest rate policy, together with the associated fiscal measures of the Stability Pact, has a profound effect upon the well-being of European citizens. If decision makers on those issues are completely detached from the processes that make them responsive to citizens, then there are reasons to be concerned about democratic citizenship and the EU.

In respect of economic and monetary policy it may be argued in reply that all that has happened is that the institutional forms of the German state, and in particular the independent role of the central bank, has been transposed to a European level. If such an institutional arrangement was compatible with a democratic order at the national level, why would it not be compatible with democratic legitimacy at the international level? Yet one difficulty with assuming that there is no problem of legitimacy is that the role and status of the Bundesbank was itself not uncontroversial. As Dyson and Featherstone (1999: 287) have pointed out, both Karl Schiller and Helmut Schmidt had difficult and strained relationships with the Bundesbank, and neither was integrated into what Dyson and Featherstone call the ordo-liberal coalition of ideas that stressed the importance to German economic prosperity of central bank policy autonomy. Moreover, even if one accepts that a strong independent monetary authority fits the circumstances of German economic policy for obvious historical reasons, it would not follow that the transposition of this form of monetary policy, with its concomitant rules for fiscal balance, was right for the EU. Again, as Dyson and Featherstone point out, it was precisely this issue that had to be resolved, most notably in France where there were strong intellectual traditions of *gouvernement économique*, in which the democratic accountability of governments for the management of the economy in a way responsive to social needs was stressed.

What is more, it is not simply issues of democratic responsiveness that are involved in the forms of EU governance, but also the means chosen by EU policy makers to achieve the goal of greater integration. In particular, since the early 1980s an important role in the transformation of the European political order has been played by the creation of the single market. From one point of view, the single market programme was simply a packaging, for the purposes of political negotiation, of measures to which the EU was already committed. Removing the non-tariff barriers to trade had been an ambition of European policy makers as soon as the customs union was achieved in the 1960s. However, the implications of single market programme are potentially extensive in terms of national democratic control. This is so directly in such areas as public procurement, where the right of member state governments to favour national champions has been abolished, but it is also important indirectly through the measures promoting the free movement of capital. In these fields, it can be argued that international trade liberalisation makes it more difficult to protect the social rights of citizens, rights that were an important achievement of post-war democratic welfare states.

Behind these problems of legitimacy, there lies a profound conceptual problem of democratic theory. If democracy rests upon the idea that a people should be able to determine the conditions of its own collective fate, so that political freedom is freedom from external domination, such freedom can only be secured if citizens have the powers to participate in the shaping of their common life. Yet the significance of this idea becomes problematic within the EU, for the concept of the people as the ultimate source of authority, let alone the concept of a people determining the conditions of its collective fate, ceases to be meaningful when we are dealing with a political association that is built upon a union of peoples. What is the meaning of democracy when there is no demos?

The shift in the locus of political authority, the centrality of the single market programme and the absence of a European demos affect the ability of states to deliver on social rights and public goods to an identifiable body of citizens. So extensive is the growth of supranational authority in the EU, and so great the reach of its powers into what have traditionally been taken to be the core functions of the nation-state, that the issue of political legitimacy cannot be avoided. Three questions, in particular, are central.

First, what reasons, if any, do democratic citizens have for accepting the legitimacy of the European Union project? This has to be taken as a genuinely open question. To be sure, the fact that the EU developed and expanded to its present form as an elite project would not of itself disqualify it from having democratic political legitimacy, just as the origin of some welfare states in the attempts by conservative ruling classes to protect themselves from political revolution does not prevent those welfare states having political legitimacy. In the case of the welfare state we have an example of a political reform that democratic citizens have reason to accept and endorse but which was not brought about by democratic action or for democratic reasons. It may be the case that the European Union falls into a similar category. It was in origin and execution an elite project, but there may still be good reasons for citizens to accept its political legitimacy.

The second question follows from the first. The process of European integration is often compared to riding a bicycle. Forward momentum needs to be maintained otherwise the project will fail. Yet, this dynamic may be questioned. Do democratic citizens have reasons to favour the deepening of European integration? It may be that, even if the present construction of the EU can find a justification in terms of the principles and values of democratic citizenship, a further growth of its powers and responsibilities would be inconsistent with those values and principles. This question can be further refined by saying that a growth of powers and responsibilities may be justified, but only if accompanied by reforms in the policy-making process that made it more democratic. Thus, deepening may be consistent with the values and principles of democratic citizenship provided only that it is accompanied by institutional reform in the decision-making process.

The third question concerns widening. Do democratic citizens have reasons for favouring the widening of European integration? Although the topicality of this question is highlighted by the accession of the ten new member states in 2004, it has a more general application. The EU can be looked at as a device for democratic consolidation, ranging from the accession of the Mediterranean states in the 1980s to the round of accessions in 2004. Can this aspect of the EU be connected to the values and principles of democratic citizenship, or is it merely incidental to the question of political legitimacy?

Note the way that I have stated the problem, namely in terms of the compatibility or incompatibility of the political order of the EU with the principles of democratic citizenship. In general form, the principal question is the extent to which the practices and institutions of the EU are compatible with the norms of democratic citizenship. This is distinct from saying that European integration requires a transformation in our conception of democratic citizenship. Such a claim is often made. For example, Kostakopoulou (2001: 6–7) contrasts civic nationalism with the political order of the European Union and argues that the diversity of the latter necessitates 'a serious rethinking of the connections between citizenship, nationality and culture'. Such an argument may well be valid, but it cannot be taken as the starting point for an enquiry. After all, it may well be that the connections between citizenship, nationality and culture require us to rethink the character of the process of European integration. Perhaps we should restrain the growth of European integration in the name of democratic citizenship. Such a possibility cannot be ignored or assumed away. To state the problem as one of incompatibility leaves open the direction in which reconceptualisation should proceed.

It might be argued at this point that, in approaching the problem of the political legitimacy of the European Union through the notion of democratic citizenship I am phrasing the question in such a way as to favour in a biased way the range of plausible answers. Democratic citizenship in the modern period is associated with nation-states, even if many nation-states have not been associated with democratic citizenship. Thus, in making the ideals of democratic citizenship so central to the evaluation of the European Union, it may be thought that there will be the danger of implicitly assuming that any political practices that threaten or undermine the integrity of the nation-state are, to that degree, suspect. If there is a strong association between democratic citizenship and the nation-state, might it not seem to be but a short step from democratic citizenship to Euroscepticism? In this context, is it not relevant that as Peter Flora notes, Stein Rokkan was probably sceptical 'about European unification or at least regarded it with mixed feelings' (Flora, Kuhnle and Urwin, 1999: 88)?

We need to be careful in appraising this line of argument, not least because it can be interpreted in different ways, not all of which are equally plausible. For example, the question might be interpreted as suggesting that Euroscepticism and a commitment to the ideals of democratic citizenship were the same thing, in effect two sides of the same coin. However, such an interpretation would misconstrue the approach that I am adopting. To be sure, I do assume that there is something valuable in the ideals of democratic citizenship. After all, such a view is part of a political position that also expresses respect and admiration for those political activists and movements that struggled to bring about democratic reforms in the states of Europe and elsewhere. Yet this is not the same as saying that upholding and extending the ideals of democratic citizenship is coextensive with maintaining or reasserting the primacy of state actors in the European political order. Some acknowledgement of the important role of state actors may follow from the ideas of democratic citizenship, as conclusion stands to premiss, but this is a far cry from saying that the two propositions are logically equivalent and function as identical or similar elements in an argument. Most obviously, the political and economic conditions under which the goods of democratic citizenship can be reliably enjoyed may, for a whole variety of reasons, require some changes in the distribution of political authority from the nation-state to other levels of governance. Indeed, on further enquiry, it may well be that the ideals of democratic citizenship can only be realised in an ever closer union of European democracies. To rule out such a possibility is to confuse the values of democracy with the manner in which those values are institutionalised in any particular political form.

Notice that all three questions of political legitimacy have a practical as well as a theoretical interpretation. Within a number of member states, it has become increasingly the case that treaty changes need to be ratified by popular referendum. Even when there is no constitutional requirement, a political decision is sometimes taken that a referendum is politically essential. Moreover, to the extent to which party competition in member states refers to issues of European integration, questions about the democratic political legitimacy of the EU are involved. I am not claiming that voting in referendums on EU treaty changes in fact involves a high level of sophisticated reasoning on the part of the average voter. But it is clear that any answer one gives to the questions of political legitimacy potentially have implications for the practical choices that individual citizens have to make about the disposition of their vote or the aim of any other political action they might take.

Given these questions, what contribution can we expect from an analysis in normative political theory? After all, we might be content to say that citizens can have varying reasons for evaluating the EU in different ways and all that is of interest is the choices they make rather than the way in which one might, in principle, reason and argue about such matters. What distinguishes an analysis in normative political theory from the sort of practical reasoning in which any citizen might engage when deciding, say, on how to cast a vote in a referendum? The next section will examine this issue.

Practical reasoning and democratic citizenship

Many problems in normative political theory have a familiar ring to them. What is the justification for punishment? Why are citizens obliged to obey the state? Do markets produce just outcomes? Is it ever right to intervene in the domestic politics of another country? The everyday familiarity of these and similar questions discussed by normative political theorists might suggest that such theorists were simply engaged in partisan exposition rather than intellectual analysis. However, this is one of those cases where appearances are deceptive. The main way in which reasoning in normative political theory is distinguished from the ordinary processes of political argument and discussion is that normative theorists typically impose a number of constraints on what counts as a valid argument when they seek to establish a conclusion about such matters. If so, then a crucial element in any theoretical analysis is formed by the constraints that the theorist imposes on admissible arguments.

The constraints that I shall accept derive from the assumption that it is possible to treat the problem of political legitimacy as one of the practical rationality of democratic citizenship. There are two elements to this central idea: that of practical rationality and that of citizenship. Practical rationality rests on the idea familiar at least since Aristotle's exposition that people act from deliberation and that they have reasons for their actions. The idea is a generic one and applies in principle to all forms of human action – from eating to voting or from marrying to going on holiday – that are not the product of reflex or habit. We reason about the best train to catch, which party to vote for at an election, where to spend our holidays, how much effort we should put into obtaining promotion, how much to save for our retirement and so on. In its most general form, all that the theory of practical rationality says is that in making such choices we engage in a consideration of reasons, and that this process of considering reasons will typically exhibit certain structural features. As Kenny (1975: 70) has noted, it is indisputable that practical reasoning takes place. The problem of analysis is how to account for it and what patterns it exhibits.

If we ask what reasons democratic citizens might have for accepting the political legitimacy of the European Union, we can interpret this question in at least two ways. In the first way, we may treat this as an empirical question. In this form we are asking what reasons are likely in practice to move people to a conclusion and decision one way or another. For example, we might consider their position in the occupational structure (are they farmers or businesspeople?), and think what reasons typically occur to people in those positions when they think about such matters. In this mode, we set out to explain someone's action by appealing to the reasons that person holds, and we make no judgement about the character or quality of the reasoning involved. In this sense of reasons, persons can just as well act from mistaken as from sound reasoning.

However, if we ask what reasons people can have for favouring a course of action or policy, we may be thinking in normative terms. What reasons ought to occur to someone when he or she is undertaking a course of action, evaluating a set of alternatives or casting a vote in an election or referendum? We sometimes mark the distinction here linguistically by talking about 'good' reasons, rather than reasons *simpliciter*. In a normative theory of democratic citizenship, we are concerned with reasoning in this 'good' reasons sense, and a central task of a normative theory is to characterise what it is that might make a set of reasons good. In discussing the political legitimacy of European integration, we are engaging in a normative argument. In particular, we are looking at the issues from the viewpoint of a normative account of democratic citizenship. Of course, citizenship is a category used in the law, but we are looking at the matter from the point of view of political theory. We are concerned not with the implications of existing legal rules, but with issues of political morality. What can count as a legitimate structure of political authority in relation to the EU?

In the present context, the relevant form of practical reasoning, I suggest, is that related to occupying a role. When we deliberate within our own soul and with others, we often do so in terms of the roles we occupy. What should I do as a parent, a teacher or a friend? Implicit in this process is the idea that roles have norms attached to them, and that, barring exceptional circumstances, the norms of the role provide reasons for action. The role of being a citizen in a democracy contains such implicit norms and by examining these norms and applying them to political questions, we can have a basis for reasoning about political issues.

We are familiar in all practical choices with reasoning about what we should do from the roles that we occupy. Roles can be thought of as a set of recognised positions, each with its own power of action, to which normative expectations and entitlements attach for occupants of those roles (compare Emmet, 1966: 138–82; Hollis and Smith, 1990: 155). One reason for approaching the problem of political legitimacy in this way is that it allows us to consider that problem in terms of the rationality of occupying a particular role, that of citizenship, on the assumption that we have some understanding about the logic of role rationality. One of the ways in which reasons can be objectivised is by appealing to the role that someone occupies. If someone asks, in relation to any particular practical matter, 'why should I undertake a particular course of action?', it is standardly part of an answer to reply that the action in question is properly something expected of someone occupying a certain role. Roles bring with them responsibilities. Consider a simple, if miscellaneous list. Parents are rightly expected to be interested in the well-being of their children; teachers are expected to follow the progress of their students; doctors are supposed to protect the confidentiality of their patients; bankers are supposed to manage the financial affairs of their clients prudently, and so on. The appeal to the normative expectations that go along with a role is a common means that persons offer to one another, and sometimes to themselves, for behaving in one way rather than another.

In highlighting the place of role-related reasoning in our understanding of practical rationality I am not supposing that such reasoning is unproblematic in all respects. If the interests or ambitions of individuals conflict with the requirements of their roles, there are a familiar range of questions that emerge about the compatibility of acting as one ought compared with acting as one wants. Where the demands of a role appear irksome or onerous, occupants of a role often ask what other reasons, apart from their role occupancy, they might have for acting in a certain way. For this reason, if no other, appeal to the obligations attached to a role may still need to be accounted for in terms of more comprehensive accounts of practical reasoning and morality. What is more, even if people are motivated solely by conscientious considerations, so that they do not feel their role obligations as such to be burdensome, the appeal to role-related reasons may become problematic when the requirements of two roles conflict with one another, so that the occupant of the role is confronted with equally pressing but incompatible obligations. Indeed, on one famous account of morality – that of Hegel (1807: 484–91) – it was just such a conflict in the case of Antigone that led to the development of a self-conscious moral system (compare Shklar, 1976: 57–95).

I do not wish to underplay either of these difficulties in making an appeal to the advantages of role-related rationality in understanding the problem of political legitimacy in terms of the notion of democratic citizenship. A full understanding of the basic principles of political morality is likely to play a key part in understanding both why one is obliged to act in accordance with the demands of the role one occupies and how to resolve the conflict of role obligations when they arise. However, I propose that it is still worthwhile exploring how far we can get with role-related practical reasoning for a number of reasons.

Note firstly that the relevant account of practical reason required is one that is aimed at citizens who are already embedded in ongoing political systems, and who see themselves as citizens of democracies living under the circumstances of democratic citizenship. We do not require an account of practical reasoning *tout court*. The question concerns the reasons that such democratic citizens might have for accepting the legitimacy of European integration, even though they might also accept that it arose by a process of permissive consensus. This makes the purely theoretical problem of practical rationality easier. We are not asking a question about rationality considered in the abstract, even though there are grounds – as the work of Gewirth (1978 and 1996; for an application to citizenship and the EU, see Dobson, 2003) and O'Neill (1989) suggests – for thinking that we can get a reasonably strong notion of practical rationality simply from an analysis of the concept of rationality as such. However, deriving reasons for action from an understanding of rationality as such is not our project here. In theoretical terms, it is the much more modest project of asking what reasons those who conceive of themselves as democratic citizens in Europe might have for accepting the legitimacy of the construction and functioning of the EU.

There is no generally accepted normative theory to which we can appeal to resolve difficult or unanswered questions about the morality of roles. It might be that Kantianism, utilitarianism or some other theory has the answer, but since there is continuing dispute about the plausibility of each of these theories appealing to any one of them is less likely to resolve first-order moral conflicts than simply raise them to a higher level of abstraction. Moreover, it is unlikely that any normative theory can be validated without use of the method of reflective equilibrium, by which the plausibility of any putative theory of normative reasoning is examined in terms of whether it yields implications that accord with our most considered convictions. These convictions will include role-related obligations, which, insofar as they are being used to provide some validation for the normative theory, will be more firmly rooted – by definition – in our thinking than any general theory of political morality is likely to be.

I have already noted that the development of the EU took place through the permissive consensus of public opinion. To say this is to say that for much of the period of its development and expansion there was no institutionalised process of public reasoning taking place in the relevant democracies. However, the point about reasons is not that they should always be offered – sometimes for example decisions have to be made too quickly or under external pressure for there to be a process of public reasoning which takes place – but rather that reasons could be offered. Thus, to treat the problem of the political legitimacy of the EU as one about the practical rationality of democratic citizenship is to ask what reasons could be offered to citizens, who took their role seriously, for accepting the legitimacy of the political order that had been created. The next chapter will examine how those reasons may be specified.

Notes

1   This account deliberately does not distinguish a realist (for example, Garrett, 1992; Hoffmann, 1966; Moravcsik, 1998 and Taylor, 1983) narrative of European integration from a functionalist one (for example, Haas, 1968; Lindberg, 1963; Mitrany, 1975; and Schmitter, 1996). Neither family of approach is stated in terms that enable the main propositions to be empirically tested (Weale *et al.*, 2000: 15–25), and in any case a functionalist process may well be an implication of realist constraints. By extension, the institutionalisation of policy principles and processes means that institutionalist accounts of how the EU works may be combined with accounts drawn from other traditions as to the origins of those institutions (Peterson, 1995a).

2
Democratic citizenship

One advantage of looking at the problem of EU legitimacy in terms of the norms of democratic citizenship is that the role of citizen has a public meaning that makes it a useful instrument of intellectual analysis. The role is a public one in a number of senses. Many of its rights and duties are legally defined, and thus have been developed through processes of legislative deliberation and refinement in the courts. Theorists of citizenship as diverse as Rousseau, John Stuart Mill and T. H. Green have stressed the extent to which the role of citizen requires individuals to extend their horizons of perception and sympathy to take into account some more general or public interest, and a precondition for this to take place is that there be some broad, if tacit, acceptance of what is a matter for public deliberation and judgement and what can be treated as a private matter. This is not to say that the boundaries between public and private are fixed; changes are taking place all the time in response to new social issues. However, such changes take place against a relatively stable background, the result of which is that there is a contrast between the role of citizen, where expectations are relatively fixed, and other roles where there may be much greater variability of judgement as to what is involved.

One way of approaching these issues is via the Rawlsian account of citizens and their powers. For Rawls (1996: 18–19), within the tradition of democratic thought, we are to think of citizens as free and equal persons. As such, citizens have two sets of powers: a capacity for a conception of the good and a capacity for a sense of justice. The fundamental idea of fair cooperation is that citizens will only advance their own conception of the good publicly to the extent to which it is fair for them to do so. In other words, they are not asked to give up on their sense of their own interests, but they are asked to restrain pursuit of those interests to the extent to which that is required for fairness. Thus, the task for a theory of citizenship is to find a form of political association in which individuals can pursue their own conception of the good without unfairly interfering with the ability of other individuals to pursue their own conception of the good.

One advantage of thinking in terms of these basic principles is that we are not tied to any particular conception of the form of political association within which the values of democratic citizenship are to be realised. Rawls's own work on *The Law of Peoples* (Rawls, 1999b) places him in a broadly civic nationalist camp, in which it is assumed that peoples constitute societies and societies in this sense provide the framework of political organisation. In this respect Rawls offers us an account of democratic citizenship that presupposes the nation-state. In contrasting the Monnet narrative of European integration with Rokkan's narrative of state-building in Europe in Chapter 1, I have already stressed the extent to which the integration narrative challenges the assumption that political association should be thought of exclusively in nation-state terms. The conception of democratic citizenship that Rawls lays out is one that presupposes forms of political association that are closer to Rokkan's narrative than they are to the integration narrative. The implication of this, discussed further in Chapter 3, is not that democratic citizenship is necessarily tied to the nation-state, but that we need to theorise adequately the general concept of a political association, rather than just remain content with conceptions of political association drawn from existing practices.

I should stress that the account I offer here takes the Rawlsian idea of the two powers of democratic citizenship as the organising framework, but does not develop it in a specifically Rawlsian way and those who wish to remain faithful to the text of Rawls will have much to dispute in my analysis. In particular, Rawls is careful to distinguish fairness from impartiality (Rawls, 1996: 16–17; 54), thinking of the latter as a form of altruism that goes beyond justice. By contrast I shall use the term 'impartiality' to designate a range of principles of fairness that may govern the relationship of citizens in a democratic order. Rawls also sees a well-ordered society as something other than an association, on the grounds that unlike an association a society is neither something that is entered into voluntarily nor does it have specific purposes of its own. By contrast, I shall designate any political order as a form of association. More substantively, I also dispute Rawls's exclusion of conceptions of the good from the scope of political deliberation. My excuse for committing these heresies relies upon Rawls's own well-known distinction between concept and conceptions. Rawls's concept of democratic citizenship as involving the two powers is an important and insightful one. Those who wish to think about the implications of citizenship in particular cases can acknowledge this without following Rawls himself in his particular conceptions.

The goods of citizenship

The first element in the Rawlsian concept of democratic citizenship is that citizens have a conception of their own good. The dominant post-war account of citizenship that I identified in Chapter 1 made civil, political and social rights central to an understanding of democratic citizenship. Why then should we approach the understanding of citizenship in the language of goods and the good, rather than in terms of the language of rights?

When Marshall spoke of the rights of citizenship, he was speaking of positive rights, primarily rights that were established through policy and legislation. In other words, his was a sociological thesis. Any claim about positive rights leaves open the issue of what normative backing there might be for such claims to positive rights. It may be correct to conceive of positive rights as receiving the backing of moral rights, but there is no necessity to do so, and if we have reasons for favouring an alternative view, there is nothing in the sociological claim that restricts us to the moral vocabulary of rights. Logically, moreover, the category of goods is more basic than that concept of rights, in the sense that to have rights is normally thought of as being to one's good, whereas not all goods are to be thought of in terms of rights. So, whereas we can define rights as a certain type of good, we cannot define all goods as particular forms of rights.

The most important goods that are not assimilable to the category of rights are public goods, like environmental protection. Environmental public goods are standardly defined as those goods or benefits from which no one can be excluded. Such benefits are not happily conceived in terms of rights distributed among individuals each of whom could, in theory, choose whether or not to exercise the right. Instead, the scope and level of environmental protection is necessarily going to be decided through a process of collective decision. It might be argued that this definitional gambit moves too quickly. There is a function of rights discourse in which it makes sense to bracket environmental protection together with the standard social and economic rights. To speak of rights is to speak of those goods to which people are entitled by virtue of their status as citizens rather than some other ground of allocation. Moreover, it is to speak of entitlements that are thought to be at a standard of provision that can be justified in terms of some principles of political morality. From this point of view, citizens can attach as much importance to environmental protection as they do to social rights. As an example, consider that for parents it is as important that when their children go swimming they can do so in safe waters as when they go to school they have a sound education. Although the good of a clean environment is public by virtue of its intrinsic characteristics, it is enjoyed at the individual level, just as is the benefits of health care or of income maintenance.

In this form of discourse the force of using the term 'right' is not that of indicating entitlements that individuals might or might not choose to take up but rather of stressing that certain benefits should be given priority in public policy and the good that is provided to individuals in terms of these benefits is particularly important. Thus, when people say that citizens have a right to a high level of environmental protection, they are not indicating that citizens individually have acquired a power that they did not have before. Rather they are saying that it is a matter of justice or high public priority that citizens be secured the benefits of environmental protection. Though a common way of speaking, I suggest that it is unhelpful to confuse the specific notion of a right with what it is right for citizens to have. For the sake of clarity, it is better to make the concept of the goods of citizenship basic, and acknowledge that some specific and important goods that democratic citizens enjoy are civil, political and social rights, while others take the form of public goods.

Taking the concept of the good as the basic category of analysis, there are broadly speaking three accounts of the notion to be found in normative political theory. Firstly, there is a subjective interpretation, in which to say that something contributes to a person's good is to say that it makes for the satisfaction of that person's preferences. However, a problem with this way of thinking is that people can adapt their preferences to their circumstances, and happy slaves might be better off changing their preferences than having them satisfied. This thought leads on to the second sense of the good as doing well according to some objective measure, like the possession of property. However, this conception can ignore differences between people in terms of their capacity to take advantage of their objective circumstances. Hence, a third conception of the good would make the capacity to take advantage of one's possessions an essential element of doing well. A satisfactory overall conception of the good would have to bring these ideas together in some coherent way.

Fortunately, in the present context, these foundational questions are not at issue. Since there is a generally accepted account of the goods of democratic citizenship, the normative question concerns the extent to which the political development of the EU threatens the achievements of what Marshall termed the democratic-welfare-capitalist society. Moreover, although goods rather than rights is the primary category of analysis, within democratic societies of the sort in mind here the concept of rights marks a distinctive form of the human good. Rights do not comprise all the goods of citizenship, but they do involve an important sub-class, and arguably define some distinctive features of citizenship in the modern state.

Here it is useful to draw on the logical parallels between legal and moral rights and in particular to draw upon Hohfeld's (1923) analysis of legal rights. According to Hohfeld, rights may be thought of as a mixture of liberties, claims, powers and immunities. Within the Hohfeldian scheme a liberty is a right to compete for some good with others who also have similar liberties, and where no party is under an obligation to allow the other to secure the right. For example, those seeking for sunken treasure have a liberty right to search, but they are not under an obligation to allow other treasure seekers to get there first. Hohfeldian claims, by contrast, are rights in which there is a corresponding duty holder who has the responsibility to ensure that the claim is met should it be exercised. The clearest example of claim rights for citizens are rights to social security, health care or education in the welfare state when these take the form of entitlements. For example, if on retirement citizens are entitled to receive an income, and the social security system is under an obligation to pay, then we may say that citizens in this respect have claim rights in the Hohfeldian sense.

The third Hohfeldian category is that of rights as powers. A power in this sense is a right to bring about some change in the world or pattern of relationships that has significance. The right to vote is a power in this sense, as is the right of the members of a jury to decide whether the accused is innocent or guilty.

There are many rights of citizenship which if not exclusively powers have a large element in them of powers in this sense, including the right to vote, the rights to freedom of association, freedom of movement and the rights to form political parties. The fourth and final element in the Hohfeldian scheme are immunities, regarded as freedoms from having duties imposed upon one from others. The freedom to practise one's religion or certain forms of freedom of expression can be viewed in this way. When the US constitution forbids Congress making a law that abridges freedom of speech, it is in effect bestowing an immunity upon citizens from the otherwise legitimate exercise of powers by Congress. Similarly, the freedom that citizens enjoy in constitutional states from arbitrary stop and search powers exercised by the police can also be regarded as an immunity.

Conceptions of citizenship correspond in part to different ways in which the rights of citizenship are specified in Hohfeldian terms. The move away from a poor law system in which public officials had the discretion to make payments depending on their assessment of the 'deservingness' of recipients, to a system in which a social security record gave one an entitlement to income, marked a sharp change in the character of the rights involved. Under poor law systems, citizens had a right to claim poor law relief, but those responsible for administering public funds were not under a duty to award relief conditional upon the claimant satisfying certain conditions. With the invention of social security systems in the mid-twentieth century, the character of the right to social security changed and this was part and parcel of a broader change in the general conception of citizenship and the way in which citizens were related to the state and to one another. Similarly, the right to work changed character in the twentieth century from the old laissez-faire notion of a right to compete with others for work if it could be found to a right to be secured work if it was feasible for governments to create the conditions of full employment (Weale, 1983: 126). Feinberg (1970) has gone so far as to say that the notion of being able to claim one's rights and insist that they be met is precisely what marks out a world with rights from a world without rights. This is perhaps another way of saying that within the category of Hohfeldian rights, claim rights are likely to be among the most politically important.

It is not a straightforward matter to know when changes in the ways that rights are conceived modify a particular conception of citizenship and when the changes are so serious or wide-ranging that they can be said to change the conception of citizenship. It would, I think, be artificial to try to come up with some general criterion in terms of which this distinction could be made. It is more a matter of considering particular transitions in the way that rights are conceived and making a judgement in those particular cases as to whether the changes are serious enough to warrant our saying that we have witnessed a shift from one conception to another as distinct from a shift within a conception. Where there is a set of wide-ranging changes in the way that rights are conceived, as happened with the rights that accompanied the rise and consolidation of the welfare state, then we may say that there has been a change in the conception of citizenship.

In discussing the goods of citizenship, I have presented them in individualist terms in the following sense. Although the goods may be provided through collective provision, and indeed in some cases – such as the right to vote – it does not make sense to think about the right apart from the social practice of which it is a part, the goods that they provide are ones that can be enjoyed by individuals and are valued because they are enjoyed by individuals. Indeed, the point of any collective provision is to enable individuals to gain access to these goods. Hence, accepting the collective dimension of provision does not imply any form of ethical collectivism in the sense that value is attached to the good of the collective in itself, for example as once it was common for some people to say that the purpose of the state was to fulfil the destiny of the nation. Rather, collective action will sometimes be the best means to secure individual benefit.

It may be argued that this takes too narrow a view of collective goods and their relation to the good of individuals. On one view, individuals can only flourish to the extent to which the collective entity in which they are embedded flourishes. However, while this may be true, it is only true empirically and not by virtue of the way in which the concept of the good functions. For those individuals who find their personal flourishing in their participation in a flourishing national culture, it will of course be true that their doing well depends upon the national culture doing well. However, there will be empirical variation in the extent to which the members of any society will define their personal good in a way that presupposes such a close relation of dependence. Within even strong national cultures there are normally sub-groups and dissidents, who will think of their good as consisting in the weakening or attenuation of the dominant national culture.

Of course it may still be argued that it is good for individuals, even dissident or minority individuals, if a national culture flourishes because the national culture will provide a context in which there are fewer social and political conflicts, and therefore the individual benefits of personal security and prosperity will be promoted. We cannot rule this possibility out, although its demonstration would require a great deal of empirical evidence to support it. What we can say is that the goods that are being aimed at, if this is the argument, are the goods of individuals and the protection of the collective good is only an indirect way of securing these. Moreover, this way of arguing stands in only an indirect relation to democratic rights. After all, the good of a national culture may be secured without democratic rights by a traditional form of political authority.

Citizenship and impartiality

The previous section focused on the goods of citizenship, conceiving them both as public goods and as the rights of citizenship taking the form of powers, rights and benefits enjoyed by individuals. But to produce the goods of citizenship requires the cooperation of citizens in forms of political association and these goods cannot be produced unless citizens undertake certain responsibilities. In a democracy this relationship of production and enjoyment takes a specific form. The fundamental idea is that a democracy is, by definition, a political system in which the principle of political equality governs the relationships between citizens. This requires citizens to treat one another as equals in their political dealings and this in turn implies an attitude of impartiality. When acting as citizens, individuals should weigh the claims of others along with their own, and they should look at public issues not from the point of view of their own special interest but from the viewpoint of the general interest.

Democratic theorists have long stressed the extent to which citizenship in a democracy requires individuals to take a larger and more encompassing point of view in making political decisions than simply consulting their own interests. For example, in his discussion of the virtues of citizens in a democracy, John Stuart Mill (1861a) assumes that democratic practice contributes to the raising of the moral character of citizens. By participating in public functions, something that everyone is expected to do on at least some occasions, democratic citizens learn to weigh interests that are not their own. They come to understand what it is to be guided by a rule or principle that does not stem from one's own partialities. They apply principles and maxims that are aimed at the common good. They benefit from associating with other minds in these public tasks. They identify with the public interest and so go beyond selfishness. Without these experiences of being a citizen acting with other citizens, persons feel themselves in competition with their neighbours and this feeling can redound to the detriment of even private morality (Mill, 1861a: 255).

It might be argued that Mill's position on these matters is over-influenced by his general account of moral psychology in which the cultivation of an active character is seen to be an essential ingredient in personal moral development. Yet, there are at least two reasons why Mill's emphasis upon impartiality makes sense in any account of democratic citizenship. The first of these stems from the empirical relation between rights and benefits on the one side and obligations and responsibilities on the other. Because the production of the rights and benefits requires citizens to have some sense of duty, citizens need to be able to weigh matters from more than one point of view. A second reason why an attitude of impartiality is implied by virtue of democratic citizenship is that citizens in a democracy are either directly or indirectly legislators. They are directly legislators when they vote in referendums, and they are indirectly legislators when they vote for representatives who are to make laws and policies for the society. There are good reasons why this task cannot properly be regarded merely as the registering of a personal preference, but instead has to be regarded as based, implicitly at least, upon the consideration of reasons that are in principle aimed at the assent of other citizens. From this point of view, exercising the rights of citizenship also involves recognising the obligation to explain and justify one's actions to others, or if not something as strong as this at least an understanding that one is not simply using the instruments of public deliberation to push for one's own narrow advantage. The obligation of impartiality applies to the reasons that citizens have individually, and distinguishes those reasons from ones that they may have from their own personal or sectional point of view.

The relevant distinctions are well expressed in the categories that Rousseau (1762) introduced when discussing the process of collective will formation. Rousseau imagines citizens as legislators, and in this role he conceives that it is possible that they can approach their task in two quite distinct frames of mind. In the first case, they undertake their legislative activity from the point of view of their 'partial wills' or, in other words, from reasons related to the sectional interests that they may have. From the second point of view, they cast their vote according to their understanding of the 'general will', or from reasons that they conceive of as being in the public interest. Note that this distinction between partial and general wills is a distinction at the level of individual voters. In this sense, we can ascribe the property of having a general will distributively to individuals. For Rousseau, the sum of partial wills results in the will of all, whereas the sum of individual general wills results in a collective general will. Only when everyone has been sincerely seeking the general will can we say that a genuine general will at the social level can emerge from voting, and it is only under these conditions that individual citizens can truly say, if they are in a minority, that they have mistaken the general will. The wills operative at the individual level determine the will operative collectively. The condition under which we can validly ascribe a general will collectively is that individuals have sought the general will as members of society.

Citizens, as individuals, are thus expected to step back from their immediate interests and perspective and take a broader point of view. Yet, this demand poses an obvious problem. To what extent and in what ways can citizens restrict and limit their own claims in a broader public interest? This problem is likely to be particularly acute within the framework of the sort of individualist theory of the good that I am presupposing more generally. Within a communitarian framework the problem is likely to seem less severe because within such a framework it is assumed that identities and interests are in large part at least constituted through one's membership of a particular community. One thinks of oneself as a citizen of this place or as an inheritor of a communal tradition. There are no such conceptual resources within an individualist framework. In the end one's good is personal, a product of the experiences and opportunities one has available. What might the obligation of impartiality mean in this context?

Chapter 3 will suggest that the stark contrast implicit here between individualism and communitarianism is misleading. Individuals may think of themselves as cooperating with one another in various ways to achieve a shared good. However, at this stage of the argument, I shall focus on the issue of the impartial attitude that is required by the role of citizenship and what it may be taken to require of individuals. Within the Rawlsian notion of the powers of citizenship, we need an account of the sense of fairness, and the task is to spell out what this sense of fairness might mean. In tackling this question, I suggest that we should not follow Rawls in being too univocal about the ways in which the idea of fair interaction can be spelt out. The notion of impartiality need not be defined in a singular way. In particular, I suggest that it be thought of as having at least four forms: non-exclusion of interests; non-exploitation; generalised reciprocity; and a willingness to compromise.

The elements of impartiality

The first element of a democratic impartialist attitude is what I shall term non-exclusion. By this I mean that in a society of democratic citizens there are no arbitrary or unfair exclusions from political and other rights. The clearest example of this principle at work is the extension of the franchise in democracies over the course of the twentieth century. Prior to the advent of mass democracy, the franchise was regarded as a privilege attendant upon property ownership. The erosion of this assumption and its replacement by the principle that all of those who had a long-term stake in the political community were entitled to some say in the running of its common affairs marks a process of democratic inclusion. Without pretending to write history on the basis of a priori reasoning, it is difficult not to see this shift as something inherent in the logic of democracy as a device for promoting the common interests of citizens. If public laws and policies affect individuals in serious ways, then it becomes extremely difficult to argue for the exclusion from political participation of any group that is resident in the political community and has a long-term stake in it.

The converse of this logic is that the exclusions that are practised are those that are consistent with the requirement that, if interests are being promoted by political means, then all who have a reasonable claim should be included. Thus, the exclusion of the young from voting can be justified on the grounds that it is not the exclusion of a group as such but an exclusion that all pass through on their way to an age when it is reasonable to assume competence. Similarly, the exclusion of short-term residents can be justified on the grounds that their interests are not as intimately bound up with the political decisions that need to be made as that of permanent or long-term residents. The logic here is one of defeasibility. We make the assumption that all who are affected in a given territorial area should be included, unless specific reasons can be shown why this assumption should be overturned.

From the point of view of citizens in general the principle of inclusion is to be seen as a requirement that citizens should impartially consider all affected interests and not arbitrarily exclude such interests from consideration in processes of public and private deliberation. If impartiality means, as Mill asserted, the weighing of interests other than one's own, then the requirement of non-exclusion is that there be no unjustifiable limits to the definition of what the relevant interests are. So, from the point of view of the responsible citizen, impartiality means not simply weighing the interests and opinions that are presented in a public debate, but also asking the question as to whether there are any other interests that may currently be marginalised that should be present in the public debate.

The second element of impartiality is the principle of non-exploitation. The rationale of this requirement is to be found in what would otherwise be a deficiency in the concept of a democratic political community. A democratic political community is one in which citizens regard one another as equals in the process of political cooperation for common interests. However, it is not enough for genuine political equality to say that citizens regard one another as equals. There must be a sense in which their respective situations are sufficiently comparable for their cooperation to be genuinely one of cooperation rather than one-sided use by one group and unwilling acquiescence by another. If it is not, then the more vulnerable groups risk being exploited by the better off group. In making this claim, I am not saying that there is a direct line of argument from political equality to economic and social equality. It is clearly possible for there to be genuine equality of political status among individuals who experience very different economic and social fortunes (though it typically takes effort on the part of the fortunate not to ascribe their good luck to their personal merits). What it is difficult to envisage is cooperation as political equals among persons some of whom are destitute and others of whom are affluent. From this point of view, the good of association with other minds, which Mill identified as part of the enlargement of individual sympathies, is lost.

In some ways this principle of non-exploitation is closely tied to the logic of inclusion, as Mill noted in his discussion of political representation. If certain classes are excluded from political representation, according to Mill, then their opinions are simply ignored or not advocated forcefully enough. If such groups are at an economic disadvantage, then any action that they take to try to improve their situation (Mill has in mind the use of the strike as an instrument of bargaining on the part of workers) will be misunderstood in public deliberation. Exclusion and exploitation thus go together. By the same token, a concern to foster background fairness in the distribution of social and economic advantages enables the participation of groups and individuals on terms of political equality, and thus enables other citizens to judge impartially the full range of relevant claims that may be advanced in respect of specific issues.

The third element of impartiality is to be found in the principle of generalised reciprocity and the best illustration of the operation of this principle is to be found in the institutional basis of the welfare state. The welfare state is a system of social insurance resting upon a contributory principle. In effect the development of welfare states in post-war Europe rested in large part on a diffusion of the German model of social insurance pioneered under Bismarck. There were of course many specific variations in respect of the implementation of the social insurance and in respect of those born with inherited disability, it has been recognised that an unmodified social insurance principle cannot apply. However, for a central range of benefits, most notably those connected with sickness and old age, the social insurance principle is what defines the terms of citizen entitlements.

The principle of social insurance, in its pure forms, rests upon the idea that redistribution is not a matter of the transfer of resources from rich to poor, but is instead the transfer of resources within income categories across the life-cycle. The general principle of insurance is that contributors make payments into the insurance fund in order to obtain the right to draw down benefits when they are needed. Social insurance makes the payments compulsory, usually only for those in work, in exchange for making the right to benefit universal. Whatever specific arrangements obtain, however, the principle at work is one of reciprocity. Citizens are behaving impartially towards one another when they make the contributions to the social insurance fund as the acknowledgement of the reciprocal obligation they owe to others for the right to make claims under the appropriate circumstances.

It may be thought that the principle of reciprocity in inadequate as an explication of the idea of impartiality. Brian Barry (1989) has urged a clear distinction between principles of impartiality and principles of reciprocity, on the grounds that the latter will ignore the unequal starting point of those entering into reciprocal obligations with one another. Barry is surely right to say that, if we made such a principle the sole basis for the distribution of benefits and social advantages, we would allow a situation in which the poor could be exploited by the rich because of the latter's unequal bargaining power. As the old Yiddish proverb has it: if the rich could pay someone to die for them, the poor could make a wonderful living.

However, Barry's line of argument, though correct in some general sense, is less telling than one might think against the interpretation of impartiality as requiring reciprocity in the welfare state. The system of reciprocity that is involved in social insurance is generalised rather than bilateral reciprocity. In turn this involves a higher degree of pooling of risks and benefits than would be true of the purely commercial sort of exchange that is built up as a result of a series of bilateral contracts in insurance markets. The compulsory nature of the scheme also means that the wealthy who might otherwise have an incentive to forgo their rights because the rights would not be justified by the expected benefits are nonetheless required to continue to contribute. Indeed, in some systems they are required to continue to contribute, even though, if they are very wealthy, they are not eligible for the benefits.

The fourth element of impartiality can be phrased in terms of a willingness to compromise where it is impossible to find widespread agreement among citizens (Bellamy, 1999: 93–114; see also Bellamy and Warleigh, 1998). In part, this obligation can be seen in the willingness of citizens in a democracy to limit the expression of their competing claims in the first place, illustrated in the norm that party competition be conducted fairly, and with limits on campaign funding. However, the willingness to compromise should also be seen in the form taken by public policy. Thus, a democratic principle of impartiality is illustrated when political parties do not design tax and public expenditure systems so as to secure rewards for their own political followers and impose burdens on those groups that support their opponents. As Bellamy stresses, compromise in this sense is not an attempt to stand in a neutral position, but to stand in a context-bound common position, or at least a position of mutual acccommodation.

Putting these four elements of impartiality together, two points in particular need to be made. The first is how undemanding in practice some of these obligations may be. Consider for example the obligation to make contributions to a common, compulsory social insurance fund. This system produced a high level of redistribution, much higher than had previously been secured in industrial societies. And yet the obligation was routinised in collection through the payroll system, in such a way that individual citizens did not need to make a choice or endorse the specific levels of payment involved. Similarly, in elections the choice of public policy effectively became a choice between competing parties and candidates, a choice that was simplified in terms of the cues that political parties were able to give about their general position in the left–right spectrum. Moreover, once television became the primary method by which voters acquired political information, they were not even required to read up on party positions, let alone familiarise themselves with the details of party programmes. Citizenship was made as user-friendly as it could be. And yet, in many ways, the political system in which this user-friendly form of citizenship was embedded was remarkably successful. Whatever else might be said about the duties of citizenship, it cannot be supposed that they are too ambitious to be promoted in political life.

The second point is that there is no reason to think that these different elements of an impartial attitude cohere with one another in a consistent way. One obvious point of tension is that between the non-exploitation and reciprocity principles, already alluded to and which will be discussed in more detail in Chapter 4. Although we may wish to assert of democracies that they are characterised by certain key ideas, there is no need to assume that these ideas form part of a fully coherent system. Indeed, in some ways the practice of politics can be seen as a way of resolving tensions that are found in the operative principles of a democratic order.

Two objections to impartiality

It can be argued that the principle of impartiality is not general to the concept of citizenship, but is instead part of a specific conception of citizenship, perhaps one identifiable with work in republican or liberal traditions of political theory. Other, less demanding, conceptions of citizenship would not impose this requirement. For example, on some interpretations, democratic pluralists do not endorse a principle of impartiality. Thus, some proponents of deliberative democracy contrast their position, which involves citizens deliberating with one another impartially in a search for the common good, with that of pluralists, who are supposed to hold that political decision making should be made by bargaining among competing social groups (Cohen, 1989: 20). The details of such a pluralist theory – if indeed there is a position that has been marked out in this way – are less important than the general conception. We might construct such a position along the following lines.

Suppose we thought, for example, that stable democratic societies were characterised by a series of cross-cutting cleavages. Thus, social groups could be thought of as divided along a series of lines (for example, workers versus owners, secularists versus the religious, and centre versus the periphery), with none of these lines of division being correlated with the others. Then, provided we thought that power was not too unevenly spread among the different social groups, we could envisage democracy not as deliberation under conditions of impartiality but rather as bargaining among those pressing their own interests and opinions within an agreed framework of legitimate competition. According to this conception members of social groups relate to one another as citizens, but only insofar as they accept common rules of political competition. There is no need for the members of these competing groups to look at issues of public policy as citizens sharing certain common interests. Putting the point in another idiom, such citizens would bargain rather than discuss with one another.

This conception is one that is often ascribed to pluralist authors such as Lipset (1963). I leave aside here the question of whether this is a plausible characterisation of Lipset's position (for the record I do not think it is), and simply note that, even if someone could use such an account to explain why certain structures of social cleavage produce stable democracies, it is a far cry to infer an evaluation from such an explanation. Moreover, there is clearly a danger in this critique of pluralism of moving fallaciously from statements about the form that competition takes within a given system to conclusions about the characteristics of the system itself. Suppose that public policy could be made through the competition of political forces within an agreed framework of rules, there would still need to be agreement on those rules and such an agreement would constitute one of the common interests of citizens. After all, the competition of interests in such a system must be the competition of interests regarded as legitimate, and so the test of legitimacy is one that in principle must be met from the point of view of all, or virtually all, citizens.

A second line of attack on an impartialist notion of citizenship comes from certain strands of feminist theory. This approach does not deny that impartiality is part of the idea of citizenship according to some conceptions, but it asserts that any such conception is gender-specific and therefore contestable. If an ethic of impartiality contains a gender bias, any conception of citizenship that rested upon or appealed to such an ethic will be deficient. Feminist ethics, it is suggested, offers ethics 'in a different voice', with a greater emphasis upon personal relationships by contrast with the impersonalism of an impartialist ethic. There are clearly a very large number of questions here, and a proper response would take more space than I have available. However, there are a number of points that need to be noted.

First, there is a useful and important distinction between first-order and second-order impartiality. The proponent of impartiality does not have to claim that people should be impartial in their dealings with everyone else, acting like a dessicated calculating machine in their interactions with others. Relations of kinship, family and friendship will make people disposed to undertake special efforts to protect and promote the interests and well-being of some others with whom they come into contact. At this first-order level, therefore, there can be extensive forms of partiality. However, it is consistent with recognising these first-order attachments that people can also recognise, at the second-order level, the requirements of impartiality. This recognition can have a number of different aspects. If I claim an entitlement to be partial towards my own children, then I am (impartially) bound to recognise that you are entitled to be partial to your children. From this it also follows that each person can recognise the boundaries of partiality. While I may be acting within my entitlements to give my child the best education, it would not be right for me to construe this entitlement as involving the permissibility of bribing the teachers at the school to give more attention or better marks to my child in preference to others. Partiality – which is just another name for special care and attention – in some respects does not imply the permissibility of partiality in all respects.

It can be argued that the distinction between first and second-order attitudes is artificial to the extent to which in practice the courses of action indicated by each conflict with one another (Mendus, 2002). We can accept that reading to one's children to support their school work is permissible and bribing the teachers is impermissible. These practices fall clearly either side of the line that is demarcated in terms of the distinction between the engagement of the parent and the recognition of social obligations by the citizen. What about more intermediate cases however? Does a concern for the impartial requirements of citizenship mean that parents should not buy a private education for their children, or must not use their superior wealth to buy a house within the catchment area of a good school? Would the demands of impartiality on citizens mean that they could not buy advantageous health care for themselves or their children, perhaps even in the case where the care was potentially life-saving? Why should we think impartiality a requirement of citizenship in the face of these questions?

In fact, as it seems to me, the existence of these sorts of dilemmas is evidence for, rather than against, the value of impartiality as constitutive of citizenship. Citizenship is a role distinct from other roles that we play in society. It would be an improbably well-ordered universe in which the obligations that went with all the roles we occupied cohered together without any conflict. That we should feel a conflict in these cases is evidence that the requirements of impartiality have independent weight; that we should feel these as pressing conflicts is evidence of the seriousness with which we take such obligations.

The argument for impartiality can be taken further by noting that it stands in a complex set of relationships with the personal attachments that make life worthwhile. As Susan James (1992) has noted, the ability of citizens to take up an impartial point of view depends upon a number of conditions being satisfied, including physical and financial security. However, it also requires an emotional security. To feel confident in making my contribution to public debate I also need to have a sufficient sense of self-esteem and self-respect to think that my views are worth being heard. However, the sense of self-esteem and self-respect is developed in the caring relationships in which the child grows up. Hence an ethic of care is needed to underpin the requirements of impartial citizenship. Here we have not an antinomy but a complementarity. In a similar vein, Mendus (2002) has argued that impartiality grows out of the moral component of the special attachments that we feel towards others. Friendship means that out of respect for their needs and interests one refrains from asking favours of one's friends that it would be difficult for them to give.

Does the appeal to an ethic of impartiality rest upon an unrealistic distinction between the public and the private sphere, however, as some forms of feminist analysis have suggested? It is certainly true that many forms of state practice have entrenched this distinction in ways that have been disadvantageous to women, with perhaps the clearest example being policies towards domestic rape and violence in many states. However, it does not follow from this observation that there can be no valid distinction between the public and the private domains, and indeed feminist demands in other areas – for example the exclusion of a woman's sexual history as evidence in rape trials – tacitly presuppose the rightfulness of such a distinction. Perhaps, however, the public character of citizenship is secured through practices that ensure the private subordination of women. Men enter the public realm having their domestic needs secured by women, just as Athenian citizens entered the public realm having had their domestic needs secured by women and slaves (see Vogel, 1991). Yet, although the empirical observation underlying this point may be valid, it is not clear what inference should be drawn. We can maintain the emphasis upon the public and impartial character of citizenship, but insist that the implication is that all citizens – both men and women – need conditions of economic and social security in place in order that they can function properly in their role as citizens.

Some general issues

Reasons of fairness can restrain individuals in the pursuit of their own good. On one approach to public deliberation, reasons of fairness or political justice can enter into public deliberation, but individuals cannot advance considerations drawn from their own conception of the good to form part of the public purpose. On this view, citizens as citizens can share a sense of fairness but not a sense of the good. In this work, I will not assume this particular restriction. There is one particular argument for adopting this more open-ended strategy. If we simply assume that citizens can deliberate with one another about public purposes and policies in terms of principles of fairness to allocate private goods, we lose the possibility of democratic discussion about public goods. Such discussion is needed because we cannot assume that there is agreement about the form and scale of provision of public goods. There is unavoidably a political choice to be made about such provision, and this in turn means that democratic discussion and decision about the good is required. Inevitably, citizens approach these decisions in the light of their own overall conception of the good.

The effect of allowing in considerations drawn from particular conceptions of the good is that one is opening up the possibility that the objectification of reasons can extend beyond fairness to accounts of the good. How far can one seek to objectify practical rationality to this extent and still remain inside a broadly liberal political theory? Clearly, there are many contemporary strands of political liberalism that are sceptical of the possibility of agreement among citizens on a single conception of the good. In consequence, theorists often suggest a strategy of privatisation in relation to such questions. Liberalism has been defined as a want-regarding political theory, upholding the view that the role of the state is to satisfy peoples' wants, whatever those wants happened to be (Barry, 1965: 66). An analogy that is often implicit in this way of thinking is that between consumer sovereignty in the marketplace and the sovereignty of citizens in the realm of political decision making. The opposite point of view is sometimes labelled perfectionism. Perfectionism can still be individualistic, since to say that a policy will be good for one's soul is still to say that it will be good for *one's* soul. So, individualism about the good need not imply anti-perfectionism.

Though often invoked in support of anti-perfectionism, the analogy between consumer and citizen sovereignty does not hold insofar as the market is the realm of purely private decision making. Politics, by contrast, is quintessentially the realm of public decision making. In an economy is which there were *per impossibile* no public goods, like defence or law and order, and no externalities of consumption or production, like pollution, then it might make sense to think about each individual's decision forming the basis for the application of a general principle of consumer sovereignty. The decision of each would express the wants of each, and so an economy in equilibrium would in some sense maximally satisfy wants. However, political decisions are by definition the realm of collective choice, and as such are sharply distinguished from this model of a market satisfying wants. Political rules have to be common rules. This does not mean, of course, that these political rules cannot be thought of in want-satisfaction terms. It does at least mean that the conception of want-satisfaction has to be different in the political case from that of the market case. Indeed, to the extent to which a democratic political association requires its citizens to internalise a democratic culture in their attitudes and beliefs, it thereby requires citizens to exercise certain virtues, in particular the virtues associated with acting impartially. However, simply saying this does not of itself solve certain important and persisting questions in the theory of citizenship.

Rawls (1996: 54–8) advances the principle that in political democracies citizens should eschew metaphysically controversial ideas. Citizens should not seek to impose upon one another morally disputed conceptions of the good. If this argument works, then democratic citizenship would be by definition anti-perfectionist. Rawls himself gets to these anti-perfectionist conclusions by means of an appeal to the importance of stability in a situation of reasonable pluralism and the circumstances of the burdens of judgement. However, it is not clear that these premises yield the conclusions that Rawls supposed.

Consider first the burdens of judgement. The burdens of judgement show that there are good reasons for holding that no one can ever be in a position to settle morally controversial questions. Certainly, it is a morally controversial issue to know what is good for someone's soul or for his or her personal development more generally. However, exactly the same line of argument can be applied to almost any aspect of public policy. Consider fundamental questions of economic policy, for example the effects of various property rights regimes or of independent monetary authorities. Able economists are typically divided, for example, about the effects of land reform in raising economic growth in developing economies or about the effects of establishing strong independent monetary authorities in an economy. Exactly the same burdens of judgement that bedevil discussions of competing conceptions of the good also bedevil the settlement of issues under these headings. However, it is clear that no political democracy can avoid making choices even in the context of a high level of uncertainty about the correct resolution of these questions.

It may be argued at this point that, in the case of many competing conceptions of the good, it is not necessary to have a public resolution of the issues, and that an anti-perfectionist politics should be pursued as far as is practically possible. However, even this move may be said to beg some questions. Some might argue that certain conceptions of the good are more easily attained in communities where public practices and policies are supportive of individual effort, whether that be a public religion or laws that require citizens to vote. Certainly, if different faith communities are territorially intermingled, it may cause problems to enforce one particular pattern of observance, but this condition might not always obtain. Where faith communities are territorially concentrated, it is possible to practise the democratic version of the politics of *cuius regio, eius religio*. By the same token, democratic perfectionists might argue for the permissibility of a politics of active citizenship at least in communities that for historic or other reasons were disposed to be sympathetic to a democratic conception of the good. For example, it would be theoretically possible to argue for institutions like the referendum and the citizens' initiative not on the grounds that they offered protection for citizens against corrupt politicians but on the grounds that the participatory practices they fostered were good for the citizens concerned. For these reasons, I do not think that ethical and methodological individualists have an argument against perfectionist versions of their claims. Such disputes have to remain within the realm of the politically contentious.

Do these considerations mean that there is nothing of importance in the claim that politics is about want-satisfaction? That would be going too far. However, this particular liberal claim is best understood, I conjecture, if it is construed as a claim about the acceptable range of goals that governments should pursue. The relevant distinction is not between actual and reflectively derived wants, but between policies that are aimed at promoting identifiable human goods, goods that could themselves be the object of wants, as distinct from goals that aim at some putative supra-individual end. Goals that would fall into this second category would include such ends as claims to the 'manifest destiny' of a nation or claims to be 'in the march of history'. In other words, the thrust of the claim that liberalism is a want-regarding political theory should be thought of as the principle that collective arrangements should serve individual purposes rather than individual purposes being shaped to serve collective – and abstractly conceived – ends.

So far I have tacitly assumed in the preceding argument that the boundaries of the political community are well-defined and that the identity of the collective agent of citizenship is clear. With the advent of the European Union, we can no longer make these assumptions. The political framework of citizenship changes, since we move from a set of relatively autonomous national systems of party competition to a system of multi-level governance. What difference does this change make to the way we think about the relationship in which citizens stand to one another and the burdens and benefits they share? Chapter 3 will set out an answer to this question.

3

Political association

So far I have argued that we are to understand the problem of democratic legitimacy in terms of the practical rationality of citizenship. From the point of view of practical rationality, citizens have two sets of reasons informing their political behaviour and shaping their collective choices. First, they have reasons that derive from their conceptions of their own good and the ways in which their good might be advanced through political action. Secondly, citizens in a democracy have reasons for political judgement deriving from a willingness to associate with others under fair terms of cooperation, a disposition that expresses a commitment to the fundamental principle of political equality. These two sets of reasons express what Rawls (1996, especially 47–88) termed the two powers of citizenship: a capacity to have a sense of one's own conception of the good and a sense of fairness.

Because these patterns of reasoning are characteristic of democratic citizenship, they pre-suppose a form of political association. The goods of citizenship are goods that depend for their production on citizens cooperating with one another in some form of political association. This is most obviously true in the case of public goods, but it applies equally to the various forms of individual goods, such as economic and social security. Indeed, the possession of political rights is strictly speaking meaningless without assuming political association. Similarly, the virtue of impartiality is a virtue exercised within a political association, one of the operative principles of which is the ideal of political equality.

The logic of political association was unproblematic in the democratic welfare states of the second half of the twentieth century. If we consider the Rokkan scheme of European state development, national identity was established before democratisation, so that democratic political systems were inheritors of the stock of political loyalty that had been built up in the pre-democratic age. Within this context, the nationalisation and expansion of welfare systems cemented the logic of identity through the added political legitimacy that they bestowed. For such states the logic of political association could be taken, by and large, as a historical given. Certainly, the rational kernel of association – the production of individual and public goods for the benefit of citizens – was embellished from time to time with the myths of primordial nationhood in the political rhetoric of these societies. There were also societies – Belgium, Spain and Italy being the most obvious examples – in which the boundaries of political association became salient elements in the political contests of the day. Yet, a striking feature of the politics of western Europe in the post-war period is the extent to which the affiliation of citizens to the nation-states of which they were members was simply a taken-for-granted assumption.

It is, of course, almost definitive of the EU that its form of political association is obscure or contested. Europe's 'would-be polity' has been categorised in a bewildering variety of ways. Dimitris Chryssochoou has been assiduous in gathering together a collection of the names that have been applied to the EU including: proto-federation, confederance, concordance system, network governance, quasi-state, *Staatenverbund*, meta-state, market polity, managed *Gesellschaft*, nascent *Gemeinschaft*, regional regime, federated republic, sympolity and confederal consocation (Chryssochoou, 2001: 23). This rush of neologisms is occasioned by the attempt of analysts to understand the workings of the EU, on the assumption that each name characterises a set of processes that define the way in which the would-be polity works. Yet, the fertility of imagination that has been displayed in the invention of such terms is not matched by the analytic consensus that has been subsequently engendered. In this maelstrom of competing categories, there does not seem to be much point in attempting another persuasive definition or in coining a new term. What is needed instead, I conjecture, is an account of the basic logic of political association. It is that task that this chapter attempts.

My assumption throughout this work is that the goods of citizenship are to be construed in individualist terms. This individualism is both a moral and a methodological individualism. The moral individualism tells us that only the goods that contribute to improving the quality of individual lives and experience are valuable. The methodological individualism tells us that we have to account for collective entities, including forms of political association, in terms of the dispositions and behaviour of individuals. Neither of these claims entails denying that there are collective entities that are independent of individuals. States, political parties, firms, universities, football teams and many other things have an existence independently of their members at any one time, in the sense that these collective entities remain the same, although the composition of their membership changes (Mellor, 1982). Thus, the British state is still the same state that it was last year, even though the make-up of the individuals who inhabit its territory has changed through death, birth and migration. Methodological individualism need not deny that collective entities exist in their own right. Rather it requires that we understand these collective entities as produced through institutionalised patterns of behaviour among individuals. Making the distinction between a collection of individuals (a set-theoretic notion) and a collective (a body having a capacity of agency as a body), the problem is how we are to define the way in which a collection can, under certain conditions, become a collective. How is it possible to give an account of collective activity in terms that are consistent with the principles of methodological individualism?

Parallel to this methodological question is a question about the associational logic of democracy. If citizens are characterised by their having a sense of their own good and a sense of fairness, what assumptions about practical rationality are we making? In answering this question I shall point to Rousseau's logic of the general will in terms of which collective decisions are made. I shall seek to reconstruct this notion by offering an account of how it is that individuals can come to share in cooperative projects via the notion of 'we-intentions'. A coherent account of collective will formation through we-intentions can be offered for a variety of associations, an account that can with suitable specification be applied to the logic of political associations. Given this, we shall be able to understand how individuals can participate in a variety of collectives, each with its own distinctive purposes. This account forms a basis for understanding political association within a multi-level polity. However, this only gives us an account of what it would mean for a group of persons to have a collective identity within the framework of a multi-level polity. There are many empirical questions that still remain to be answered.

Associations and we-intentions

Looking at democratic citizenship in terms of practical rationality, citizens as potential legislators have to think of rules and policies not only from their own point of view, but from the point of view of the association as a whole. In Rousseau's (1762: Book 2) terms, they have to seek a general will, and not merely assert a partial will. This is more than the reciprocity of mutual advantage. It involves a willingness to balance interests and this in turn involves assigning roles and duties in a common purpose. The notion of a general will carries two senses in Rousseau's thought. On the one hand, it is a property of individuals within society, each of whom is seeking to answer the question of what is best for the body of citizens from an impartial perspective. In this sense, it is to be understood distributively, as a property that can be assigned to individuals. On the other hand, it names the results of citizens' voting, and in this sense it is to be understood non-distributively as a social property ascribable to the collectivity of citizens. In Rousseau's account, citizens recognise the general will when they can affirm that the collectively agreed decision should inform their own choices, even if this means that they have to revise their own original conception of what the general will is.

Rousseau places a great deal of emphasis upon the act of voting in discovering the collective general will from the individual conceptions of the general will, and in particular claims that majority voting will discover the collective general will through a process in which the pluses cancel the minuses (Rousseau, 1762: book 2, chapter 3). Much puzzlement has been caused by this formula, typified by Plamenatz's (1963: 393) exasperated remark that we should beware of political philosophers who use mathematics, no matter how simple, to illustrate their meaning. However, recent scholarship has suggested that Rousseau here may be alluding to Condorcet's jury theorem, in which it can be shown that if all citizens have an equal, better than even, chance of being right, then the majority of citizens have a higher chance of being right than any one of them (Grofman and Feld, 1988). Moreover, Rousseau's faith in majority voting is made more intelligible once we realise that he held to a conventionalist view of political morality, in which what is right is what is agreed by a group of citizens. For example, the rightness or wrongness of the death penalty is decided by each citizen weighing up the benefits for them of its deterrent powers with the risk that they will suffer the penalty. Like any other convention, the question is not one of determining what is the right thing to do in virtue of some general moral principle, but what in practice others will agree to do. Voting simply determines the balance of opinion that in turn determines for each individual where the point of convergence is.

Rousseau's thought, and the traditions of democratic thought it has influenced, are sometimes taken to be totalitarian in effect if not in intention. There is no knock-down answer to this interpretation, but one way in which it can be met is to ask whether we can we provide an account of political association that is consistent with ethical and methodological individualism. Conceptually, the key move here has been made by Tuomela and it involves introducing the notion of 'we-intentions'. The purpose of using this notion is to show how a collective enterprise is both possible and consistent with the assumption that collective entities rest upon continuing patterns of individual behaviour. In the twenty-five or so years that Tuomela has been working on this idea, he has refined and modified the strict formulation of the definition of we-intentions, and related ideas like 'we-attitudes'. However, the core methodological thought remains the same: agents have we-intentions if they belong to a group, share the intentions of that group, believe others share the intentions of the group and believe that there is a mutual belief in such we-intentions.

We can present this idea more explicitly by drawing on a recent formulation of Tuomela (2000: 6). In particular, we say that a member Ai of a collective G, we-intends to do X, if and only if:

i Ai intends to do his or her part of X;
ii Ai believes that the conditions for G to do X obtain;
iii Ai believes that there is a mutual belief among the members of G that the conditions for doing X obtain; and
iv Ai intends to do his or her part of X because of (ii) and (iii).

(Compare Tuomela, 1984: 35; 1995: 145–6; 2000: 64.) In other words, the defining feature of a collective is a shared set of intentions on the part of individuals in relation to common courses of action, where the intentions are underpinned by interlocking mutual sets of belief on the part of those individuals. Where these interlocking beliefs and intentions exist, we may say that we have the conditions for the individuals to play their part in the collective action.

It is an important part of the idea of we-intentions that an individual's sharing a collective purpose involves making his or her action depend upon the collective behaviour of others, regarding those others as part of the collective. This is more than simply making one's behaviour conditional upon how others behave, as happens in bilateral market exchanges, where there is no requirement for participating agents to look at the collectivity of market traders as distinct from weighing up the advantages and disadvantages of a particular offer made by another individual trader. We-intentions, by contrast, require individuals to see themselves as contributing to a shared purpose.

We can illustrate the importance of this distinction by contrasting a market equilibrium with collective behaviour strictly so called, for example a group of people playing in an orchestra. Market equilibrium emerges from a series of bilateral exchanges among individuals, none of whom needs to have any conception that there is a market equilibrium to be attained. In a perfectly functioning market, no one needs to intend an equilibrium in order for one to emerge. Indeed, it is possible to read the critique of centrally planned economies, which asserts that no central planner has enough information to allocate resources efficiently, as showing that if anyone were to aim at an equilibrium they would be bound to fail. Contrast now the case of the orchestra. To attain the requisite standard of performance, each individual member needs to understand him or herself as engaged in a complex co-performance with others. This need not involve everyone having the same understanding and interpretation of the work that is being played. But it does require everyone to be willing to play his or her part according to some particular interpretation, which is the interpretation that the collective aspires to achieve. Thus, the notion of playing one's part in a set of actions that one shares with others must enter into the decision premises of the individuals involved. To say that an association can act collectively is to say that its members have the requisite interlocking set of beliefs.

Note that although we are talking about the beliefs of individuals, the content of those beliefs makes essential reference to social entities. If each player in the orchestra wishes to play his or her part in the performance, then they are conceptualising what they are doing in terms of the activities of the orchestra, which is a collective entity. However, although the content of the beliefs is social in this sense, this does not impugn the methodologically individualist character of the approach. It is still individuals who have interlocking sets of beliefs about a social entity, and without that interlocking set of beliefs the collectivity would cease to exist.

It might be thought that in conceding this essential reference to the beliefs of individuals as to how the social entity will behave that I have not conceded enough, since in order for the beliefs to be well-founded, it must be the case that the social entity exists, in some sense, prior to the individuals. In order to think that the members of the orchestra have the requisite interlocking intentions to turn up to play, I must have the idea of the orchestra. Do I not thereby have an idea of a collective entity? In some sense, this is undoubtedly so, but even this does not damage the methodologically individualist character of the account. The methodological individualist is not committed to the claim that collective entities are the same as the set of individuals who make them up, otherwise there could be no continuing collective entity when membership turns over. Rather the methodological individualist is committed to the claim that we analyse recurrent patterns of collective behaviour in terms of the interlocking intentions and beliefs of individuals.

The logic of we-intentions is the most general logic of association. One might think that its obvious application is to situations in which individuals have to work physically together to play a piece of music or lift a heavy object, and these are the sorts of examples that Tuomela often uses by way of illustration. However, following Nida-Rümelin (1997) as well as hints in the work of Tuomela (1995: 176) himself, the same logic can be transferred to the case of political associations. Thus, if we suppose that a political association can act as a collective agent in pursuit of its members' common purposes, then we shall need to give an account of such agency. If that account is to be consistent with methodological individualism, then it will need the concept of we-intentions, or some logical equivalent.

There is a strand of thinking in political theory that distinguishes between the idea of a political association and that of a collective agent. Michael Oakeshott (1975: 108–84) argued that a proper understanding of the state requires us to think about it as a civil association rather than an enterprise association. A civil association, by contrast with an enterprise association, has no purposes of its own. It is simply a form of association among individuals, each of whom is willing to acknowledge a certain set of rules as conditioning the performance of their own actions. I have argued elsewhere (Weale, 1999: 47–53) that to construe the idea of a political association along these lines requires us to suppose a very particular set of circumstances to obtain, including the condition that all legislation takes the form of customary law in which there is no legislative intent. Once we allow that explicit legislation can be enacted for specific purposes, then the idea that we can model political association on the principles of civil association makes no sense. Indeed, it only takes one such instance to render the logical equation untenable. Moreover, it is extremely difficult, if not impossible, to see how states could enter into international agreements with one another, if we did not allow for states to have purposes that they pursued in their actions.

There is one principal difficulty with relating the logic of we-intentions to a Rousseauian understanding of the practical rationality of democratic citizenship, particularly if the notion of we-intentions is being used to explicate the notion of the general will. This is the question of representation. In Rousseau's thought world, political representation cannot take place. In Chapter 15 of Book 3 of the *Social Contract*, Rousseau famously asserted that though the English people think they are free, they are wrong. They are only free at the point at which they elect their parliament. Between elections, they are slaves. In support of this position, Rousseau offers a number of arguments. He makes his usual appeal to the claim that in societies in which prosperity and civilisation are valued, and therefore citizens find it expedient to let representatives take on the tasks of legislation, there is little concern for the public interest and in the end representatives sell the country. It is for this reason that he regards the corvée as less opposed to liberty than taxes.

But, apart from the knock-about stuff on the dispiriting effects of general prosperity, Rousseau has one important conceptual argument. The sovereignty of the people cannot be represented because it consists in the general will and 'will does not admit of representation' (Rousseau, 1762: 240). Why might one think that the will cannot be represented, and that, as Rousseau goes on to say, the will is either itself or something else, without there being any intermediate possibility? One possible answer to this question is as follows. Rousseau inherits a Cartesian theory of the will, probably through Malebranche (compare Wokler, 2001: 85), in which the exercise of the will is an inner occurrence in the mental history of persons. If to be free is to exercise one's own will and not be subject to the will of another, it follows that one ceases to be free when one ceases to exercise one's will. Since the will, by definition, is an inner event in one's own mental life, it follows that only by exercising one's own will in pursuit of the general good can one be free.

This Cartesian inner occurrence theory of the will was notoriously criticised by Ryle (1949: 61–7) as an extension of the fallacious theory of the ghost in the machine. There were many arguments that Ryle advanced to show that such a theory was riddled with contradictions and anomalies. For example, the phenomenology of acts of will is extremely obscure, particularly when we consider these mental events are supposed to be so frequent and common: no one dates their inner mental life in terms of when acts of will occurred. Moreover, if the exercise of the will were an inner event, an action in one's mental life, then like all actions it should be brought about by another act of will, but there would quickly develop an infinite regress. Insofar, therefore, as Rousseau did rely upon a Cartesian theory of the will to ground an argument for the impossibility of political representation, he was founding his argument upon a false premiss.

The problem, however, does not lie in Rousseau's voluntarism – any theory of democracy has to be voluntarist to some degree about political morality – but in the form his voluntarism took. There is no generally accepted account of the will in the philosophy of action, but there are many grounds for thinking that an adequate theory will not make the will an inner occurrence, but rather a way of designating an ensemble of intelligent human action. As Kenny (1975: 26) puts it, volitions are not motions of the mind, but states of the mind, and states in which reasoned deliberation determines the choices that people make. On this account, the expression of a general will is not the outward manifestation of an inner impulse, but the uncoerced affirmation of a reasoned choice, where the notion of affirmation is to be understood on the pattern of a speech-act.

From this point of view, it is possible to see both that one person can politically represent another, and what might be involved in such an act of representation. If the will is understood as expressed in the affirmation of a reasoned choice, then someone else represents me when they make a choice on my behalf that I would have reason to make were I making the choice. Of course, this formula is merely formal. It states what is conceptually involved in one person representing another and in practice what is involved in such representation requires us to understand how the represented comes to know the reasons that are offered, can verify that the representative is acting in an appropriate way and can modify the representative's behaviour in cases of poor representation. But, even on this formal account, it is clear that a person can represent the will of another if the will is understood in an appropriate way.

However, there is a further sense of representation, of which Rousseau would no doubt have been sceptical, and that is the sense of representation that consists of an empowerment to go beyond the reasoned choices that have been expressed. This is representation as authorisation. I authorise a representative in this sense not when I ask them to express my reasoned choices in the forums of democratic deliberation, but when I grant them powers to make commitments on my behalf, perhaps to create institutions, practices and relations that will give me reasons for actions in the future. It is in this sense of representation that political representatives enter into domestic and international agreements on behalf of their constituents, without it being the case that those constituents have themselves chosen those agreements.

The main reason why it can make sense for citizens to authorise representatives in this way is that it can be to the good of citizens, as individuals, to belong to collectivities that can commit all the members of the collectivity to a common course of action. The most obvious example here is that of international agreements. For example, it can be to the advantage of individuals that their states can enter into international agreements to reduce cross-boundary pollution, even though those citizens may not have thought about the details of the policies involved. The reason why it can be to the advantage of individuals arises from the logic of assurance games in such cases. International agreements of this sort exhibit an assurance logic. The signatories to an international agreement typically express a willingness to undertake a course of action, conditional upon other signatories doing the same. Unless other states have the assurance that the members of your society will undertake the burdens that are involved in the agreement, they will not have reason to enter it. It follows that it can be to your good to authorise someone to bind you, so that the relevant common purposes can be realised.

Representation has another aspect, which is well brought out by considering what exactly is Rousseau's claim that one is freer as a citizen undertaking the corvée than paying taxes. I have noted that Tuomela's standard examples of situations in which we-intentions emerge are those in which individuals have to act physically together, for example lifting a table or playing in an orchestra. All cases in which individuals have to act physically together involve an opportunity cost, in the sense that they take time and effort that could be given to other things. For many such activities the opportunity cost is not worth giving up one's preferred common activity for, playing in orchestras or sports teams being obvious examples for many people. But it is difficult to mount such an argument for the activities involved in political association. Certainly, if as with Rousseau, one stresses that the alternative activities to political cooperation are simply frivolous, then political cooperation can be made to seem more worthy. But the alternatives are not always frivolous, and though political activity has sometimes to be burdensome, it makes little sense to design forms of political association that make it so burdensome as to prevent citizens from developing their human excellences in other ways. A system of political representation reduces the burdens of political association in a number of ways. Most obviously it is political representatives who take on the burdens of practically coordinating the tasks of legislation and decision.

So far, then, I have argued that we can use the logic of we-intentions to spell out the practical rationality of democratic citizenship in a political association. If we think that citizens have the two powers of having a conception of their own good and also abiding by fair terms of cooperation, we can show how this is possible via the logic of we-intentions. This also gives sense to the idea that citizens can have a general will. The logic of we-intentions shows not only that these ideas are coherent, but also that they can be expressed within a framework of analysis that is methodologically individualist.

At this point, however, it will be argued that the problem of citizenship in political associations does not relate to the logical coherence of the idea but to its empirical plausibility. Tuomela has been criticised for not having any theory of where common beliefs come from (Miller, 1985) and failing to deal with the game-theoretic puzzle of explaining how individuals could want to play their part in a collective action (Bardsley, 2001: 179). To the first, he has replied (Tuomela, 1985) that Miller's criticism confuses the semantic issue of what it means to say that collective action exists with the empirical question of under what psychological and social conditions individuals will act on the purposes that they share. The same reply, it seems to me, holds for the game-theoretic puzzle. Yet, the questions, though not damaging to the semantic issue are important in themselves. To deal with them, we need to pass from the logical analysis of what it means for the members of a collectivity to have we-intentions to a discussion of the empirical conditions under which political associations are able to rely upon the behaviour and dispositions of their citizens to create such we-intentions.

Empirical conditions of we-intentions

The notion of we-intentions enables us to understand what is involved in the logic of citizens' having a general will, and therefore it enables us to understand the basic logic of democratic citizenship. On the Rousseauian account, in a well-functioning polity every member is seeking the general will and thinks that all other members are also seeking the general will. On these assumptions, each member is prepared to concede that he or she has mistaken the general will should they turn out to be in a minority. However, this is clearly a special and idealised account. In practice, even in a well-functioning political association, there may be important departures from the assumptions that can be made about the conditions under which collective will formation takes place and we can investigate these via the logic of we-intentions.

To undertake this investigation, all we need to do is to consider Tuomela's conditions for we-intentions, and ask what happens if one or more of these conditions is missing. Those conditions, it will be recalled, involve individuals intending to play their part in a scheme of cooperation believing that the conditions obtain for their doing this and that others also intend to play their part, all parties being bound by mutually interlocking sets of belief. Hence, if we are looking at the conditions that give rise to failures of cooperative action, we need to look at the cases where one or other of the relevant conditions is not satisfied. For example, some individuals might think that not enough others would be willing to play their part in a collective action. Alternatively, some individuals may wish to free-ride on the willingness of others to play their part. Some individuals may be uncertain about whether others are or are not willing to play their part. Or there may be insufficient information, by way of shared or common beliefs, for individuals to form a view about what others are likely to do. When one or more of these conditions is not satisfied, there cannot be the mutual assurance of collective action that is required for we-intentions to arise. How empirically might these departures from the standard case be corrected and what sort of political devices are involved?

The first and most obvious device is the institution of an authoritative rule-maker who can impose punishments upon those individuals who do not make their behaviour conform to the collective requirements. This is of course the Hobbesian insight and the insight that has informed that tradition of political theory influenced by Hobbes. One important element in that tradition is to stress that the authoritative sovereign does not achieve its effects of inducing cooperative behaviour merely by punishing individuals who defect from playing their part in collective activity. Rather, the system of punishment gives each individual the assurance that his or her contribution will not be futile because it will be matched by the requisite performance of others. As Hart pointed out in his discussion of the 'minimum content of natural law', penalties are needed 'not as the normal motive for obedience, but as a *guarantee* that those who would voluntarily obey shall not be sacrificed to those who would not' (Hart, 1961: 193; see also Barry, 1968, both cited in Taylor, 1976: 107).

This does not mean that a system of penalties is not needed for individuals supplying them with a motive for obedience, since as Taylor (1976: 109) pointed out, penalties cannot just serve the function of giving individuals the assurance that others will cooperate. If that was their sole use, they would have the effect of raising the incentives for individuals *not* to cooperate, since a system of penalties that told someone that everyone else will cooperate will make it more rational for that person to free-ride. Thus, for the system of authoritative rule-making to work, each individual needs to think that the penalties will be applied against his or herself in the case of breach of common obligations, or at least that there is sufficient probability of this happening to constitute a sufficient deterrent. As has most recently been pointed out by Goodin (1992: 25), the willingness to see oneself as a potential recipient of penalties, under the right circumstances, can be in one's own interests, since it provides a signal to others that you are more likely to perform your part of the collective action. Those tempted to free-ride might think that what is good for all is not good for each, but if they did think this they would be wrong. It is only if enough people think that there is a credible system of penalties that will apply to *anyone* who seeks to free-ride that enough people will have the requisite belief.

In saying that a credible system of penalties makes for the possibility of collective action, it might be thought that all I am doing is pushing the problem one stage back, since it cannot be assumed that any system of rule-enforcement backed by the threat of force makes for cooperative social arrangements. There are many examples of authoritarian systems that have amassed considerable capacity to impose penalties and yet in which compliance is low and performance in the securing of public goods is poor. Indeed, there is one sense of the phrase that those governments are best which govern least, namely that when political authorities have to rely excessively on the threat of penalties to secure compliance among their populations, they are normally demonstrating a weakness in their perceived sense of legitimacy by the population whom they are governing. There has to be some acceptance of the system of rule-making by those subject to the rules if the credibility of penalties is to be maintained.

One way in which such congruence may be secured is through participation in a common culture. Individuals will not act on their we-intentions unless they believe that a sufficient number of other individuals will also act on the same we-intention, and this requirement of interlocking reinforcement is a feature for all relevant individuals. In effect, for such individuals we-intentions only make sense if they have the assurance that a sufficient number of other individuals will act in accordance with the same we-intention. If we now ask under what conditions such individuals could have such assurance, one obvious answer is that each individual has been socialised into a set of cultural norms that cue the behaviour under the appropriate circumstances, and the fact of this socialisation is common knowledge. In effect, each individual is able to use him or herself as an analogue computer to predict the behaviour of others (an analogy I owe to J.C.C. Smart). Such cultural conditioning supplements the process of authoritative rule-making in at least two respects. Firstly, it economises on the need for the scarce resource of authoritative rule-making, by raising the level of voluntary compliance with the contributions that individuals can make to collective action by making socialised norms the motive for behaviour. Secondly, it heightens the chance that when penalties are imposed they will be seen as rightful or legitimate and not merely as the expression of political force.

Culture from this point of view serves as an assurance mechanism, rather than as an identify-constituting process. More colloquially, culture need not go 'all the way down' and persons do not need to be over-socialised in order for culture to play its part. So long as it provides evidence reassuring the members of a collection that they can act in common, that is sufficient. The precise sense in which this is so needs to be understood, however, for there is one sense in which culture, in the sense of shared beliefs, is constitutive. In a system in which I have been socialised into certain norms of behaviour, I have the beliefs that I do because I have been brought up in that culture or have come to acquire it in some other way. This is not to say that I cannot distance myself from this culture by thinking that some other set of norms would be better for myself and others. Thus, many women in traditional cultures know how to behave in 'feminine' ways in those cultures, and therefore in one sense interact quite successfully according to the norms of those cultures, without thinking that those cultures are the best for them or for human relations in general. It is in this sense that culture does not go all the way down.

There is another limit in culture, namely that it does not go 'all the way across', so that it does not constitute a collective identity as distinct from create the conditions in which individuals share a set of we-intentions that are constitutive of a collective identity. Consider the case of any collective. Then to say that a culture constituted the identity of that collective, without reference to the beliefs of the typical individuals who shared in that culture, would be to hold to a methodologically wholist position. On this account collective identity constituted by culture would be the prior entity and collective purposes defined by a culture would take place 'behind the backs' of individuals. Such an account would render one important political phenomenon unintelligible, namely the conscious promotion of a common culture by means of the instruments of state power and resources. Consider as an instance the phenomenon named by Eugene Weber (1979) as the transformation of peasants into Frenchmen in the nineteenth century. In the middle of the nineteenth century less than half of all French schoolchildren spoke French. In response the French government instituted a series of policies, most notably in education, the effect of which was to instil in citizens a political identification through participation in a common culture. Here we have the conscious use of culture by policy makers to form affective sentiments within the population to nation and to state. It would be impossible to account for such policy strategies if we took the culture to be the primary unit and individuals the bearers of the culture from one generation to another.

Moreover, the pattern through which the nation was constructed by means of the instruments of cultural policy is not of merely marginal significance. The work of Rokkan makes it clear that this process was common to many European polities. In Rokkan's account, state formation precedes nation building, which is in part a process generated by social and economic changes, but in large part a process that depends upon political choices and policy strategies. Although the details vary from place to place, the political measures include the privileging of a particular dialect or language as the official language, making pre-eminent one particular city by contrast with a periphery and standardising culture and sometimes religion. Democratic practices are built upon this political construction of nationhood.

In making these points about the limits of socialisation and cultural autonomy, I am not saying that individuals stand in a purely instrumental or external relation to the culture in which they participate. Clearly, one of the important mechanisms by which culture works in associating individuals together is that it provides a set of taken-for-granted assumptions that form the background against which individuals make their everyday decisions. If it did not do this, it could not function as the coordinating device that I am supposing in the emergence of we-intentions. However, there is no reason to think that, though cultures may have effects, they can do so only by being hard-wired into those who participate in them, without those who participate in the culture also having the capacity to reflect upon their decisions and on occasions distance themselves from their culture.

The third element in securing we-intentions is organisation. Suppose we have a collective group, the members of which share an interest in common, and where the securing of that interest requires collective action taking the form of we-intentions. Then organisation consists of some agent, possibly but not necessarily a sub-set of the group, doing such things as the following: identifying the opportunity for collective action, reminding or informing individuals of the part they have to play in the collective action, maintaining lines of communication between the members of the collective and acting as the ambassador to external collective agents where necessary. In one idiom this is known as political mobilisation and in another as political entrepreneurship. There are, of course, many questions about why agents would undertake such organisational roles, but for our purposes they do not matter. All that it is necessary to do in the present case is remind ourselves that this organisational function does have to be performed – at least under some circumstances – if the collective action resulting from we-intentions is to take place.

The reason for examining the logic of political association was to consider the distinctive political form of the EU. What happens, then, if we apply this logic to the EU?

The EU and political association

So far I have referred to political associations, and the most obvious political association to have in mind is that of the nation-state. However, although the state may be taken as a paradigmatic political association, it is not the only form of political association to exhibit the logic of we-intentions. Consider, for example, international regimes on the one hand or self-regulation by professional and corporate entities on the other. Such associations share with the state the political characteristic that they can make binding rules for those over whom they have authority. In other words, the theory of we-intentions can be applied to the logic of political association more generally than simply to the case of the nation-state.

The similarities among the forms of association are obscured by a Weberian approach that defines the state in terms of its monopoly of the legitimate use of coercive force within a given territorial area. To be sure, this is a good account of those states in which territorial control is important and the financing of armies by means of taxation is crucial to security. Yet, even in these contexts, the focus upon force can be misleading, as David Hume pointed out, over a hundred years before Weber, in his remark that, though the soldan of Egypt or the emperor of Rome might drive harmless subjects against their will, marmalukes and praetorian bands must be led by opinion (Hume, 1742: 110). This is not to deny that coercion does have a place in the construction of political authority. Nor is it to deny that the state is the pre-eminent form of political association. But it is to deny that the best way to understand political association in general is through the specific form of the state.

In the most general case, a political association has the ability to make rules that are treated as authoritative for the members of a collectivity. Democratic political association, in this general case, arises when those binding rules are the product, according to some recognised process, of the expressed opinions of the members of the collectivity, either directly or through representatives. From this point of view, the core notion of representation is that of authorisation, in the sense that the represented accept the decisions of representatives as being the rules that are binding.

One advantage of looking at the logic of political association in the general case is that we can also see, following Nida-Rümelin, how that logic can work for the EU as a multi-level system of governance (Nida-Rümelin, 1997). As an individual I may participate in a large number of collectives, that is to say that I can share we-intentions with a wide range of groups. The political collective of which I am a part will not coincide with the religious collective of which I am a part, which will not coincide with the sporting collective of which I am a part, which will not coincide with the collective with whom I make music. And so on. The reason why I can participate in many collectives in this way is that the spheres of social action to which these collectives relate are typically distinct and non-overlapping. Indeed, role conflict sometimes, perhaps often, occurs when the spheres of action of the different collectives with which someone may be associated overlap but with divergent purposes, as when religious organisations find themselves in conflict with the decision of a government to go to war. Yet, even allowing for such role conflict, there is no problem with the thought that I can participate in various collective enterprises, with those different enterprises relating to different spheres of social life. The idea here is informal and intuitive, but no less clear for all that.

Nida-Rümelin transfers this thought to multi-level governance in the EU. For the purposes for which the EU has competence, I can conceive of myself as a member of the collectivity in which all other EU citizens participate, and I can ask myself what we-intentions are and ought to be shared by members of that collectivity. For the purposes that are under the control of member states, I can conceive of myself as a citizen of that state, and consider the set of we-intentions that citizens of that state share or ought to share. Indeed, in states with strong regional or local identities that find political expression, I may conceive of myself as a local citizen, participating in a collectivity of relevant we-intentions with others. In order to explicate the notion of citizenship in a scheme of multi-level governance, therefore, all we need is the idea that political collectives relate to different spheres of political responsibility and activity, just as in the general case other forms of collective relate to different spheres of social activity.

To be sure, the thoughts that I have in relation specifically to the EU need to be somewhat more complex than this, because the allocation of competences in the EU is not one in which spheres of political responsibility are exclusively assigned to one level of political organisation or another. The most common division of responsibility is the one in which rules are made at the EU level and implemented at the member state level. This in turn means that, as a citizen, I must conceive of the relevant we-intentions in respect of rule-making in relation to one collectivity and to another collectivity in respect of rule-implementation. I doubt if many EU citizens have the time or the inclination to entertain such thoughts, but that implicitly is what the rule-making process invites them to do, and certainly there is a division of labour among their representatives in which this is what is done. In short, there is nothing incoherent in the theory of we-intentions when applied to a system of multi-level governance. Just as the we-intentions of any one individual are tied to the different collectivities of which he or she is a part, so the we-intentions of EU citizens vary depending on the political collectivity with which they are associated.

In terms of the definition we are working with, what this requires is an expansion in the definition, such that the relevant collection is relativised to a particular set of actions. In other words, when we say in Tuomela's formula that Ai is a member of G, G is not treated as a constant but as a variable, taking different possible values in relation to different sets of collective action. Suppose, for example, that one collective action is to pay one's taxes to the local authority and the other collective action is to pay one's taxes to the national government. In this case the theory of we-intentions says that the collection of individuals in respect of one action is made up of the citizens of the local authority, whereas the collection of individuals in the second case in made up of all nationals. As individuals we belong to many different collections of individuals. By virtue of we-intentions, we can transform this membership of a *collection* into member of a *collective*, insofar as the conditions of we-intentions are satisfied.

Citizens join in common action to provide collective or public goods for themselves. It is simply a feature of such goods that they need to be provided at different levels of social organisation. Protection of the environment may require action at the local, regional, national or continental level. Hence different collections of citizens will be involved in the provision of public goods at these different levels. The approach via we-intentions shows how these different collections of individuals can form different collectives, typically organised in different layers of government. Indeed, it is a strength of methodological individualism that it shows how the complexity of organisation is possible.

We can here link the principle of representation with the logic of multiple we-intentions. One of the advantages that is gained through a system of authoritative representation is that the members of one collectivity can enter into binding agreements with other collectivities with some assurance that any contribution that they make to the overarching collective activity will be reciprocated by other associations. In other words, one important form of political association is that of an association of associations. Both federations and international organisations conform to this pattern. The entering into multiple commitments within a logic of we-intentions is made easier for citizens if the obligations and plans are agreed by their representatives, in situations where representatives have the capacity to bind the collectivity to the performance of what has been promised. The individualist character of this analysis can be maintained, once we see that it can be to the advantage of individuals to be members of an association that can bind all of its members to a common course of action in respect of other associations. In short, the EU can be regarded as a political association in which both the individual citizens and the political associations to which they belong, the member states, are participants in a system of political authority that defined the purposes of the larger association. Yet, although EU citizens might be able to entertain the we-intentions of the complex sort that I have suggested, is there any reason to expect that they will do so? One way of answering this question is to see whether the empirical conditions that facilitate the emergence of we-intentions in political associations in general can be expected to operate in the EU.

The first condition that I identified was that of authoritative rulemaking. When this condition is satisfied, individuals have some assurance that the contribution which they make to a collective effort will be reciprocated by others. Individuals also make their own commitment more credible by virtue of their willingness to incur penalties should they fail to play their proper part. I also pointed out that essential to this condition was a notion of legitimate or rightful power, since penalties have a different meaning if they are imposed rightfully rather than arbitrarily. Treated as a rule-making and rule-enforcing body, the EU has established rightful authority in its domain of competence. This is not to say that exercises of the authority go unchallenged, nor that compliance with the rules that are issued is as good as it should be. I am merely making the point that in terms of its general practice, the authority of the EU is regarded as legitimate, and it is worth noting that this legitimacy is at least as high as many states around the world. The EU also has enforcement powers. Admittedly these are powers that are applied to member states rather than having direct effect on citizens, but this is simply part of the modus operandi of the Union. Insofar as citizens need some assurance that their contribution to any collective action will be reciprocated by others, the structure of EU authority and its rule-making contributes to this. Moreover, opinion poll evidence suggests that citizens at the individual level have positive views about those responsibilities it is sensible for the EU to undertake (Sinnott, 1995), views that are not inconsistent with the EU acquiring legitimate authority in some areas.

Shared culture may seem to pose a greater challenge. However, even in relation to this point, there are reasons for thinking that the conditions for we-intentions are sometimes met. For example, there is opinion poll evidence that values and attitudes on key public policy questions are similarly distributed among the member states. The median voter in each member state is somewhat to the centre left on the scope of government in policy (Roller, 1995), and a John Stuart Mill liberal on matters of censorship (Golding and van Snippenburg, 1995). Variance in values and attitudes within member states is high relative to variance between member states. Moreover, the party systems of member states are organised around similar cleavages, reinforcing the view that the cultural conditions for we-intentions across the EU would not preclude cooperative activity. It certainly does not follow from these simple observations that there is sufficient cultural identification among the citizens of the EU to sustain the full range of political and policy purposes associated with conventional states, and one aspect of this problem – related to the possibility of economic redistribution – will be examined in Chapter 4. However, if culture is interpreted as political attitudes and orientation, then there is a sense in which the citizens of the EU share a civic culture.

Political attitudes and orientation are only one aspect of culture, however, and there is one obvious point of cultural difference among the peoples of Europe that is relevant, namely language. How significant is this likely to be? To examine this question, I shall consider an argument drawn from Charles Taylor. Charles Taylor's argument for basing political association on national identity arises from the position of French-speakers in Canada and in particular with the relation between Quebec and the rest of Canada. However, it also seeks to offer a general account of political identity and it is this general account that we will be concerned with here. In particular, the question of how far language is constitutive of political identity, such that questions of political values are determined by language. Of course, it is obvious that differences of language pose practical problems of communication and such problems are clearly of policy relevance. However, an absolutely decisive consideration would be to show that political associations presupposed an homogeneity of language and it is this latter claim that we will examine.

Taylor's argument has three premises (see Taylor, 1993, especially pp. 40–58). The first is that individuals are not social atoms and that successful functioning as a human being requires an identity from communal membership of some kind. The second is that an obvious 'pole of self-identity' for a speaking animal is that of language. The third is that, for those who have been emancipated through the processes of modernisation, identification with the nation as the locus of self-rule is appropriate. Note that all three premises are needed to deliver the conclusion that the nation should be a sovereign state. For example, with only the first two premises, it would be consistent to say that political association could be principally based at a local level, perhaps with some loose overarching form of political authority, like the traditional empires of Europe, to maintain peace between these communal or local forms of association.

Taylor's insistence on the importance of identity in this context is particularly important, because of his commitment to the ideal of democracy, and in particular to that version of democracy that is associated with the tradition of civic humanism. For Taylor, democracy is a form of government in which the people rule themselves. Self-determination of this sort is only possible if people are grouped in their *patriae*, so that the ideal of civic humanism requires that each *patria* be given some form of political personality. Once the process of modernisation has emancipated people from local and communal ties, the next stage up the ladder of personality, so to speak, is the nation.

Yet, Taylor himself recognises that the institutional implications of his theoretical position are ambiguous. There is no essential link between the nation as a state and the idea of republican self-rule. Although the claims of an identity-giving culture need embodiment in public institutions, if that culture is to be a rich and healthy one, there is no reason why these public institutions should be those of the nation-state. Republican self-rule is compatible both with the nation-state and with a high degree of political autonomy as a constituent unit within a federation. The political expression of nationhood could be the modern sovereign state, but it could equally be a federal set of relations between nations. Thus, Taylor's own preference within Canada is for a federal solution: indeed, according to him, Quebec has republican self-rule within the existing Canadian federation. This Canadian example might suggest that the argument linking identity and national self-government proves too much in making language a primary pole of political identity. Conversely, it may show too little by taking only language as the basis for political identity.

Whatever else may be true, we cannot take absence of a common language as negating the possibility of identity. Consider the case of Belgium. A series of constitutional reforms have considerably decentralised power to the three language groups. Each of these three language groups could be linked to linguistic groups in France, the Netherlands and Germany. Yet, despite the differences of language, there is a distinct Belgian identity, which has found its focal point in institutions like the monarchy and the national football team. Conversely, language by itself is not the basis for political identity. Scottish nationalism, for example, is not confined to the very small Gaelic-speaking parts of the country. Similarly, Germany and Austria have distinct national identities, despite their common language. To take language as a 'paradigm pole of self-identity' is to neglect all those identity forming processes that take place within language groups.

Language, then, is neither a necessary nor a sufficient condition for national, and by extension political, identity. We can find states like Germany and Austria in which language does not bind into a nation, and nations like Belgium in which differences of language do not prevent the achievement of nationhood. The most I think we can say about language is that it is one potential basis for social and political identity along with a whole number of others, including religion, common historical experience and ethnic origins, and that it is likely to be most potent when a minority language group feels threatened by a larger, more powerful and different language group.

Two conclusions follow from the observation that language and national identity are not always coextensive. The first is that there need be no basic 'social fact' or deep social structural condition that binds a people together. Instead we should see the conditions of political association as comprised of partially overlapping characteristics, of which in some cases, like Belgium, the mere historical contingencies of shared experience are the most important element. The second observation is that, despite the absence of any 'deep structure', the habits and expectations that gather round a shared set of norms and practices may sometimes be sufficient to constitute a people as a nation, and more generally to constitute the circumstances in which we-intentions, sufficient for authoritative political rule, can be maintained. There is a natural tendency to think that there must be something more to political association than shared participation in a common set of political practices. On this 'deeper' account, if a sense of nationhood exists, it will always seek to find political expression, and encouragement in this way of thinking derives from the extent to which the modern doctrine of nationalism owes its origins to popular struggles against imperial rule. But this is only one account of political identity. As well as being a striving for institutional expression, nationhood can itself be a consequence of established political institutions.

This is not of itself to weaken the claims of nationhood on the loyalties of citizens. One persistent fallacy to which people are liable in this area is to think that unless nationhood were rooted in some basic characteristic like language, religion or culture then the preservation of nationhood would have less of a moral and political claim upon us. On this view it is as though something that were as a consequence of human institutions somehow had less value than something that was a cause of institutions. But this view has only to be stated clearly for its weakness to be revealed. Simply because habits and expectations have emerged from norms and practices, there is no reason to think that their maintenance is less valuable than if they had arisen from some pre-political source.

What I have said so far is intended to be no more than an updating of Sidgwick's (1891: 213–15) argument about nationhood to the effect that all we need for a sense of nationhood is a collective willingness of a people to hang together apart from their formal political obligations, so that in the event of war or revolution, where the operations of normal government were suspended, there would still be willingness of the members of a nation to act as one. This, it seems to me is all that is strictly necessary for nationhood but it also illustrates the conditions for politically significant we-intentions. As I have argued, the logic of we-intentions shows how this is possible within nations, but it also shows how it is possible for collectives other than nations.

There are three conclusions we can draw from this consideration of the relation between the idea of nationality, political association and we-intentions more generally. Firstly, there may be circumstances in which a distinctive cultural form of life needs to find expression in autonomous political institutions, particularly when that form of life is under potential threat from a rival dominant culture, as is the case with French speakers in Canada. Secondly, this is, however, only a special case of a more general phenomenon, namely the conditions of political association. Political association may rest upon the expression of a culturally distinct form of life, but there are other ways in which political identity can be established.

Thirdly, the creation of political association around the norms and practices of a particular set of institutions should not be taken to imply only a weak commitment to the nation-state. Even nation-states formed out of culturally diverse elements may be fierce in their wish to preserve their national autonomy. The problem is that in the context of the competitive rivalries of the international system, this attempt to preserve autonomy may well set up destructive military and security tensions that overwhelm the collection of nation-states unless there are international organisations to control and tame these destructive rivalries. The circumstances of political identity in Europe, and almost certainly elsewhere in the world may require the creation of international organisations like the European Union if these collectively self-destructive impulses are to be constrained.

So far I have argued that the general form of political association rests upon the logic of we-intentions, of which conventional states are but one example. It is, of course, important that our conception of democratic citizenship has evolved in the context of such states, and it would be a mistake to suppose that we can transfer our understanding of the practical rationality of citizenship straightfowardly from the nation-state to the political association of the EU. We need to examine, case by case, what the powers, claims and benefits of democratic citizenship might be within the EU. This involves looking at the effects of the EU on the important components of democratic citizenship. Chapter 4 will begin that task.

4

Social rights beyond the single market?

Citizenship in post-war European states involved social and economic rights (social rights for short) to goods like income security and medical care, goods thought to be valuable in themselves and as complementing the civil and political rights of citizens in a democracy. This was Rokkan's fourth stage of political development in which nation-building is consolidated through the creation of the rights of social citizenship. The effect was to create for citizens systems of social protection from the vagaries of market fluctuations and the risks associated with participation in the labour market. If anything has a claim to be at the heart of what is sometimes called Europe's social model, it is these social rights.

The assertion that it is possible to balance the demands of a productive economy with protection for social rights has often been challenged. From the 1970s onwards there has developed a literature on the 'crisis of the welfare state' (Gough, 1979; O'Connor, 1973; and Offe, 1984). According to this view, welfare states are caught between two contradictory imperatives. On the one hand, they need to secure conditions for capital accumulation, and thus they need to maintain the conditions for the profitability of firms and businesses. On the other hand, they need to secure democratic legitimacy through public spending to protect social rights, but the demands that this spending places on the economy jeopardises the need to maintain profitability. Because states are trapped between these contradictory imperatives, a crisis of sustainability is likely.

Although this view has been popular with some commentators on the welfare state, it is a misleading way of characterising the issues. As Rudolf Klein (1996: 305–16) has pointed out, the identification of contradictory 'imperatives' is merely another way of saying that policy makers are faced with competing objectives that they have to balance off against one another. Though true, this thought is hardly an index of crisis. Moreover, systematic analysis of public opinion survey evidence across Europe has shown populations to be supportive of a wide range of policies for maintaining social rights. Although there are cross-currents of opinion, reliable sampling evidence still shows strong and deep support for the institutions of the welfare state among mass electorates (Pettersen, 1995; Ross, 2000: 19). Moreover, if health care coverage is taken to be an objective measure of well-being, European citizens have enjoyed higher levels of such well-being than, say, citizens of the US. Whatever may be the standing of the welfare state in discussions in political theory, there is no doubt as to the democratic support that welfare state institutions in general receive from citizens.

The early development of the European Union took off at the same place that the rights of social citizenship were being consolidated in post-war European welfare states. Yet, as European integration has relied upon market integration, there are those who hold that the logic of European integration through the creation of a single market is in conflict with the social solidarity that is necessary in welfare states to maintain and enhance social rights. To secure social rights, it may be argued, states require the use of policy instruments that enable public control of key economic decisions, including investment, business location and levels of taxation, all of which are undermined legally and in economic logic by the creation of the single market. Moreover, it may be argued, to the extent to which European integration moves the locus of political authority from the national level to the European level, policy makers lose the ability to rely upon sentiments of civic identification in mass populations that provide the basis upon which redistribution can be rationalised within a political culture.

For an account of the practical rationality of democratic citizenship there are obviously important questions at issue here. Given the value and importance of social citizenship, what reasons might citizens who were supportive of democratic welfare states have for favouring European integration and all that goes with it? Is there a problem of political legitimacy for the EU if we look at it from the point of view of those who value the national welfare state? What use is a Europe that cannot secure the long-term survival of Europe's distinctive social model?

There is one important point of definition that needs to be cleared up before looking at these questions in detail. In the policy discourses of the European Union, the term 'social policy' is used to cover a wide variety of issues, including anti-poverty measures, health and safety at work, community development, works councils in business firms, issues of gender equality, the portability or otherwise of rights to benefits for Union citizens travelling across borders and a number of other policies besides. Some of the variety of this heterogeneous list is to be accounted for in terms of a logic of pre-emption, in which the role of the member states in providing systems of social security predominates in the policy process (Pierson and Leibfried, 1995: 20–4). However, since it is precisely these systems of social security that critics of European integration feel are threatened, it is these I shall concentrate upon here. Indeed, I shall be even more focused, by concentrating primarily upon the logic of social insurance within the post-war welfare state, since whatever the variety of forms of welfare state in Europe, the logic of social insurance is central to the issues of political principle, and hence to the practical rationality of democratic citizenship.

Welfare states and social rights

Public authorities have accepted responsibility for dealing with poverty and destitution for centuries. Policies aimed at relieving destitution are not new. What was new in the development of the European welfare state, from its origins in Bismarck's system of social insurance, was the attempt 'to provide economic security, to prevent people from falling into destitution rather than rescuing them after they had already fallen' (Marmor, Mashaw and Harvey, 1990: 26–7). In other words, the welfare state should not be seen as having merely an anti-poverty objective, though this is certainly one element, but should also be seen as aiming at economic and social security more broadly conceived.

No two European welfare states are the same, but there are some common elements that stand out. Firstly, there is the issue of policy instruments. The supplementing of the anti-poverty objective with the economic security objective was accomplished by the extension and consolidation of schemes of social insurance, schemes in which benefits in times of need were available to those who had contributed to the social insurance fund during their working lives (Flora and Alber, 1981). The details of social insurance varied from state to state, but the principle of benefits earned through contributions – no matter how tightly or loosely the two were tied in strict actuarial terms – was central. The instrument of social insurance was supplemented by that of social assistance, discretionary benefits administered by public officials to deal with those cases of income deficiency that were not covered by social insurance. In addition, welfare states provided additional income to certain citizens falling into particular categories, for example those with children or the disabled, as well as a range of public and social services.

Alongside income maintenance, the second important area of social protection has been the socialisation of the financial risks of health care. In this case, the two main organisational forms used have been social insurance, where the German model stands as the exemplar, and general taxation, where the UK model stands as the exemplar (White, 1995). The key element in terms of social rights was a reduction and in most cases an elimination of the financial barriers to access to health care in times of need. Public policy thus provided a form of security for citizens in respect of a crucial dimension of their well-being. This is not to say that the socialisation of health care succeeded in eliminating inequalities of health status among citizens. Indeed, a long-standing topic of debate in the relevant social science has been the extent to which the sources of ill health outside of the formal health care system operate with uneven effects on citizens. But this is to say that in accomplishing significant benefits, health policies did not accomplish all that needs to be done.

Social insurance may be defined as any scheme of social benefits in which receipt of the benefit is made conditional upon having contributed to a social insurance scheme, either one run directly by the state or one under state regulation and control and in which it is compulsory for earners to contribute. Within welfare states, pensions, sickness and accident cover and unemployment cover are the main benefits that are so supplied. In some systems, this is also the pattern for health and long-term care. Although social insurance schemes limit benefits on the basis of contribution, and therefore it might seem as though they were not based on a principle of citizenship, appearances are misleading. Since social insurance benefits typically take into account variable family size, they cannot be assimilated simply to a category of state-run actuarial insurance. The 'blanketing in' of family members is not a practice that would spring from a market-based system of insurance. Moreover, the relationship between benefits and contributions is not as direct as it would be under private insurance. Indeed, in continental schemes of earnings-related benefits, there is a relationship between what workers contribute and what entitlements they receive, but the relationship is nested in subsidies, both explicit and implicit, from the public purse to ensure that benefits are suitably uprated in line with general earnings in the economy. Hence, although the device of social insurance depends upon a scheme of reciprocity, it tends towards generalised reciprocity within the set of citizens rather than the specific reciprocity that a market would yield.

It is an interesting historical and political question as to what the conditions were that encouraged the emergence of such systems. As Robert Goodin (1992) has pointed out, this is a case where the motivational causes of an institutional arrangement need not correspond with the reasons that can be offered that would justify that arrangement. His own candidate, following a suggestion of Titmuss (1950: 506), is the experience of war and in particular aerial bombardment, which induced in policy makers an understanding that damage to homes and civilians was indiscriminate. An alternative view is that the system of social insurance solved, with its contributions condition, a problem that was implicit both in poor law arrangements and in mutual self-insurance arrangements among workers, namely the difficulty of knowing whether a claim was a valid one or merely represented a case of shirking or defect of moral character. As Abram de Swaan has noted, the mutuals faced many problems. When dealing with claims for benefits, they found it hard to screen the claims, distinguishing between those that were valid and those that arose from malingering. Similarly, they found it difficult to operate according to principles of procedural fairness and rationality, treating like cases as like. They were also prone to internal conflicts and pressures arising from fraud and mismanagement (de Swaan, 1988: 145–6).

There is one further important element in the logic of social insurance that needs to be understood in the context of the welfare state and this can be illustrated best in the case of pensions. From the point of view of the individual, a social insurance based pension scheme is a means by which the right to benefit is earned through having made contributions. However, pension schemes in European welfare states were typically based on the 'pay-as-you-go' principle, according to which current contributions finance current benefits. Thus, if we consider such schemes from the collective point of view, social insurance constitutes a device by which current workers finance the consumption of those past working age, in the form of an inter-generational transfer. In a classic paper Samuelson

(1958) explained the logic of this arrangement as an implicit three-party inter-generational contract, under which the present generation of workers finances the retirement consumption of the elderly on condition that their own retirement is financed from the next generation of workers. Successive generations are therefore locked into a process of 'pass-the-parcel', by which the obligation to finance the consumption of the retired is passed down the line.

So far, I have described European welfare states as a group. Certainly, they share many similarities, and they stand out by comparison with the USA in terms of the dependence of the programmes upon public finance. The under-developed welfare state of the USA is really a reflection of the fact that US policy makers have been willing to rely upon private, occupationally based insurance to provide for health and pensions to a much greater degree than its European counterparts (Hacker, 2002: 5–27). Moroever, we reinforce the sense of distinctiveness, if we compare these European developments with developments in Australasia, where social insurance did not develop. The extensive use of social insurance, rather than general tax revenues, reflected a relative weakness of the labour movement in Europe compared to Australia and New Zealand. In Australia and New Zealand, the relative shortage of labour and high degree of working-class political mobilisation meant that instruments of state policy were used to protect the rights of the working man, to which social insurance was thought to be hostile (Castles, 1985). Social insurance in Europe as an instrument of policy seems to reflect a political balance between capital and labour, contrasting with the US, where working-class mobilisation at crucial times was relatively weak and Australasia, where working-class mobilisation at crucial times was relatively strong.

Yet, in stressing the similarities among European welfare states, it is important not to neglect the differences. There is a significant strand of analysis that has been concerned to highlight these differences and to evaluate the extent to which differences in welfare state performance are associated with differences in the organisational form and underlying logics of different types of welfare state. In particular, building on Titmuss's distinction between institutional and residual welfare states, Esping-Andersen (1990) has argued that it is important to distinguish 'three worlds of welfare capitalism'. The first of these is the Anglo-Saxon model of residual provision, aimed at those citizens who cannot otherwise provide for themselves. The second is the German or continental model of social insurance tied to occupational categorisation. And the third is the Scandinavian model of universalism in which the basic principle is the inclusion of all citizens on the same terms in a common form of provision.

The important feature of this categorisation in the present context is that, although all European states use the instruments of social insurance to protect some social rights, the exact form this use takes and the purposes to which the measures are aimed can vary significantly with implications for social citizenship. For example, in the Anglo-Saxon model, social insurance in pensions has been largely tied to a principle of minimum income provision, in which the function of the state is to provide a basic income and if citizens wish to go beyond this

minimum, then the implicit principle is that they are free to use market arrangements. In a Bismarckian system of social insurance, by contrast, pensions are associated with forms of social insurance that are tightly tied to occupation and in
which long-term work participation is a necessary condition for building up an
entitlement to a pension that is related to life-time earnings. In the Nordic model
as exemplified by Sweden, by further contrast, the social insurance basis for pensions was supplemented in an important reform of 1960 by tax support, which
allowed both a high minimum pension payment as well as earnings related benefits in retirement.

Esping-Andersen's classification has been subject to various forms of criticism in the empirical literature. In particular, it has been argued that it ignored
the 'fourth world' of the Mediterranean rim. Moreover, it can be argued that the
right unit of analysis is not the whole of a welfare regime, but the component
programmes of all such regimes. On this latter analysis, any particular welfare
regime in any particular country can be a mixture of elements combining universalistic, occupational and residual features to different degrees. Thus, for example,
the UK's universalistic National Health Service sits alongside its residual pension
provision, and no single classification is going to capture the particular combination of features that it contains. Whatever the merits of these empirical and methodological criticisms of welfare regimes approach, that approach does at least serve
to highlight the variation in the extent to which social rights have been detached
from labour market position. We thus need to see European welfare states as being characterised by differences as well as similarities. They are similar in that they
detach financial security, particularly in respect of health and retirement, from
labour market position by means of a mixture of social insurance and tax-funded
provision. They are different in the degree to which they do this and the extent to
which they assume that the responsibility of the state is to maintain more than a
minimum level of provision.

What values have been served by these policies and what issues of democratic
principle are raised by welfare state programmes? As Marshall (1950) stressed, the
conception of citizenship that came to predominate in the post-war welfare state
was one in which social rights, or entitlements to the benefits of social programmes,
came to be seen as an integral part of democratic citizenship. This was so for two
related reasons. The first was that by suspending or modifying the influence of the
market in respect of certain goods and services like health care and education the
grounds for allocation ceased to be ability to pay and came to be related to membership of the political community. This decommodification – to use the ugly but
useful phrase – was not simply an absence of market; it was simultaneously the
assertion of an alternative ground of allocation, to be found in the idea of membership and the rights and obligations that membership entailed. Secondly, citizenship was important because typically the benefits required a long-term
association with the political community that had organised the supply. To be
sure, guest workers could avail themselves of the services and in some cases, as
with the UK's National Health Service, even temporary visitors could enjoy the

benefits. But, by and large, citizenship was the key condition, and when not citizenship it was its closest cousin, namely long-term working residence.

The goods that these social rights provide are the goods of economic and social security, or protection from the contingencies of the labour market and fluctuations in the business cycle. By socialising the costs associated with the provision of these benefits, financial burdens are lifted upon any one particular individual or household. Because these rights are concerned with the provision of securities, it is important that, in Hohfeld's (1923) language, they take the form of claims, that is to say demands upon which the right-holder can insist. Indeed, unless the goods did take the form of such claims, their value would be diminished. The contrast between social insurance and social assistance was that in the latter a large element of discretion remained with public officials in terms of a judgement about the eligibility of citizens for benefit, whereas in social insurance programmes the principle was that specific events – illness, an accident or reaching retirement age – should trigger an entitlement to the benefit. In terms of a conception of democratic citizenship, therefore, the values that are served are those of independence, dignity and self-respect. Those who can insist upon their rights, because they have earned them through their contributions, are not dependent upon the judgement of others for their security. In being less vulnerable, they are made more independent.

What forms of impartiality are involved in welfare state programmes? Here we need to make the distinction between horizontal and vertical redistribution. Some of the redistribution that occurs within the welfare state is between different income classes. However, much of it takes place within income classes but across the life-cycle, shifting income from people when they are relatively affluent in the prime of their working life to when they are relatively poor in times of ill health or old age. This 'pay now, receive later' maxim is best understood on the model of reciprocity, although it is a form of generalised reciprocity, since the link between benefits and contributions is not strict in actuarial terms.

What then of fairness as non-exploitation or the provision of minimum standards of provision? To the extent to which the horizontal redistribution of social insurance also provides protection against destitution, it achieves fairness understood as both reciprocity and non-exploitation. However, social insurance does not prevent exploitation for those cases where its contribution requirement means that some groups are uncovered or are covered only inadequately. Indeed, ever since the inception of the welfare state there have been those (for example Meade, 1948) who have argued that social insurance is inadequate as a device for achieving social citizenship and that what is needed is some form of basic citizens' income or demogrant scheme that would ensure that all citizens had at least a minimum income guarantee that would be independent of any further condition they would have to meet.

This is not simply a question of the non-exploitation principle supplementing the reciprocity principle. The two aspects of fairness can pull in opposite directions, as can be seen in the question of whether a work test should be imposed on citizens as a condition for receiving certain benefits such as unemployment compensation or disability benefit. The social insurance principle requires that those who are able to make a contribution should do so as a condition of being entitled to receive. The social minimum principle says that people are entitled to receive independently of any contribution that they make. If the non-exploitation principle is given priority, then there is a direct argument for income maintenance schemes including an element that provides a minimum income unconditionally as a way of preventing poverty. Such a payment would be made independently of a work test and would therefore by given to the 'work-shy' as well as those involuntarily unemployed. A reciprocity test by contrast would make a willingness to work a condition for receiving benefit, or at least would demand some test of social participation, say in the form of voluntary work or the provision of personal care to relatives or dependants. In practice, welfare states have given priority to the reciprocity principle, although Goodin (2001) has pointed out that the Netherlands in the 1990s came to approximate to a system of unconditional income guarantees.

The single market: a race to the bottom?

Although welfare policies brought about a form of social citizenship, they also required economic growth in order to develop. Why might this be so? The answer is probably contained in Crosland's (1956) conjecture that high levels of redistribution are easier to sustain in economies that are growing strongly than in economies that are sluggish. Those who incur the costs of redistribution (even if on the principle of reciprocity they are going to gain later) find it easier to make payments if their own personal income is growing at the same time. Conversely, when contributions to social welfare involve a drop in personal consumption, it is more likely that some sort of tax revolt or resistance will emerge.

The significance of this dependence on economic growth underpinning social rights can be explained as follows. The social rights of national welfare states provided important social goods to citizens, most obviously some measure of economic and financial security in the face of fluctuations in fortunes. However, these policies presupposed the success of other macro-economic policies. When these macro-economic policies were successful, then the future of the welfare state was secure at the national level. However, if conditions emerged under which those policies encountered difficulties, this in turn would have implications for the future of welfare. Thus, after the Mitterrand government's failed attempts at redistributive Keynesianism upon their election in 1981, it became clear to the French government that it could not bring about a strengthening of social welfare by means of its own domestic policy instruments alone. The foreign exchange problems that had plagued the UK Labour government in the 1960s were replicated in the French socialist experience of the 1980s (Hall, 1986).

It was this experience that provided the background to the creation and implementation of the single market programme and the common currency. As Dyson and Featherstone (1999: 124–201) have shown, there was a turning point in French economic policy making when Mitterrand might have abandoned plans for European monetary union. However, having realised that it was not going to be possible to protect and enhance social rights through national policies, an essential building block in the inter-governmental coalition between France and Germany for the single currency was put in place. Yet, it is the strategy of integration through the single market and the creation of the single currency that looks as though it is one of the forces threatening the integrity of national welfare states and their programmes of social and environmental protection. As Pierson and Leibfried (1995: 32) put it, the success of the single market programme seems to be predicated on a lowest common denominator policy, which is precisely the agenda most feared by European social policy advocates. If this is so, then there appears to be a sharp contradiction between the demands of European integration and the protection of social rights in the welfare state (compare Kleinman, 2002).

Why might the single market and the common currency be a threat to national welfare state regimes? In theory at least, we can pick out three reasons. The first relates to the differential mobility of the factors of production. Capital is more mobile than labour. So the implementation of freedom of movement for both capital and labour – central planks in the single market programme – might be expected to have differential effects on the two factors of production. If owners or controllers of capital are seeking the highest rate of return on their investments, then they will move their assets to the most profitable location, wherever that might be, assuming that the risks are equal. Labour by contrast is made up of individual men and women and their families, and for a whole variety of reasons is not as mobile, even in the aggregate, as capital.

In this context, it is important that social insurance is typically based on payroll taxes in a number of states. Owners or controllers of capital therefore incur the costs of financing these expenditures, even when it does not directly contribute to their own profitability. In these circumstances the rational response from enterprises is to see how far they can invest more profitably outside of their own national economy in locations where the same burdens of social insurance do not exist, or to reduce the number of workers that they take on to reduce payroll costs. Such a reduction in labour demand will increase unemployment and therefore increase the expenditure of social insurance funds, thus worsening their income and expenditure accounts in what could be a downward spiral.

If national governments respond to the pressures set up by these effects, then one obvious approach is to seek to reduce payroll taxes either by shifting the burden of taxation into other revenue accounts, by reducing benefits or by some combination of both strategies. To the extent to which different national systems of social protection are in competition with one another within the EU, the overall effect of these moves is to exert downward pressure on measures of social protection. Benefit levels will be cut and entitlement conditions tightened. The main point of reference will be the countries with the lowest levels of social protection, since they are the ones that are hypothesised to provide the most attractive locations for investors.

The second theoretical reason for thinking that market integration is bad for welfare policy arises from the effects of the Growth and Stability Pact. The rules for national debt and budgetary balance limit the extent to which national governments can engage in counter-cyclical spending. One of the main arguments for social welfare spending has turned on its ability to provide built-in stabilisers for the economy. In the absence of social expenditures, if the business cycle starts to move the economy into recession, workers will be laid off and their drop in income will worsen the recession by reducing their demand for goods. However, these effects will be mitigated, if not entirely avoided, by automatic payments to laid-off workers. Demand will not drop as much as it otherwise would and the recession will therefore be shallower.

It is these counter-cyclical effects that the Stability Pact threatens (ironically in view of its name). As workers are laid off, government revenues fall, thus worsening their budgetary position. Under the Stability Pact, if the deficit goes above 3 per cent of national income, governments are in breach of the rules, and they are then under increased pressure to cut expenditure to stay within limits. However, such a cut is likely to deepen the recession rather than mitigate it. For obvious reasons, these effects are unattractive to governments, which is precisely why both France and Germany have been unwilling to take the necessary corrective action in recent years to avoid falling foul of the Stability Pact. Nevertheless, for other countries the counter-inflationary discipline of the Stability Pact is important, which is why there are considerable political pressures on both France and Germany to come into line.

A third possible source of pressure, at least in theoretical terms, has been suggested by Scharpf (2003), who has pointed to the pre-eminence that integration through the market gives to competition law. One of the principal features of social insurance is the compulsory inclusion of all citizens in schemes of reciprocal benefit. Scharpf invites us to imagine the situation in which private insurers seek to set up in competition with social insurance systems in Nordic welfare states. These state systems tend to be vertically strongly redistributive. If private insurers could secure competition on terms that perhaps involved tax subsidies to those taking out cover, it is possible that they would be able to entice away better-off workers from the state scheme, leading to a situation like that in US health care in which insurance cover is fragmented. This would not only damage social citizenship, it would also be likely to push up overall costs, since the experience of the fragmented US health care insurance market is that it is both inequitable in social terms and expensive in financial terms.

These three anticipated sorts of effects are purely theoretical. Even if they occur, the key question is the extent to which they occur. However, the dynamic to which they point does indicate the reasons why someone supportive of the national welfare state would be sceptical of European integration. If the only way in which European integration can be advanced is by measures the effect of which is to threaten the integrity of the welfare state, that would pose difficulties. Between the choice of European integration and welfare protection, someone who took seriously their responsibilities as a citizen of a democracy might well incline to the latter.

The starting point for an evaluation has first to be an assessment of the link between the growth of welfare state expenditure and techniques of Keynesian demand management. A key assumption of many commentators on the Keynesian era is that governments during this period were able to manipulate real aggregates in the economy, in particular rates of growth and the level of unemployment, by suitable adjustments to public taxation and spending and it was these demand management techniques that provided the background to the institutionalisation of social rights. This was the supposedly golden age of the welfare state, the *trente glorieuses*. After the golden age, as Esping-Andersen has put it, 'non-inflationary demand-led growth within one country appears impossible …' (Esping-Andersen, 1996: 3). Yet to assume that there was a high degree of government control in the economies of Europe is to ignore the way in which those economies were linked through the Bretton Woods system to the policies of the US. Because European countries were tied to US policy making though a commitment to fixed exchange rates, monetary discipline from the US was conveyed in the form of balance of payments deficits. Within the US itself the reception of Keynesian ideas was late, and anti-inflationary objectives remained important.

In consequence of the Bretton Woods linkage, as Samuel Brittan (1983: 93) has pointed out, it came to seem that the constraints on faster growth were imposed by exchange considerations, rather than any potentially inflationary implications of increased public spending. In fact, what was happening was the monetary discipline was being imposed by the foreign exchange markets. Only when dollar convertability was abandoned by the Nixon administration in 1971 did it become apparent that restrictions on stimulating growth might stem from the effects of any stimulus being dissipated in higher prices rather than boosting demand (Brittan, 1995: 128–31). The corollary was that the relatively fast growth of European economies between 1945 and 1975 was less of a consequence of redistributive Keynsianism than a pre-condition for those policies.

Behind this point about the significance of exchange rate stability for the domestic agenda of policy in the Keynesian period, there lies a more general point. For any economy there is an inconsistent triad of institutional arrangements within which economic management can take place. These three institutions are fixed exchange rates, the free movement of capital and an independent domestic monetary policy (Mundell, 1963; Quiggin, 2001). To say that these are an inconsistent triad is to say that it is possible to institutionalise any two of these arrangements at the same time, but not all three. Thus, the nineteenth and early twentieth-century gold standard maintained fixed exchange rates and the free movement of capital, but left little scope for independent domestic monetary policy. By contrast, the Bretton Woods arrangements maintained fixed exchange rates and domestic monetary autonomy, but restricted the free movement of capital. Finally, UK economic policy in the early 1980s allowed the free movement of capital and upheld an independent monetary policy, but allowed the pound to fluctuate on the foreign exchange markets.

Within the single currency participating countries no longer have the possibility to introduce competitive devaluations. With the free movement of capital across borders, this in turn means that they have to give up setting their own interest rates. It might therefore look as though it is the free movement of capital that is undermining national control, rather than the productivity of the national economy. But this is where appearances are deceptive, since under the Bretton Woods regime, although governments imposed restrictions on the outward flow of capital, they could not easily attract foreign investment nor could they guarantee to maintain any particular currency parity, if public spending became inflationary. These constraints, built into the Bretton Woods regime, undermine the view that national governments could freely engage in welfare spending. In consequence, we cannot assume that the single currency and the measures that go with it, including the control of public budgets, necessarily impose greater constraints than was true under Bretton Woods, during the so called golden age.

This, however, is a negative argument. It says that integration through the single market may not be as damaging to the welfare state as is often assumed. However, there may be a more positive argument about the relationship between social rights and economic performance. From the theoretical point of view, there may be positive effects on productivity from expenditure on social rights. In the first place, the mobility of capital will need to take into account labour productivity and there are reasons to think that this is enhanced by social expenditures. High labour cost economies are also economies in which workers are likely to be better educated and more capable of adapting to new production demands. The security provided by social programmes means that workers can absorb changes more easily. There is in any case the phenomenon of asset specificity (Williamson, 1985: 52–6), meaning the way in which production is organised may require workers with particular skills, experience and cultural orientation. Labour is not a homogeneous commodity, but is typically differentiated in terms of skills and ability, so that those who control capital may not find it so easy to reproduce the same conditions of production as elsewhere. These are, of course, only theoretical possibilities, and it is an empirical question as to how the balance of advantages and disadvantages plays itself out in respect of capital investment. But we should not confuse the incentives that some controllers of capital might have when taking decisions with predictions about the likely behaviour of capital investments as a whole.

Moreover, relatively high levels of public expenditure can be compatible with high levels of economic performance, at least when the social cost of alternatives is properly accounted for. From the social point of view, what matters is not whether the expenditure is public or private but what the total cost is of supplying economic and financial security to mass populations. As the experience of US health care demonstrates, private solutions may turn out to be more costly than public solutions (White, 1995). This point is relevant to Scharpf's conjecture about the possible effects of competition law. Of course, it is hazardous to second guess how the European Court of Justice would decide in any particular field. However, is it being too fanciful to assume that some rationality will operate in the process, such that if it can be shown that an element of market competition would lead to higher social costs then the Court would decide that there was ground not to liberalise?

In political terms, so far, European welfare states have remained robust in the face of the regime of freely moving capital flows. Summarising work on the post-Keynesian experience up to the early 1990s, van Keesbergen (2000: 22) noted that the 'conclusion of most of the studies is that the European welfare state is not being abandoned, but adjusted incrementally and reconstructed partially'. Subsequent empirical assessment suggests that the race to the bottom has not been a conspicuous effect arising from the creation of the single market. Indeed, social expenditures have come under pressure, both from the comparative sluggishness of the European economy in the 1990s and the demands of the Stability Pact, but in overall terms what is most striking is the extent to which savings are being made at the margins of programmes which are quite large in themselves. For example, a survey of welfare state experience over the 1990s suggested that the Nordic model had been robust in the face of challenges, even given the high unemployment generated by the economic downturn of the early 1990s (Kuhnle, 2000). Of course, UK policy makers have done a good job in creating a mess of pensions policy, but they started to do this before the single market programme got going and have not needed to join the single currency in order to keep up the effort.

The massive political fact, as Pierson and others have shown, is that there is considerable in-built resistance in democratic societies to serious cuts in popular public expenditure programmes of the sort that form the core of the welfare state (Pierson, 1994; Pierson, 2001). Even in the US, where the conditions for maintaining public expenditure are less favourable than in Europe, it has not been possible to make deep cuts in the social security budget, despite some inflated rhetoric at various times about the crisis of social security. In part, the existence of these political constraints is one explanation of the willingness of national governments to breach the terms of the Stability Pact in order to maintain social protection in the face of persistent unemployment.

It is in any case important not to ascribe all the reasons that there might be for belt-tightening in the welfare state to the effects of market integration. Some change in the terms and conditions of such schemes would almost certainly have occurred without the creation of the single market, and to the extent to which the single market has dynamic effects on the economy at large, it is possible that it makes the scale of the adjustments needed smaller rather than larger. For example, in respect of pensions provision (which is the largest single item of expenditure under income maintenance programmes), the pay-as-you-go principle was rationalisable in terms of a three generational social contract, with the working generation paying for the older generation on condition that younger generations in turn made their contribution. In terms of the principle of reciprocity, this can be understood as a fair arrangement, at least if one treats a generation as a collective entity. Yet, the model also highlights the extent to which such social insurance rests upon the assumption of a community, in which inter-generational transactions take place within fixed boundaries. But clearly such a model assumes a demographic balance between the relevant generations, both in terms of numbers and in terms of the proportion of their lifetimes that a retiring generation has worked. So, while it may promise to deliver the value of economic security in old age, such an arrangement is going to be sensitive to changes in population balance, in particular declining birth rates or greater longevity.

It is not surprising in this context, then, that Sweden reformed its generous pension scheme, in order to maintain its solvency. Key elements of the reform in the mid-1990s (see Ståhlberg, 1997, for details) included moving from a defined benefits scheme to a defined contributions scheme, in which pension rights are defined by the actuarial estimate of how long an average member of that generation has to live, combined with extra contributions. The effect of all the changes was to reduce the pension entitlement of someone with a full contribution record from around 65 per cent of average earnings to 60 per cent. This is significant, but can hardly be said to be an attack on the heart of the welfare state. There was, moreover, one small but interesting element of the Swedish reforms. A portion of pension contributions has been shifted from the pay-as-you-go scheme to capital investment. One advantage of shifting the funding in this way is that overseas capital markets are opened up, and citizens become less dependent upon the particular demography of their own country. There are of course many ethical issues implied by such a policy, including the responsibility with which investments are targeted. However, what we seem to be seeing here is not an ending of the welfare state but a transformation of the policy instruments by which its traditional aims are achieved in changed circumstances.

It is possible to catalogue a series of reforms across welfare states purely in terms of negative trends (for an exercise in this mode, see Bonoli, George and Taylor-Gooby, 2000). However, this is to ignore those reforms that might be thought more positive from the point of view of democratic citizenship. For example, in a summary of changes in three welfare states, Clasen and van Oorschot (2002) point out that recent reforms have included equal rights for men and women in pension and the universalisation of child allowances in the Netherlands and credits in pension insurance for carers in German pensions. What is more, even if we focus on cut-backs, what is one to make of the former scheme in the Italian pension system by which public officials could retire on full pension after twenty years in service? For some, there will be doubts as to whether this is the best example of citizenship rights to defend.

Even if, in general, the goods secured through social rights are independence and dignity, we cannot make a general inference from social rights to democratic values, without also noticing that there are respects in which such rights as they are institutionalised in social insurance could be exclusionary rather than inclusionary. As the contrast with the US and Australasia show, programmes of social insurance in the European welfare state reflect a class politics, in which the fundamental struggle is between capital and labour and in which economic security is the main issue. By institutionalising a system of contributory benefits financed through payroll taxation, the terms of the class struggle could be modified and the issue of economic security resolved in a way that was mutually acceptable to capital and labour. But, as critics have pointed out, this institutionalisation risks creating a division between insiders and outsiders among citizens in the welfare state. Whereas mainly male, full-time workers with large employers are benefited, there are other groups who find it hard or impossible to meet the contribution conditions. These include many women who take time out from the labour market to rear children, and especially female lone parents. They also include part-time or other marginal workers, as well as those disabled early in their lives. Even if one supports the general principle of social insurance, therefore, it does not follow that all policies that are pursued under a regime of social insurance are justified in particular cases. This is not, of course, to endorse any particular policy – since more detail is required in individual cases than can be dealt with here – but it is to say that, though the principle of social insurance has typically functioned as an expression of the principle of reciprocity, its operation will some times not be entirely coincident with it.

To summarise the argument so far, someone valuing social rights as goods would have no intrinsic reason to be hostile to European integration. European integration in and of itself cannot be said to threaten the national welfare state. Of course, democratic citizens might well want to be assured that the political mechanisms are in place to control developments that would threaten welfare state achievements, but as long as the principal link between political decision makers and their populations is national elections, the political mechanisms sustaining welfare state programmes are likely to stay in place. There is no unambiguous chain of reasoning from the creation of the single market to the lowering of social standards. Of course, it can be argued that it is too early to know how far the creation of the single market and single currency is exerting downward pressure on social expenditure. Perhaps the effects can only be felt after some twenty years of policy developments, each of which might look relatively small in itself but the cumulative effect of which would be significant. Only time will tell and it is difficult to settle a current argument on the basis of appeal to future conjectures. Yet, quite apart from appealing to such conjectures, there is a further move the defender of the national welfare state can make. It can be argued that the positive case for upholding national economic control comes from the importance of political community in the ethical life of individual citizens.

National social solidarity?

In discussing the logic of political association, I have asserted that methodological individualism does not deny the existence of collective entities like nations and communities. Given that collective entities exist over and above the individuals who compose them, and, following Taylor (1993), given also that individuals require there to be such collective entities in order to be able to engage in socially recognisable acts of self-referring, there is likely to be some collective entity which acts as a focal point for political self-identification. For many, the relevant entity in the modern world is the nation-state. The implication is that individuals in general will give their loyalty and support to the national collective entity over others. The nation-state should not be seen merely as a convenient device for the pursuit and enhancement of interests. Rather the nation-state helps individuals to define what their interests and their obligations are and this view is sometimes thought to have implications for social rights. David Miller (1995) has sought to offer the most plausible theoretical account of this last claim, and given the sophistication of his position, it is worthwhile examining in some detail. In particular, Miller claims that in understanding a political system we need more than the juridical concept of citizenship of a state. We need in addition an account of nationality, which shows how the ethical life of individuals can be rooted in their national community.

A nation for Miller is distinguished by five characteristics. It is in the first place constituted by a set of beliefs. Its members recognise one another as compatriots. Secondly, a nation embodies some historical continuity. Thirdly, the identity that a nation bestows upon an individual is to be thought of as an active identity. On this account, nations are communities that do things together, and take certain decisions about their conduct. Fourthly, national identity connects a group of people to a particular territory. As Miller himself puts it, a 'nation must have a homeland' (Miller, 1995: 24). Fifthly, national identity requires that the members of a political community share a common political culture. Miller is clear that this public culture can be fluid and complex. It may well be made up of overlapping elements from different sources. But it is equally clear that he thinks that this public culture must be rich enough to provide the reference points for political decisions and public policy commitments.

In addition to this account of what is involved in the idea of national identity, Miller also offers an account of the ethics of nationality. Here he is concerned to argue that compatriots can have special obligations to one another, obligations that cannot simply be regarded as convenient allocations of universal duties given the circumstances of social and political life (Miller, 1995: 62–3, criticising Goodin, 1988). The crucial move in the argument is the claim that the ethics of community enhances voluntary compliance in respect of obligations towards others, partly because, given the identification story laid out above, individuals do not make a sharp distinction between themselves as persons and the obligations they have towards others, and partly because in a community individuals have the assurance of reciprocity from others. Moreover, political associations may formalise the informal patterns of obligations that grow up in communities, thus strengthening the social bonds of their members with one another. The national community is well placed to do this through the establishment of public institutions and policies. The special obligations that compatriots owe to one another are therefore an outgrowth of the general ethics of community, fixed in a particular form by the practices of politics.

Let me begin the examination of why there might be a difficulty with something as strong as Miller's nationality principle by drawing attention to one of its particular conceptual features. This is the role that the idea of a public culture plays in the argument. The notion of a public culture both accounts for how individuals relate to the national community of which they are a part and explains particular policy configurations in different countries. For example, it is an evident problem with the Miller thesis that a strong national identity like that in the US does not produce a stronger form of redistributive politics, say by comparison with Canada which is divided in its national cultures. If the argument that it is a common public culture which in part constitutes nationhood is correct, and if nationhood fosters social cooperation, then it would seem that a strong sense of nationhood should foster a strong sense of social cooperation. In public policy terms, this logic would be embodied in the institutions of the welfare state. Yet, the US is conventionally regarded as a welfare state laggard, and so something must have happened to the logic of nationhood.

Miller commendably acknowledges this problem, and seeks to deal with it explicitly. He argues that the difference between Canada and the US in respect of their welfare politics is to be understood in terms of the distinction between the strength of a public culture and the character of a public culture (Miller, 1995: 94). US public culture may be strong, but its character is individualistic, and this is invoked to account for the weakness of US welfare policy. The difficulty is that this is all too quick a move to make. In the first place it ignores the extent to which there is a culture of collectivism in the US, at least in respect of the popularity of certain welfare measures like social security. Secondly, it assigns no role to institutional variables in understanding public policy developments, so that culture is seen to have an unmediated role in explaining policy outcomes. Yet, this assumption of a direct relation between culture and policy choice runs counter to a significant body of work in comparative public policy.

The comparison between Canada and the US is instructive here. At the risk of offending any Canadians who may be reading this chapter (and I express the point as accurately as I can), the society with the culture closest to that of the US is Canada. A high proportion of Canadians live close the US border and there is generally a great deal of cultural interchange between the two societies (Marmor and Klein, 1986: 117–18). More importantly in the present context is the fact that up until the early 1970s Canada and the US had similar health care systems, with almost identical trends in terms of cost-escalation – the two things being related because health costs reflect underlying institutional arrangements. When Canada introduced its single-payer health care reforms in 1971, its pattern of health care delivery began to diverge from that of the US (Evans, 1982).

How was it that Canada was able to 'socialise medicine' in a way that had not been possible in the US since Roosevelt first contemplated a federal scheme in the 1930s? The answer that is common in the political science analysis turns on the institutional features of US policy making. In particular, the US policy-making system is characterised by a number of 'veto points' that could and have been exploited by those interests opposed to some form of federal health insurance scheme (Hacker, 2004). The contrast here with social security – in comparative terms a relatively early and generous US federal government income transfer scheme – is supportive evidence for the role of institutions. If an individualistic culture were the crucial explanatory variable, then the US social security system ought to be extremely unpopular. In fact, the opposite is the case, and attempts to undermine it have faced the constraints of popular resistance and, as important, the logic of anticipated reactions among policy makers. (George Bush looks as though he is going to make social security reform an important part of his second term agenda, so the elements of the explanation offered here will receive a crucial test in the next few years.)

Why do we need to make this excursion into the recesses of comparative public policy? It is not to deny the role of public culture in the making of public policy. The political culture of a society, and in particular the specific policy cultures of the political class, will play a role in providing the accepted stock of ideas and arguments in terms of which policy choices are justified and defended. But a public culture does not express itself directly and in an unmediated way in public policy. Instead, the key ideas have to be taken up, refined and sometimes refashioned by policy entrepreneurs and advocates before they can become politically effective. What is more, members of a society do not only define themselves in terms of the public culture in which they participate, they also can distance themselves from the political institutions within which they have to argue. Whatever her politics, Mrs Thatcher was being a good political scientist when she complained that she and her party had not defeated socialism in the UK to see it introduced via Brussels. Once the trades unions saw that they could make little or no headway with Mrs Thatcher's government, their next logical step was to exploit the institutions and policy competences of the European Union in order to advance their interests. If a constitutive public culture were conceptually tied to the institutions of the national political community, such political manoeuvring would not make any sense. But of course it does.

The general point, of which this is a particular illustration, can be put as follows. We can accept that the public culture of a national society is in part constitutive of the identities of the members of that society. This does not mean, however, that those same citizens cannot take an intelligently formed instrumental view about how far those institutions help further or hinder their interests or indeed their basic political values. Indeed, political actors will sometimes seek to displace political conflicts from one level of political authority to another precisely because they think that the likely outcome is going to be closer to their preferred point than fighting the matter out where they are. Faced with such an experience, it is clearly possible for actors to conclude that the right alternative was economic autarchy, in which an economy retreats behind protective barriers in order to secure the conditions under which greater social justice can be brought about. (Interestingly, Miller (1995: 102–3) seems to think that this is the right policy from the point of view of one who takes seriously the principle of national self-determination.) However, the same actors might democratically decide to take another course. They might think – and they would have good reason for doing so – that economic autarchy might leave all too little to redistribute. They might therefore come to the conclusion that the only context in which they can hope to secure goals of social protection is by means of an internationalisation of economic policy making. In other words, in order to secure the goods that a number of nation-states have aspired to provide, the institutions of the nation-state were no longer sufficient. In the case of economic policy, this would mean going beyond the standard arrangements of international cooperation to a pooling of sovereignty. In other words, there is a chain of reasoning from a concern with protection of the welfare state to a willingness to internationalise economic policy. Rather than pose a problem for social rights, European integration may well be the condition for their maintenance. Such a line of reasoning is at least open to those concerned with the practical rationality of democratic citizenship.

A European demogrant?

There is a contrasting line of argument to the civic nationalist case just considered. It can be argued that maintaining that defenders of the national welfare state do not have anything intrinsically to fear from European integration takes too cautious an attitude from the point of view of democratic citizens. Perhaps such citizens in member states have positive reasons for favouring European integration. After all, such integration provides the organisational capacity that could enable enhancements of social rights to take place.

There are reasons for thinking that the development of social policy at the European level would be advantageous if social rights are thought to be valuable. If we consider the US social security programme, it operates on a continental scale, and has considerable advantages as a result, by virtue of the fact that the risks of coverage can be spread across a large number of contributors. Moreover, and as already noted, the Social Security programme is popular in the US. Might this example provide evidence, or at least some working model, of the claim that it ought to be possible to develop social policy programmes at the European level? After all, if we are looking to the development of political loyalty and affect among citizens in the EU, the prospect of a European social security cheque being deposited in the bank account might provide very tangible evidence of the benefits of European integration.

There clearly is a line of argument to the effect that in an increasingly integrated market, it makes sense to share the costs of the flanking measures as widely as possible. Moreover, a unified social security system across Europe would help compensate for asymmetric shocks affecting some country economies in the euro area more seriously than others. However, democratic citizens have to recognise the limits of the feasible, and in this case considerations of a practical kind are going to be decisive. The creation of the US social security programme took place *de novo*; it did not seek to harmonise or reconcile existing systems of social insurance. The same would not be true in the European context. Indeed, despite the similarity of function that I have identified among EU member states, there is clearly great dissimilarity of structure. It is not possible to envisage bringing these systems together. There is a political logic of pre-emption at work, as detailed by Pierson and Leibfried (1995: 33), by which EU social policy initiatives take place around the edges of national cores, and such initiatives lack the legitimating potential of national welfare state programmes.

However, it might be argued that an ambitious scheme of income maintenance could be developed at the European level not in relation to the social insurance component of income maintenance programmes but in relation to the residual income maintenance programmes that go under various names in the member states. In particular, Phillipe Van Parijs (1997) has argued for the introduction of at least a partial basic income scheme at the European level. From the point of view of democratic citizenship, such a scheme, Van Parijs argues, has a number of advantages: it avoids intrusion into the private lives of citizens; it prevents citizens being caught in the employment trap of means tested benefits; it avoids the problems associated with reductions in working time or subsidising employers; and it provides a form of European freedom. The proposed Eurogrant could be introduced at a basic level, paid to every adult permanently resident in the EU and financed from a common European tax, for example on energy.

If such a scheme could be introduced, it could well be argued that it would enhance, rather than diminish, the social rights secured by the national welfare state. Since it would only supplement, not incorporate, the social insurance schemes of member states, it would not encounter the practical objections detailed above. Of course, it may have considerable administrative difficulties considered in its own terms, but for the purposes of evaluation, these will be disregarded here. Moreover, there is redistribution currently in the EU across countries, but it takes the form of agricultural subsidies or the regional and structural funds. From the point of view of those citizens being asked to make a tax contribution to a Eurogrant, it might well seem better to contribute to a transparent scheme aimed at the reduction of poverty than a complex set of transfers that may simply have the effect of augmenting the incomes of those who are already well off. If this line of argument is accepted, it might well be argued from the point of view of democratic citizenship, such a European demogrant would be very attractive.

Yet, there are grounds that would make one sceptical of the proposal. Let me sketch what such grounds might be. As I have already noted, the principles of fairness that are built into present-day welfare state arrangements involve two distinct sets of principles. The first is the principle of non-exploitation. This is the principle that suggests 'pure' redistribution from rich to poor, or at least to the poorest. This is the 'Robin Hood' component of the welfare state. The other component is the 'Beveridge' principle, by which redistribution is a matter of transfers across the lifecycle. Such redistribution is best thought of as corresponding to an agreement based on the principle of reciprocity among citizens. Obviously, in practice, these rationales are mixed, but in theory we can distinguish them as two quite distinct grounds for redistribution.

How should democratic citizens, either individually or collectively, balance these two principles against one another when they are thinking about the role and place of alternative schemes of distribution? The answer to this question is quite obvious: there is no general consideration that will suggest a tilt towards one principle rather than the other. Instead, when considering alternatives, citizens have to weigh a number of different claims. For example, proponents of a pure basic income scheme argue that there is a strong case for a basic income that is not made conditional upon a work test or other form of social participation. All citizens, on this view, have an entitlement to a minimum income guarantee, whatever their circumstances and willingness to work. However, there are those who argue that even at the basic level it is right to impose some reciprocity test, at least insofar as this takes the form of a work test (White, 2000). In other words, from this critical position, we cannot assume away the implications of the reciprocity principle.

Given this disagreement about how to balance conflicting applications of the non-exploitation and reciprocity principles, one wants to lodge the balancing that does take place in the public space which is at the most appropriate level. For a variety of reasons, this is likely to be the national level. In the first place, policies for a social minimum will need to be thought through in relation to the social insurance scheme and these schemes have complex regulations that operate at the national level. Secondly, information and understanding are more likely to be found at the national level, if only for reasons of language. Finally, national political communities will already have arrived at some balance between the two principles, and it does not make sense to disrupt such balances. Institutionalised reciprocity has value simply by virtue of the fact that it is institutionalised. These normative considerations reinforce the logic of pre-emption that has a powerful effect on limiting developments anyway. Taken together they argue for not seeking to expand in a radical the scope or extent of EU social policy, particularly in the core areas of the welfare state. This is not to say, of course, that there is not a case for enhancing reciprocal rights between systems most notably in the area of tax policy. But EU citizens should neither expect nor hope for a European welfare state to complement the European single market. However, this is not to say that the social agenda is entirely closed, as we shall see in Chapter 5 in the case of environmental policy.

5

Environmental protection

The economic growth that underlay the development and consolidation of social rights in the national welfare states of Europe brought problems in its wake. In particular, the growth of commodity consumption meant the risk of combining private affluence with public squalor. For many the warning evidence came from the United States, and Galbraith's amusing, if poignant, description of the effects of mass affluence provided a glimpse of what might happen in Europe unless corrective action was taken:

> The family which takes its mauve and cerise, air-conditioned, power-steered, and power-braked car out for a tour passes through a series of cities that are badly paved, made hideous by litter, blighted buildings, billboards, and posts for wires that should long since have been put underground. They pass on into a countyside that has been rendered largely invisible by commercial art ... They picnic on exquisitely packaged food from a portable icebox by a polluted stream and go on to spend the night at a park which is a menace to public health and morals. Just before dozing off on an air-mattress, beneath a nylon tent, amid the stench of decaying refuse, they may reflect vaguely on the curious unevenness of their blessings. (Galbraith, 1970: 208–9)

In fact, by the late 1960s and early 1970s there were significant political movements in all developed societies that pressed for public action to control pollution and increase environmental protection. What is striking is the extent to which in the late 1960s and early 1970s there were parallel policy developments for environmental protection across a range of democratic welfare states (Weale, 1992: 10–23). Although the definitive political science of the politics of this period has still to be written, it is possible to identify some of the main political forces that were influential in raising the priority of environmental issues on the political agenda.

In the first place, for some political parties a concern for environmental issues could be seen as compatible with existing policy orientations. In the German

Federal Republic, for example, the Social Democrats had already taken up in the early 1960s the slogan of 'blue skies over the Ruhr', in a campaign that reflected an awareness of the public health effects of the dust that was routinely discharged into the atmosphere (Spelsberg, 1984: 205). In Sweden the Agrarian Party was able to take up environmental issues quickly, because its rural base meant that its ideology did not fit unambiguously into a left–right spectrum, and it benefited considerably in the election of 1976 (Kronsell, 1997: 50). By contrast, in cases where strands of party thinking were sympathetic to industry, as with the Austrian Social Democrats, environmental issues were not taken up until the 1980s (Lauber, 1997: 90).

Secondly, there was a clear influence from advocacy groups, including both the traditional nature protection associations and the newer groups, like Friends of the Earth, that formed in the 1960s. Specific events, like the grounding of the oil supertanker *Torrey Canyon* in 1967, provided a catalyst for protest activity and focused public and political attention on issues of environmental protection. Moreover, there were social commentaries that led to a general questioning of the benefits of material affluence and the productive system that underlay it. Sometimes these critiques were widely popular. It is striking for example how many accounts draw attention to the role of Rachel Carson's 1962 book, *Silent Spring*, but the activities of key scientists were also significant, for example that of Svante Odén in Sweden who drew attention to the widespread nature of the problems of acidification.

However, there had been damaging environmental incidents before, for example the London smog of 1952, that had not led to the widespread upsurge of interest that was characteristic of the late 1960s and early 1970s. For this reason, although its role is disputed, it is difficult to tell the story of the politics of pollution in democratic welfare states without mentioning generational change and the rise of post-materialist values (Inglehart, 1977). As affluence on a mass scale came to be the norm, rather than an aspiration, sensitivity to issues of environmental quality could find greater resonance among democratic populations.

The timing of developments is important when considering the Europeanisation of policy. Because environmental issues did not make their way seriously onto political agendas until the late 1960s and early 1970s, the logic of pre-emption that operated in respect of social insurance and social rights did not apply with the same force. This is not to deny that there were established features of national policy systems that resisted EU policy developments, but they did so partly in terms of the environmental rule-making system that emerged within the EU and partly in terms of their resistance to implementation. The whole-scale pre-emption of an area of policy did not take place. Moreover, environmental protection measures typically use the instruments of administrative regulation rather than public spending, instruments that are the quintessential policy mode of the EU (Majone, 1996). So, rather than competing with national welfare states on the terrain of public spending, a terrain on which national political leaders had a great deal of political capital invested, it was possible for the EU to develop an environmental policy capacity at the same time that national systems were developing their own capacity at the national level.

Speculatively, one may go further. It is difficult not to see in the early development of EU environmental policy an attempt to secure some democratic legitimacy on the part of EU leaders. When the first environmental programme was inaugurated in 1972, there was not even a treaty basis for European action in this field. If, as Rokkan claimed, the development of social rights cemented political legitimacy in the democratic national welfare state, it is not too fanciful to see the EU's development of environmental policy as a bid for democratic legitimacy at the international level. And since, as the saying has it, pollution knows no boundaries, there was a certain plausibility to this position. In consequence, the political logic of environmental policy in respect of its national and EU dimensions is quite different from that of social policy.

The depth and extent of policy developments since 1972 is impressive by any standards (Weale *et al.*, 2000: 2–5). By the end of the 1990s some three hundred environmental policy measures were in operation, largely in the form of regulations and directives. The EU stipulated standards of pollution control for major discharges to air and water. It regulated waste disposal policy. It had policies in the field of nature conservation, particularly in respect of birds. It not only set standards for polluting emissions itself but also stipulated requirements for the way in which standards were set and implemented in member states, for example in respect of public access to environmental information or the auditing of firms' pollution controls. The EU represents the member states on major international bodies concerned with environmental protection, most notably the Kyoto treaty, where it is seen by some (Sbragia and Damro, 1999) as a leader in supporting stringent controls on climate change gases. In sum, as Zito (2000: 2) has pointed out, EU environmental legislation and activity stands out as a notable achievement compared to other issue areas.

It might be thought that these developments have taken place because environmental questions are valence issues, and so not matters of political controversy. Everyone agrees, so it may be argued, that the environment needs protection and the only questions that arise are technical ones about the most appropriate methods for achieving an agreed goal or the speed at which improvements can be implemented. At one time this view appears to have prevailed in some national capitals. Jordan (2002: 195–6) has noted that this was the view among UK policy makers in the 1970s and it was only in the 1980s that policy makers began to wake up to the environmental policy agenda that had developed in Germany and the Netherlands, an agenda that for much of UK industry threatened high and possibly unsustainable costs.

Yet, questions such as the control of acidification, river basin and estuarine pollution and the control of dispersed chemicals in the environment, while technical in terms of the specification of policy options, are not uncontroversial in terms of the reallocation of economic and political resources they occasion. Not all political parties were equally fast to take up environmental issues. Some on the left saw the environmental agenda as threatening the basis of mass affluence, and some on the right were protective of the profitability of industry. Indeed, as Paul Sabatier (1987) has nicely put it, the advocacy coalitions that gather around environmental policy across all democracies may be divided into an environmental protection grouping and an economic feasibility grouping. We should not assume that environment issues are uncontentious in democratic politics.

Although the EU was able to develop its extensive range of measures in part because, unlike the case of social insurance, national policy competences were not rigidly established in a form that would brook no challenge, this is not to say that Europeanisation has been complete. In terms of implementation, national policy administrations have responded differently. Empirical work to date on this question is limited, but there appears to be a contrast between the UK and Germany in this regard. Whereas for a variety of reasons the content and instruments of policy have changed extensively in the UK, leading to a substantial Europeanisation, the same processes were not operative in Germany, where administrative resistance limited the effects of the measures (Jordan, 2002; Knill, 2001). Yet, in a way, even in the case of Germany, problems of implementation confirm the importance of the EU's environmental policy, for it is one thing for a nation-state to be the norm-setter for its own environmental standards, quite another for it to be resisting in implementation a process that has been established at a higher level of political authority.

Practical rationality and environmental protection

So far I have considered the issue of environmental policy in Europe from an empirical point of view. What happens when we consider the issues from the viewpoint of the practical rationality of democratic citizenship?

The benefits of environmental protection cover a wide variety of goods. They include mental and physical health by means of protection from toxic substances; access to such goods as clean air, fresh water and a flourishing countryside; protection of the urban fabric; and such intangible goods as reassurance that species and natural habitats are being preserved, even if one does not have direct experience oneself of the species or habitats in question. Although these goods are diverse, they share the characteristic that they cannot be produced for purely private consumption. They are, in the strict sense in which economists use the phrase, public goods, defined as goods in which 'each individual's consumption leads to no subtraction from any other individual's consumption of that good' (Samuelson, 1954). For example, if I live in an area where the air is clean, then my enjoyment of that clean air is not purchased at the expense of the others' enjoyment. Similarly, if a species is preserved for any, it is preserved for all. This is not to say that the enjoyment of the good occurs at a supra-individual level. It is still individual experiences or individual states of body and mind that constitute the goods in question. It is simply that such good cannot be made available at the individual level without their also being made available collectively.

This feature of environmental goods suggests that the logic of we-intentions rapidly comes into play, for by definition the provision of any such good has to be thought of from the public point of view, and this raises the question of how individuals may play their part in a cooperative practice to ensure the production of environmental goods. Another reason for introducing the logic of we-intentions is that environmental damage is typically the unintended by-product of activities that are otherwise perfectly legitimate, including farming, industry and transport (Underdal, 1980). Such activities usually follow the logic of a market equilibrium, in which the outcome for the collective is the unintended product of a myriad of individual interactions in which all the parties are seeking for legitimate mutual advantage. However, there is no reason to suppose that this process will produce an outcome that any of the participating parites would have willed, let alone that any of the parties could propose as a justifiable we-intention.

These public and collective features of the goods secured by environmental protection lead to standard arguments in economics about the justification for public action in the field of environmental policy. These arguments derive from the insight that it is not possible fully to satisfy wants by processes of purely market exchange in the presence of these public features. Those arguments will be set out here, but I will also suggest that they need to be complemented by further arguments concerned with non-market values and the assertion of public standards of the good.

The principle of economic efficiency is that the wants of citizens, as consumers, should be satisfied to the maximum extent possible. This notion can be defined as equivalent to an allocation in the economy in which no one can be made better off without making someone else worse off, the so called Pareto optimum. One of the standard justifications for the use of markets in an economy is that the market allocation of resources in equilibrium is efficient in this sense. However, it is generally recognised that this result only holds under certain conditions, of which one is that there be no externalities. An externality exists when one person's economic activity affects another person's welfare, either favourably or adversely. The bee keeper's bees that pollinate the flower grower's flowers is an example of a favourable or positive externality. The factory's emissions that pollute a river fishery is an example of an adverse or negative externality.

In the case of pollution, where there is a negative externality, it is possible that there is a loss of economic efficiency in the following sense. If the victims of the pollution would find that they could pay the polluter to stop polluting and they would still be better off, then there is a potential gain from trade that is not being achieved. Not all the profitable opportunities in the economy are being used up. Economic efficiency, by definition, requires that there are no further gains from trade, and hence it follows that if there are externalities of this sort, the market outcome is inefficient. Note one important feature of this result. The test of the loss of efficiency is the willingness of the victims to pay the polluters to reduce their pollution. From a common-sense point of view, this seems counter-intuitive. Why should victims of pollution be expected to pay polluters to reduce the damage that they are causing? However, the counter-intuitive result follows simply from the fact that it is only a test of economic efficiency that is being applied and not a test of liability. All that the test of economic efficiency is concerned with is whether there are potential further gains from trade to be made. If there are not, then the test of economic efficiency is satisfied.

However, the mere introduction of the notion of liability is insufficient, by itself, to produce a situation in which the polluters are required to change their behaviour without any compensation from the victims of pollution. In a justly famous paper, Coase (1960) showed that, in the absence of transactions costs, the optimal level of production in an economy was unaffected by the liability regime in place for pollution. It makes no difference to the optimal level of production whether polluters have to pay victims for the right to pollute or whether victims have to bribe polluters to reduce their emissions. The choice of liability regime will of course make a difference to the distribution of income in an economy. When the liability is placed on polluters, they will be poorer in equilibrium than when the liability is placed upon victims. But in terms of the mix of goods in the economy there is no effect.

It is an important feature of the Coase result that it holds only the absence of transactions costs. Where there are transactions costs, we may well have a guide as to how liability is to be allocated. The obvious rule would be that liability should be assigned in such a way as to minimise the transactions costs required in order to secure potential gains from trade. However, although this might often lead to a situation in which it is polluters who have the liability, there is no guarantee that it will do so. For example, where there are a few point sources of pollution and a large number of people are adversely affected, it generally makes sense to assign liability to the polluter, since control measures can be more easily monitored. However, where there are a large number of dispersed sources of pollution, it may be necessary for the community as a whole to pay for clean-up costs. (Indeed, some public policy systems, as in Germany, explicitly recognise the 'community burden' principle alongside the producer pays principle as principles of public policy, see Weale, O'Riordan and Kramme, 1991: 115.)

What is the link between the principle of economic efficiency and the idea of democratic citizenship? Central to the idea of democratic citizenship is that it is the task of political associations to promote the good of their citizens and one way of achieving this objective is to meet whatever wants citizens happen to have. For a wide range of goods and commodities, a relatively freely functioning market system will meet wants in an efficient way, so that citizens as consumers are doing as well as they can do, within the budgets that are available to them. However, under certain conditions, including the existence of negative externalities, freely functioning markets will not be efficient in this way. Some form of market correcting policy needs to be considered.

None of this leads inevitably to the conclusion that the public authorities should regulate or control any particular form of economic activity. For any pollution problem there may be in practice a variety of possible solutions. Public action may involve regulation that modifies or suspends market relations, but it may also involve organising markets, for example markets in waste products, for the purpose of ensuring that the cumulative unintended outcomes of market activity are consistent with the overall interests of citizens. Whatever the precise content of the measures the existence of externalities is a reason for saying that the public authorities have a responsibility to ensure that the good of environmental protection is provided.

There is a way of supplementing these considerations based upon a somewhat different notion of efficiency from that of Paretian efficiency. This argument begins with the observation that, in the absence of public action, victims of pollution will resort to private law remedies, including tort and breaches of common law duties of care. For many products and processes a succession of separate legal actions, in which individuals separately sue for damages is more costly than the public authorities establishing a regulatory regime that controls the production of hazards in the first place. These costs are transactions costs, defined as the costs of running the market. The benefit of public action therefore can be to reduce these transactions costs and public action is a way of securing economies of scale in what would otherwise be dispersed individual action.

The argument so far can be stated as follows. Environmental protection takes the form of a public good. It typically involves protection from the negative externalities of others, including those that take the form of the cumulative, unintended consequences of the actions of others. Taking the satisfaction of the wants that citizens happen to have as part of their good, we find in such situations that market mechanisms are usually unable to satisfy these wants to the maximum extent. Uncoordinated activity in the market produces, in Rousseau's terms, the sum of the will of all rather than a general will. It produces, that is to say, a collection of I-intentions, related to other I-intentions through mutual gains from trade, but it does not produce a we-intention that anyone can endorse. We want the private affluence, but we do not want it at the expense of the public squalor.

A common, and often insightful, way of putting this point is to say that underlying problems of environmental protection is an n-person prisoners' dilemma (Hardin, 1982). Acting on principles of individual rationality, each person wants the best for him or herself, but this leads to attempts to free-ride on others in ways that turn out to be self-defeating. If I use scarce water for my plants in a time of drought, hoping that others will conserve, I am ignoring the fact that what is rational for me is rational for others as well. If my fleet fishes the scarce stocks in the sea, hoping that others will conserve, I am ignoring the incentive others have to fish as intensively as they can. If I drive to work, hoping that others will take the bus, I am ignoring their reasons for driving also, and we shall all be caught in the traffic jam. If I have reason to stand on tiptoe, hoping to see better, so does everyone else. In these circumstances, what is rational for each is not rational for all.

There are clearly cases where the logic of environmental protection is the logic of a prisoners' dilemma, but it is a merit of the we-intentions approach that the problems do not have to be seen in this way. They can be seen as problems taking the form of assurance games, and such problems produce a less vicious set of traps than do prisoners' dilemmas (see Sen, 1982: 78–80). In a prisoners' dilemma each individual has an incentive to free-ride upon the cooperative behaviour of others. If others are conserving water, then my best course of action is to use it freely. If others are conserving fish stocks, then my best course of action is to fish as intensively as possible. In assurance games, by contrast, we find a different structure of incentives. In assurance problems, each person wishes to cooperate with others only provided that he or she can be assured that enough others are willing to cooperate on their part.

One of the empirical conditions in which the preferences of actors are likely to take this assurance form is that there is a prevalent norm of fairness, by which each person wishes to play his or her part in a cooperative scheme to general advantage (Hart, 1955). Another possible condition is that some authoritative public body is able to punish defectors from the cooperative scheme to the point where it is not worthwhile defecting, thus turning a prisoners' dilemma into an assurance game. The point of analytic interest is that the production of public goods in the general case should be thought of as a case of how we-intentions are to be produced, whether we think of the underlying problem structure in prisoners' dilemma or assurance game terms.

The arguments summarised here for public intervention have sometimes been presented as reasons for state intervention, but the varying levels of cooperation required for the production of different public goods mean that there is no direct inference from market failure to state. What is more, there can be state failure as well as market failure. Sometimes state failure exists when national states fail to deal adequately with their own problems because they are too responsive to well-organised special interests who displace problems onto others, for example by loading pollution control costs onto public budgets instead of their being assigned to those responsible for the pollution, as has arguably happened for water clean-up costs from the over-use of agricultural fertilisers. However, state failure can also occur when problems at the national level are displaced onto higher levels, as when countries in the 1950s and 1960s solved their national air pollution problems from factories and electricity generating plants by building higher chimneys, the effect of which was to carry pollutants across boundaries. Finally, we cannot assume that the inference is from environmental protection as a public good to state action when we are dealing with problems that arise in the international commons, such as the open seas or the global atmosphere.

EU environmental policy

The goods of environmental protection may be found at different levels of social organisation. For example, some goods are local, providing benefits for citizens of a city, town or commune but not for those outside. A safe and effective system of waste management or system of public transport for a city would be examples. Some forms of environmental protection may be required at the regional level, for example in the management of a river basin. Some forms may be required at the national level and yet others at the continental or global levels. For any one individual, therefore, the relevant group whose members need to cooperate to produce the relevant set of we-intentions is not fixed but will vary with the problem at hand. In some cases it will be citizens of one's town or region, in other cases it will be members of the national community, and in yet other cases the production of the public good will require cooperation by citizens across national boundaries. Of course, the practical problems of obtaining sufficient assurance that others will act cooperatively may be more difficult at some levels of organisation than others, but the problems of supplying such assurance arise precisely because cooperation is needed across variously constituted groups.

It would seem that, so far, there is a coincidence between the empirical conditions underlying the development of environmental policy in Europe and the normative justification for public action for environmental protection that can be offered within the practical rationality of democratic citizenship. In normative terms, if environmental protection is needed at a number of different levels of social organisation, this would appear to provide a clear justification for action at the EU level. Empirically speaking, because the logic of pre-emption did not operate as strongly in the case of environmental protection as in the case of social insurance, policy competences could be more easily developed within the EU. Such an allocation of policy competences between different levels of governance is implied by the recognition that the production of we-intentions in differing levels of political association was required by the character of the problems being dealt with.

However, this appearance of seemingly happy coincidence between empirical process and justifying logic needs to be qualified. What the argument from scale shows is that some form of international association is needed to deal with some problems of environmental protection. If state failure spills over onto the citizens of other states, then it is clear why the victims would want to make agreements with the perpetrators. However, why seek to institutionalise international environmental cooperation so extensively within the EU? There is an alternative way of dealing with cross-boundary issues. This would involve nation-states dealing with problems at their level of organisation and cooperating with another in international regimes for problems on a larger scale. After all, within Europe many international pollution problems have concerned countries both inside and outside the EU, and international agreements, like those concerned with long-range transboundary pollutants have been negotiated and compliance mechanisms established. Thus, during the 1970s and 1980s there was widespread international concern about sulphur dioxide emissions from electricity generating plants and similar large stationary sources. In the 1980s concerns about global climate change, as well as a large number of other problems, also emerged, and there was a general recognition that some form of international policy coordination was needed if such problems were to be dealt with effectively. What additional advantage, if any, might flow to citizens by institutionalising an environmental policy capacity in the EU?

The core of the answer to this question turns on the single market. Although a variety of international environmental control regimes exist in Europe, the distinctive reason for the EU acquiring environmental policy capacity relates to the single market. In particular, in the absence of an environmental policy capacity in the EU, environmental standards in Europe might otherwise have been threatened by the extension of free trade within the single market. In other words, given that the method chosen to promote European integration was through the creation of the single market, there was always the danger that standards would have been lower after the single market than before.

What are the general reasons for thinking that European integration through the single market could lead to a loss of environmental protection? Since the single market is a liberalising measure, one part of the answer to this question turns on arguments about the relationship between environmental protection and free trade generally. Here, as with social policy, the reasons are not clearcut in either direction. As Brack (1995) has argued, there are respects in which free trade can be good for the environment and respects in which it can encourage environmental deterioration. Insofar as it facilitates the efficient use of resources, free trade is likely to be good for the environment. It also promotes transparent pricing, which makes it difficult to maintain environmentally damaging subsidies. Free trade also opens economies to the use of new technologies, which are generally less environmentally damaging than traditional ones. Free trade can promote clean production, product diversification and better use of natural resources.

Moreover, there are particular reasons why we might not expect the single market to create a race to the bottom (compare Weale, 1994). As far as products are concerned, if there is a rising demand for goods that meet high environmental standards, then the structure of demand in the market will act to maintain quality. The same can even be true of processes, insofar as process features enter into an assessment of the characteristics by which consumers judge the value of commodities or their development provides a 'first-mover' advantage to the country that mandates their use. What is more, governments are not unitary actors, but collections of organisations, each with their own specific policy orientation and policy paradigm. Economic ministries concerned about the costs of production will either have to negotiate with environment ministries concerned about environmental quality or take the dispute to a political level in which cabinet colleagues have to resolve their differences. Finally, the single market provides an incentive to governments to ensure that other countries are meeting high environmental standards, in order to assure themselves that the costs of meeting environmental standards are being fairly shared.

On the other hand, we also have to recognise the factors that incline free trade to be bad for the environment. Although pollution per unit of output may be lower with the more efficient use of resources, the overall increase in the total volume of production can contribute to environmental stress, as any driver suffering the effects of congestion will know. The higher returns derived from improved trading opportunities may not be devoted to environmental improvement.

Moreover, to the extent that pollution control measures require increased invest-ment, the demands they create will make a demand on funds that otherwise could have been put to more profitable uses. Again, with capital being more mobile than labour, and certainly more mobile than the physical environment, the effect of strin-gent environmental regulations in one country will lead entrepreneurs to look at opportunities elsewhere. So the freedom of movement of capital will create a down-ward movement on the stringency of national environmental regulations.

These conflicting arguments and the political forces with which they were associated were played out in practice in the development of environmental policy in the wake of the creation of the single market (Weale, *et al.*, 2000: 29–52). Envi-ronmental policy developed in the European Union in part because, as pollution control standards can also constitute non-tariff barriers to trade, there was an explicit link with the logic of the single market and in part because EU policy makers saw environmental policy as one way to enhance the legitimacy of the EU. Although it is impossible to know definitively whether the state of the environ-ment in the member states is better or worse than it would have been without European integration, it is possible to find some examples where EU environ-mental policy has either limited pollution control measures that particular coun-tries wished to introduce or has threatened to do so. The leading example here is the Danish law to try to control the disposal of drinks containers, although the European Court of Justice (ECJ) did in the end uphold the right of the Danish government to implement the measure. More common, however, is the tendency of EU legislation to put pressure on environmental laggards to improve their per-formance. Of course, it is always possible to argue that a smaller group of leader states could have forged ahead had they not had the requirement to secure agree-ment through the EU legislative process, but conjecture at that point gets very speculative. The balance of effect seems to be that EU environmental policy has raised standards throughout the Union as a whole, even taking into account the inevitable implementation failures. Certainly, there was a slowing down in the pace of environmental regulation in the 1990s compared to the 1980s and early 1990s, but that may be attributed to the downturn in the economy, which tends to have a depressing effect on environmental zeal.

However, there is another reason, related to but distinct from the single mar-ket, as to why an environmental capacity at EU level might contribute to the pro-duction of public goods of benefit to citizens. Consider the feature of environmental problems discussed earlier, namely the fact that environmental problems are typically a by-product of otherwise legitimate activities like indus-try, transport and agriculture. The inference that environmental policy analysts have drawn from this observation is that environmental concerns should not be thought of as a discrete area of public policy but should be integrated into a broad range of public policies. Hence, it would seem to follow that as the EU acquired more policy-making responsibilities, it needed to ensure that the environmental implications of policy making in this expanded set of competencies were being addressed. Indeed, the Single European Act itself recognised environmental standards as relevant to a wide range of policies and asserted the principle that environmental protection requirements should be 'a component of the Community's other policies' and this approach was strengthened in the Treaty on European Union by the formulation that environmental 'protection requirements must be integrated into the definition and implementation of other Community policies' (Weale *et al.*, 2000: 70).

One advantage that is often claimed for such integration is that it makes it easier to develop preventive and comprehensive policy strategies. Consider, as an example, the case of air pollution from road vehicles. It is possible to regulate the emission values of vehicles, with the intention of reducing emissions per vehicle. However, if the total number of passenger journeys increases significantly, the value of the individual vehicle reduction can be more than off-set by the value of the cumulative effects. What is then needed, so it is argued, is an ability to design systems of transport that reduce these overall effects, and this in turn requires an expansion of policy competencies at a suitable level.

In theory there is a great deal to be said in favour of this approach. However, its exact significance in practice is difficult to estimate, and there are reasons for thinking that environmental policy integration is less decisive an argument in favour of an EU environmental policy capacity than one might think. In the first place, there is a well-known phenomenon of limited attention span within policy-making institutions, which means that policy makers in sectors other than environment will find it difficult in cognitive terms to integrate environmental decision-making into their policy calculations. Moreover, there may be considerable political investments in certain policies, of which in the EU the most obvious would be the Common Agricultural Policy, making it difficult for those with environmental concerns to change priorities in sectors that are causing environmental damage. One can argue that even the rhetorical commitment to environmental policy integration is helpful to those seeking to end wasteful or polluting practices, but it is difficult to base a whole case for an EU environmental capacity on the importance of integration given the record to date.

There is an argument for the superiority of the EU's environmental capacity over international regimes, if we consider the fairness aspect of environmental protection. As already pointed out, fairness in relation to environmental protection depends upon more than the identification of liability and the enforcement of the polluter pays principle, since those liable for environmental damage may themselves be economically vulnerable. Hence, what is needed are means by which compensating transfers can be secured in order to protect the position of the vulnerable. Although not impossible, as the example of technology transfer arrangements under the Climate Change Treaty shows, it is difficult in general to secure such transfers. The standard pattern of international agreements on pollution control, for example, consists of reductions in pollutants from a base-line figure, where the responsibility for reduction is allocated in proportion to the volume of pollutant being emitted. In situations where the contracting parties are of roughly equal economic standing, no distributional issue arises from such a form of agreement. However, where there are distributional issues, then compensation mechanisms can become important. The advantage of the EU is that the structural and regional funds can be used as compensating devices to off-set the obligations that member states might have under pollution control measures. The potential for issue linkage in this way is integral to the case for favouring an explicit environmental policy capacity in the EU.

European environmental ideals?

Sometimes within the EU it is difficult to match the actual assignment of competences with the principles of assignment that would seem to be implied by the practical rationality of democratic citizenship. From this point of view, there is a mismatch between the actual evolution of EU environmental policy and its justifying rationale. Thus, a familiar argument about EU environmental policy is that it is over-intrusive into domains that should really be the concerns of the member states, or perhaps even of regions within the member states. Consider the case of the bathing waters directive. This regulates the quality of designated bathing waters and seeks to apply common standards of quality across the whole of the EU. Although the object at which it aims is limited, it has led to considerable costs being incurred in order to install waste-water treatment facilities sufficient to meet its requirements. Yet, on any reasonable account, bathing waters are clearly only a local public good. It is hardly plausible to argue that the quality of the beaches in Scarborough or Blackpool is of great concern to the inhabitants of Helsinki or Athens and indeed at the time the original directive was passed ministers in both Britain and Germany thought that its main benefits would be in the Mediterranean (Wurzel, 2002: 201). One common rule in welfare economics is that the level at which the provision of public goods should be decided is the level sufficiently large to have internalised the externalities. Application of this principle to this case would mean that it would cease to be a responsibility carried out at the European level. More local communities would have to decide on the quality of bathing waters that they wished to maintain.

If the arguments were solely about correcting for market failure and meeting the criterion of efficiency, then this conclusion would be the correct one, and no more need be said on the matter. However, this would be too quick a move. For although the regulation of any environmental problem involves an irreducible technical element, there is inevitably also a set of issues about public values raised in the setting of standards. The original bathing waters directive had little scientific evidence to support the limit values that it included, as became clear when the Commission sought to revise the directive in the 1990s (Wurzel, 2002: 243–51). However, it was also clear from the revision process that the positions of national governments were liable to criticism, even those like the UK which claimed that their position was based upon a scientifically validated approach. Indeed, as has been argued by the UK's Royal Commission on Environmental Pollution

(1998), the setting of environmental standards is likely always to involve a consideration of public values as well as a concern for technical matters. From this point of view, even policies for local public goods provide a forum within which wider discussions can take place about standards that should be applied within a political association.

Looked at in this way, EU environmental policy is about increasing the deliberative space within which policy arguments are developed. Part of that increase in deliberative capacity is to allow for ideal-regarding arguments to be heard in the formulation of we-intentions, where the 'we' ranges over a group of citizens larger than a local community or a nation-state. In this particular case, it is sometimes argued that all citizens in the EU are entitled to be able to allow their children to swim in clean bathing waters. In other words, the debate is transformed from one about the most effective way to meet preferences antecedently given, and becomes one about the appropriate standards in terms of which those preferences are formed. The challenge is not solely about how best to organise decision making for pollution control so as to meet local views, but whether those local views can withstand the test of deliberative challenge.

Note that this argument is distinct from the one that can be developed within a conventional welfare economic framework and which has been well laid out by Wils (1994). Wils notes that the preferences that citizens in one member state have about the practices of citizens in another member state have relevance if the EU is concerned to maximise citizen welfare, as would be suggested by the conventional argument of public environmental protection. For example, UK citizens feel strongly about the protection of animal welfare in other member states, and it might well be that welfare in the EU as a whole would be raised if those external preferences were taken into consideration when making policy. In other words, if to the categories of physical and economic spill-overs, we add the category of psychic spill-overs, then we can see that otherwise local environmental issues actually had a broader scope and interest. Yet, this is not the argument I am seeking to develop at this point. It is not so much a question of how to make policy so as to satisfy pre-existing preferences – no matter how broadly held in geographical terms – as of thinking about how the activities of the EU as a political association provide a context within which citizens can reflect upon and develop their preferences.

One way of seeing this point is to note how, within a democratic political association, arguments for public action move beyond a neutral want-regarding form and begin to involve ideal-regarding considerations, to use Barry's (1965) distinction. To see the pattern of this development, consider the familiar idea that it is a legitimate function of the state to prevent the harm that one person or agent causes to another. It is well know that this harm principle cannot stand on its own, since there are many circumstances in which it is appropriate to allow harms to occur, as for example in cases of economic competition, when the successful pricing strategy of one business will harm the business of a competitor. As long ago as John Stuart Mill (1859), it has been recognised that the harms from which persons should be protected are those where there is some moral claim to protection. Similarly, there may be non-harms from which persons should be protected, the most obvious examples being offensive nuisances of the sort that often occur in pollution control, for example protection from offensive odours. A breach of these protected harms may be called a wrong, and in that sense the task of public policy is to prevent wrongs.

The question now arises as to whether it is only wrongful harms that are a justified target of public action. In particular, might there be activities in relation to the use of environmental resources that are wrong independently of any harm that they might cause to other persons? In this connection, consider the obligation, as some people see it, to avoid wasting natural resources. Although the waste of natural resources is often associated with wrongs towards others, most obviously the wrong of an unjust appropriation of resources from some common stock of goods, there is no reason why it need take this form. Someone might waste resources but pay sufficient by way of compensation to mean that there is no loss to others. It might be held that people should not litter, even if they are prepared to pay other people to pick their waste up after them.

If we argue for environmental policy measures in this way, we are invoking very different sorts of considerations from those that are advanced under the heading of efficiency. When we argue in terms of efficiency, we are taking existing wants, or at least some close cousin like enlightened preferences, and asking what social and economic institutions are best able to deliver maximum satisfaction of those wants. By contrast, if we say that public policy should aim at the reduction of waste, in and of itself, then we are arguing in an ideal-regarding way. There are a number of reasons why a liberal polity might not allow an ideal-regarding argument, but the same is not true in a democratic polity. It is difficult to find a principle of democracy that would prevent citizens from legislating according to ideal-regarding considerations, if that is what they choose. I suspect the reason why this does not happen more often is that many ideal-regarding considerations are morally contentious especially in any large-scale society where value pluralism is likely to be found. Nevertheless, the bathing waters issue can be conceived in ideal-regarding terms, and the scope of such arguments can be extended more generally.

Of course, we cannot avoid the fact that the issues are as much to do with the substantive merits of the standards as with the question of local control. The levels of quality that are being aimed at are very high, with such dilute concentrations of some pollutants that standards may be breached simply by natural phenomena like droppings from sea-birds. In this sort of case, much of the discussion turns on questions about the marginal value of increased expenditure on water cleanliness. In other words, unless we can make a categorical distinction between what is safe and what is unsafe, it is difficult to say that there is an entitlement being breached that has some absolute force. There is one aspect of the difficulty of using the language of rights in the context of social provision that comes in graded quantities of less or more, a point that Brian Barry (1965: 149–50) made many years ago. This is not to deny that environmental protection has the status of a claim that can be made on resources and policy priorities. It is to say that in pursuit of that claim it will be necessary to undertake some balancing of conflicting considerations.

In terms of the practical choices that might be made about where to assign responsibility for decision making on local public goods, this argument about the extension of the deliberative space need not be decisive. One can still argue that the deliberative challenge could be opened up without assigning decision making to the highest level of effective political association. For example, someone might argue that given the competition for attention from policy makers and decision-making forums, it was better to enable the EU to focus on the problems where it had a distinct advantage, and that would be in the field of international public goods, rather than local public goods. Crowded policy agendas do not make for good policy choices. However, whatever the merits of this argument, it is still less an argument of principle than the argument that says that it is constitutionally wrong for higher levels of decision making to become involved with lower levels of decision making.

Conclusion

Public goods provide one of the main elements of the goods of citizenship. They contribute to well-being and complement the social rights that also play a strategic role in enabling citizens to advance their own conception of the good. Public goods are also essential components in the maintenance of a civilised life, that is to say a life free from intrusive nuisances, which though they might not be fundamentally threatening to human well-being affect our sense of how well life goes for us.

In this chapter, I have argued that, though it is a simple matter of observation that public goods occur at different levels of social and political organisation, this of itself is not an argument for EU environmental policy. Instead, we need to see that policy as strengthening the political rights of citizenship, in providing a means of representation and a forum within which high standards of policy performance can be discussed and debated. Through this process, the policy task of improving the supply of public goods feeds back to the conception of political citizenship in the EU. The purposes of the emerging political association that is the EU become redefined and reformulated, and in this sense the political association is itself redefined and reformulated. The general logic at work here is the extension of the range of 'we' in the concept of we-intentions.

6

Security policy

Protection from external threat is the paradigm of a public good supplied through political association. In the absence of such protection, human groups stand in a state of nature with respect to one another. Production and reproduction are made difficult or impossible. As Hobbes memorably put it, not only is there no place for industry, there is no place for the arts and sciences: 'no commodious building; no instruments of moving and removing, such things as require much force; no knowledge of the face of the earth; no account of time; no arts; no letters; no society' (Hobbes, 1651, Chapter 13). In the absence of security, therefore, human life will not flourish and there will be no exercise of the higher capacities of which human beings are capable. In extreme circumstances, where individuals have no secure protection at all from the force of others, survival itself is at stake, so that in Hobbes's words, there is 'continual fear, and danger of violent death; and the life of man, solitary, poor, nasty, brutish, and short'.

The conventional lesson to draw from the absence of security in a state of nature is the need to form a political association that is capable of enforcing law and order upon citizens who would otherwise be at war with one another. This was the lesson that Hobbes himself drew, using it as justification for the establishment of a leviathan holding individuals in awe, a lesson that has been echoed by many others subsequently. However, there is a sceptical tradition in respect of this argument, a position taken by Rousseau in *L'Etat de Guerre*, who argued that in ending the state of nature among individuals, political associations created a state of nature among themselves. In the absence of a common sovereign to govern such associations, the conditions existed for international war. These wars would be more threatening to the security of individuals than the original state of nature, because of the increased military power that nations possessed compared to individuals. In modern times, this Rousseauian argument has been taken up by Michael Taylor (1976: 131), who has suggested that states established at the national level to rescue people from the threats of war may cause a security dilemma to emerge at the international level.

In the twentieth century, European citizens had had occasion to learn this Rousseauian lesson well. By 1945, France and Germany had fought their third war in less than eighty years, and the rest of the world had been drawn in to the latter two. But even prior to this period, the European state system had not managed to find a peaceful equilibrium. This was not simply a matter of the need to tidy up the national boundaries that had remained ragged or disputed in the dynastic politics of the middle ages and early modern period. It was also a consequence of the nationalism that had emerged with the creation of the European state system itself, spilling out as it did into the Napoleonic wars. Rokkan's stages of state and nation building, which were important in creating the conditions for representative democratic government in western Europe, also created the conditions for nationalist wars in Europe, as well as the expansion of European states into imperial ambitions overseas.

Although the politics and policy of the European Union often seems preoccupied with detailed matters of economic and social regulation, we should not forget that one of its primary rationales was historically to be found in the desire to avoid further nationalistic wars in Europe. Indeed, the creation of the European Union, through the initial development of the Coal and Steel Community can be seen as an attempt to suppress the rivalries of inter-state politics. Coal and steel were important because whoever controlled their production controlled one of the primary means of manufacturing military equipment. Placing their production under supranational control was intended as a way of reducing the capacity of Germany to engage in war. Of course, we cannot assume that the emergence and growth of the European Union historically served the purpose of quelling ancient feuds. Rousseauian gloom is still possible in the face of European integration, as Stanley Hoffmann illustrated during the Cold War in an essay on Rousseau on international relations, when he pointed out, in respect of the suspension of force among west European nations, that 'the reason why such an oasis of peace can bloom is not that world peace is getting nearer, but that an external danger has brought threatened nations together' (Hoffmann, 1965: 85). Yet, whatever the balance of historical forces at work, security issues have not been far from the central concerns of EU integration.

Moreover, there are clearly large questions about the future of security in Europe after the end of the Cold War. The EU was embedded in the security protection provided by NATO, the original purpose of which ended with the collapse of communism in central and eastern Europe. It is common to argue in this context that not only did the identity of the enemy change with the ending of the Cold War, but so too did the character of the security threats themselves. In place of conventional and nuclear wars, so it is argued, we should see the threats as coming from non-state actors willing to practise terrorism. Indeed, in some versions of this account, the notion of there being threats that are related to military capacity is regarded as being inadequate. Threats to security, so it is argued, can take a whole variety of forms, including migration, environmental pollution, attacks on business IT capacity, disease and other harms.

To some extent, a redefinition of security is inevitable after the Cold War, but as Ole Wæver (1996: 108) has pointed out, one problem with this broadening of the security agenda is that, though it is intended to give priority to certain issues like the need for environmental protection, it can also bestow an unjustified priority to certain putative solutions, including giving a privileged place to centralising policy instruments, which may not be the right ones to use for the problem at hand. Moreover, there is always some advantage in seeking to be clear in one's use of key terms and in the logic of concept formation. Accordingly, I shall invoke the distinction (going back to Hart, 1961: 156; Perelman, 1963; and Rawls, 1999a: 5) between concepts and conceptions. A concept is the general form of an idea; and conceptions are specific formulations. Thus, to take one example, the concept of justice can be specified in the requirement that there be no arbitrary distinctions among people in the making and implementation of public policy. We turn to particular theories of justice to find a specification of what counts as an arbitrary distinction, thus determining distinct conceptions of justice.

Seen from this point of view, the concept of security names a three-place relation taking the following form: an agent is secured from some threat in respect of their particular goods or interests. Particular conceptions of security spell out distinct specifications of this concept, in which the agent, the threat and the interests are detailed according to the theory in question. Thus the agent can be individuals, peoples, states, firms or many other types of agent. Threats can be military, environmental or cultural. The interests or goods can be personal integrity of life and limb, property and possessions or the cultural life of a people. In terms of this logic, when people call for new security concepts, they are in fact calling for the replacement or supplementing of the traditional military conception of security with other conceptions.

Hobbesian security can be defined as the conception that individuals have a basic interest in being free from the fear of violence. In turn, this is seen to involve the protection of the life and possession of citizens through military and other instruments of force and in practice this requires the protection of the integrity of the state. Such a conception of security has traditionally raised special problems in political theory. The reason is that the use of force is generally taken to require strong reasons in support, and there is always the worry that measures that were intended to be for the protection of citizens in fact turn out to their disadvantage. So, this chapter will be concerned with the principles that govern this Hobbesian conception of security, that is to say those aspects of security that may need to be addressed by means of military force. This is not to deny that there are other threats to other forms of security, nor is it to imply that a Hobbesian – or in modern terms realist – general theoretical framework is the right one with which to approach such problems. It is merely to acknowledge that the Hobbesian conception of security raises a distinctive set of issues and to accept that the practical rationality of democratic citizenship faces particular problems when questions of security in this sense are raised.

European security issues

In the immediate aftermath of the Allied victory in the Second World War, it was not clear what form the new security arrangements in Europe would take. In particular, the future arrangements for the government of Germany were unclear or disputed in quite fundamental respects, including the extent to which Germany was to be treated as an integrated country or the extent to which it should be allowed to re-industrialise. Yet, by 1950, the fundamental balance of forces and institutions of the Cold War era were in place. The iron curtain divided Europe between east and west and in each half communist and capitalist regimes were established, in line with Stalin's principle: 'Whoever occupies a territory also imposes on it his own social system. Everyone imposes his own social system as far as his army can reach' (cited in Trachtenberg, 1999: 36). Germany was divided between the Soviet-controlled east and the Allied-controlled west at the point where Stalin's principle met its greatest test. The founding of the German Federal Republic in 1949 in effect institutionalised this division, as did the establishment of NATO as an alliance to protect the territorial integrity of western Europe. Finally, although the security of Europe rested upon the US possession of nuclear weapons, the fact that the Soviet Union also had developed a nuclear capability, meant that the European theatre was one of the key areas in relation to which the US/USSR arms race would develop.

Yet, within this broad balance of forces and institutions, there were many fundamental issues still to be worked out, as Trachtenberg (1999) has shown. Fully to construct the peace of Europe required a number of basic questions to be confronted. How far could Europe develop an autonomous military capacity at a supra-national level, something that the US was particularly keen to promote? What role would Germany play in the new security arrangements? In particular, how was the question of whether or not there should be a German nuclear capability to be resolved? How much political control could realistically be exercised over military commanders in what might turn out to be a pre-emptive use of military weapons? How would the economic burden of Europe's defence be shared between the US on the one side and its European partners on the other? None of these questions were easy to answer at the time, and to some extent contemporary issues are framed by the legacy of the answers finally given.

With the failure in 1954 to create the European Defence Community and the expansion of NATO at Eden's initiative to include Germany and Italy (Duke, 1996: 168), NATO came to assume the leading role in the provision of European security throughout the period of the Cold War. This in turn had implications for the form that European integration would take. As Anne Deighton has put it, the European Union 'essentially remained a nested organization that was in practice protected by Nato, and by states' own defence regimes' (Deighton, 2003: 277). So, as far as the European Union was concerned, security issues were off the agenda, and the logic of European integration occurred not in the high politics of military policy but in the low politics of market integration. When governments faced opposition to the implications of these defence arrangements, for example in the 1980s over the up-grading of nuclear missile capability, they did so as national governments committed to NATO and not as members of the European Union. Conversely, with the accession of neutral states like Ireland, Austria, Finland and Sweden to the Union, the security issues were made more difficult to handle rather than less.

What are the implications of these historical legacies in the context of the post-Cold War world? Clearly, the logic of Stalin's principle has been ended, and in theory at least all sides to the former conflict became committed to the principle of democratic self-determination. In other words, there was a return to the aspirations of Woodrow Wilson after the First World War for the norm of self-determination to replace the imperial suppression of nations in Europe. However, rather than adding to the security of European states, the new era ushered in new problems, just as Robert Lansing, Woodrow Wilson's Secretary of State, predicted of its original use when he said that it was loaded with dynamite and would 'raise hopes which can never be realized' (quoted in Franck, 1992: 53). The problem here is inescapable, for the principle of self-determination is only uncontroversial where the identity of the collective 'self' at issue is itself uncontroversial. In the absence of this condition, the application of the principle is, in Lansing's word, 'dynamite'. In particular, this was to be so in the former Yugoslavia, and, as the constituent units of the federation sought for independence, bloodshed ensued. The European Union was badly equipped to deal with the situation, and not until US intervention was it possible to create the conditions within which peacekeeping could occur. In short, the ending of the Cold War meant that the countries of the European Union acquired a problem of how to deal with the consequences of civil war and ethnic cleansing in the heart of Europe itself.

The ending of the Cold War also affected global security issues, particularly in the field of humanitarian intervention. Such issues had been around throughout the latter part of the twentieth century, for example in relation to Tanzania's invasion of Uganda inspired by humanitarian aims and India's military intervention into what was to become Bangladesh. However, for the most part, during the Cold War intervention had mainly taken the form of super-power support for particular political factions within a country. This was quite a distinct case from that of humanitarian intervention, which is concerned to protect vulnerable populations from their own governments or the exercise of force from powerful groups within the population. After the Cold War and the wave of global democratisation, it became more difficult for decision makers to resist the argument that intervention may sometimes be needed to protect vulnerable populations. Unfortunately, the performance did not match the aspiration, as was so conspicuously demonstrated in Rwanda, where in 1994 the minority Tutsis would have welcomed protection from the majority Hutus had members of the international community been willing to intervene.

The third security issue to emerge has been that of terrorism. For some EU member states, the UK and Spain in particular, the issue of terrorism had been on the security policy agenda for a number of years. Clearly, however, after the attacks on the Twin Towers in New York on 11 September 2001, the problems were seen to increase in scope and extent. Moreover, the stance of the US was to align these problems with the issue of failed or rogue states, with the claim that three states in particular were intent on developing weapons of mass destruction. This interpretation of the situation was not shared by many member states in the EU, and the dissent from the Bush administration's decision to invade Iraq was obviously a major fault-line in the western alliance. How to deal with the threat of terrorist activity from various groups became therefore not only a problem in itself but a problem as to how to handle the problem in the western alliance.

The emergence of these new questions poses basic questions in relation to the process of European integration. The security arrangements of the Cold War arose in part because it was not possible for European countries to agree among themselves on a supranational way of organising their military capabilities. Nesting the EU in NATO turned out to be a way of dealing with this problem, which had the additional advantage that it left the EU to integrate along economic lines while its security needs were catered for. Yet, the NATO arrangement was obviously geared to the specific type of threats associated with the territorial struggle for Europe. Indeed, NATO has managed since the end of the Cold War to redefine its mission and its field of activities, particularly by means of its partnership for peace. Yet, those developments heighten, if anything, the important questions about any future military dimension of the EU.

Security and democratic citizenship

Can principles of democratic citizenship be applied to security policy? Traditionally, a central theme in republican versions of democratic theory has been a stress upon the virtues that citizens display by being willing to serve in a citizens' militia. Thus, the role of citizens in both the hoplite army and in the Athenian navy has often been noted, as has the role of the Roman citizen in the army (Lakoff: 1996: 54–5, 65–6). Rousseau's admiration for Sparta has often been a topic for critics and admirers alike. There seems to be at least an elective affinity between an insistence that the virtues of citizenship are displayed in a willingness to serve one's community in a military role and a commitment to a strong notion of democracy with its stress upon the importance of personal participation on the part of citizens in the defence of their community.

For Rousseau, and for writers in the republican tradition, it is of crucial importance that the military service be personal and undertaken by citizens themselves rather than produced through the agency of an alien state. As Hoffmann (1965: 62–3) among others has noted, the reason why for Rousseau the development of military forces by the state is no solution to the Hobbesian security problem is that those same military forces can simply be used by rulers to oppress their own citizens. Moreover, the international system breeds more insecurity than the state of nature among individuals, since the powers that are amassed are considerably greater. Although this pessimistic interpretation of Rousseau has been questioned (Roosevelt, 1990), there clearly is a line of argument that, outside of the framework of a direct democracy in which individual citizens stand ready to defend the patria, any provision for security is an illusion. This problem is one aspect of the generally negative account of representation that pervades Rousseau's account of democracy. To be represented, for Rousseau, is to alienate your will. Such an act of alienation is strictly impossible. Yet, citizens may nonetheless have the belief that it is possible. As a result citizens are in a state of illusion, a state of illusion that is reinforced in any political system in which prosperity and civilisation are made objects of desire.

There is an interesting echo of this position in Rawls's *The Law of Peoples*, in which it is argued that a justified normative theory of the international order ought to be constructed on the basis not of relationships among states but on relationships among peoples (Rawls, 1999b: 23–30). On the assumption that the notion of 'a people' could be well defined, Rawls argued that to construe the relationship as being one among states allowed too much influence from realist ideas of state sovereignty. In particular, he argued, such realist ideas of inter-state relations gave states the power to use the instrument of warfare to further their own purposes, whereas a relationship construed between peoples would not have this effect. States cannot arrogate to themselves the power to make war in the international realm, nor can they derive such a power from those whom they govern.

It is difficult to know exactly what to make of this argument. From one point of view, it is not clear that it is anything other than a simple verbal manoeuvre. It is central to Rawls's own approach that there are two forms of contractual relation, that among citizens to form systems of political authority and that among those systems of political authority to form the rules of the international order. Rawls (1999b: 32) is clear that this latter contract is between 'the rational representatives of liberal peoples', and so it is not a contract among peoples except insofar as their representatives take part. Such representatives look as though they are going to be – shall we say – state-like entities, at least in the sense that they are corporate bodies with a persisting existence over time. Moreover, it is difficult to appeal to the argument that, by phrasing the issues in terms of inter-state relations, we are giving power to states to wage war for their own purposes, when as Rawls himself pointed out, the trend in international law has been to restrict the conditions under which states can wage war (Rawls, 1999b: 27).

The question of representation is central to both these lines of argument. Rawls assumes that representation is possible, otherwise liberal peoples could not enter into relationships with one another. Implicitly he is posing the question of how far that representation can adequately be carried out by states. Rousseau's scepticism is more radical, because for him the very idea of representation is problematic. Rousseau thought that citizens would be unfree if they allowed political representatives to make decisions on their behalf, a position that I argued in Chapter

3 is best made intelligible if we assume that Rousseau was working with a Cartesian theory of the will, in which an exercise of the will was an event in the inner life of individuals. If, by contrast, we think, along with Kenny (1975: 26), of the will not as a motion of the mind but a state of the mind in which reasoned deliberation determines the choices that people make, then we can see how legitimate political representation is possible.

If we can allow for a notion of representation on the model of reasoned deliberation, then political representatives act properly when they act on the balance of reasons where the reasons are drawn from an understanding of the goods of citizens impartially advanced. In the case of defence and security policy, the goods are those that maintain the peaceable conditions of social life, the Hobbesian conception of security. This does not mean that political representatives are enjoined to maintain peace at any price. There may well be circumstances in which, for their own long-run security, it is better for a body of citizens to resist an enemy than to give in to force or pressure. What is required, however, is that the good be considered impartially. To be a justified act of political representation, any decision to use force in response to security threats needs to reflect the general or public interest rather than any sectional interest of society.

Democratic representation carries the idea that the representative body acts from the authority of its principal. In a democracy the citizens are the principal and the state the agent. The agent acts in the name of the principal. In an interdependent world citizens have an interest in the faithful representation of their interests, and this in turn means that they have an interest in promoting the international conditions that will contribute to the promotion of their interests (Weale, 1991: 162–3). Citizens can thus will that the principle of impartiality be carried over from the domestic to the international arena. Just as a democracy rests upon fair terms of association among its citizens, so a democratically justifiable international order rests upon the principle of fair terms of cooperation among member states. This does not imply that the obligations that citizens have towards non-citizens are as extensive as the obligations that they have towards one another, but it does imply that citizens cannot reasonably expect other states and their citizens to behave towards them in ways that they would not be prepared to reciprocate under appropriate conditions. In effect, this is to view states as standing in the same relation to one another in the international order as individuals do in the domestic. From this point of view, the international system constitutes a sphere of relations to be governed by certain rules or norms.

What then might be the relevant set of rules? One obvious candidate, because they have some standing in tradition, is to be found in the Grotian principles of the international order. These principles include the equality of states in the international system, the duty of non-intervention and respect for the territorial integrity of states, the duty to abide by the terms of international treaties freely entered into and the duty not to hinder or molest the citizens of another state lawfully residing in or visiting one's territory. Sidgwick (1891: 230) offered the important thought that these duties correspond at an international level among states to the arrangements that minimal state liberal individualists have recommended for the relations among citizens in the state.

Notice that, though on this construction the duties are the duties of non-interference, they are still duties, that is to say they provide reasons for limiting the freedom of action of states in the conduct of their international relations. For example, the Grotian norms do not forbid the use of warfare as a means of state policy, but they limit the circumstances under which resort to wars can be justified. Why might states be thought to have such duties? To answer this question we need the notion of fair cooperation among states and in particular we need to spell out what impartiality as reciprocity might mean in the international context. One possible way to think about the matter is to see the rules of impartiality as those that would emerge from a multi-party security contract among states. Thus, if each state wishes to ensure its own security, then it can be argued that it would prudently agree to rules in which it respects the territorial integrity and associated interests of other states on condition that those other states respected its territorial integrity. This is not to say, of course, that such an international contract was ever formulated and explicitly agreed. It is to say that the rules are those that would be agreed by prudent representatives of states were such a contract to be formulated and proposed.

To think of the issues in terms of a multi-party security contract also brings out that aspect of democratic representation that is concerned with authorisation. In order to have their interests protected in the international order, citizens need their state to be able to enter into collective commitments that bind all members of a society. In the absence of the capacity of a state to be able to make binding collective commitments, other states have no reason to forgo any advantages that they might have. For a non-democratic state, what is required is the capacity to generate among other states a belief in its willingness and ability to implement its agreements. In a system of democratic states, there is extra assurance generated when there is mutual knowledge among the states participating in international agreements that those with whom they are negotiating have democratic authorisation to make binding commitments. For in those circumstances, decision makers have reason to believe that promises will be carried out, not just because states have the power to make commitments but because they have the authority to do so as well.

However, the scope of reasons that operate among states may only have general and not universal force. In many ways, the underlying logic of association in the international order in respect of security questions is more akin to a prisoners' dilemma than to an assurance game. Unlike biological individuals, states lack a natural sociability, and it is such sociability that often makes it attractive for individuals to participate in common activities, whereas with states the impulse to Hobbesian eminence is likely to be stronger. It is this difference that is at the heart of the modern debate among realists and their opponents, when the issue is framed in terms of relative or absolute gains. (The debate is usefully collected in Baldwin, 1993.) The value of power for an actor is a relative matter, in the sense that the likelihood of success from force is dependent upon the reaction that the exercise of force will meet. Realists erect this principle into a generalisation that is thought to be so fundamental that states will not enter into agreements that would be to their benefit when those agreements enhance the relative power of another.

Such a generalisation, if it could be maintained, would be sufficient to establish the relevance of the prisoners' dilemma rather than assurance game model to international security issues. To be sure, in this context, there is much in Sidgwick's (1891: 286) thought that it is important not to exaggerate the difference between the interests of any particular state and the general interest of the community of nations. However, even Sidgwick had to admit that sometimes the two principles could come into conflict with one another, although he did think that when they did come into conflict it was the duty of the state to prefer the general to the particular interest. This line of reasoning suggests that the principles of international duty should not be conceived as always being in the interests of all participants according to a simple model of a multi-party contract, but instead has to be constrained by some independent principle of impartiality. Here again we have an analogy to the principles of domestic political association. In the case of domestic political association, the principle of impartiality as reciprocity needs to be supplemented by the principle of impartiality as non-exploitation. At the international level, the equivalent requirement is that states with superior power do not use that power to violate the rights of more vulnerable states in the international system. Thus, the willingness of the British and German governments in the Hoare-Laval pact of 1935 to accede to the Italian invasion of Abyssinia provoked considerable outcry, precisely because it allowed a weaker country to be annexed by a stronger one, for no other reason than that the aggressor was stronger than the victim.

A further implication of the transfer of the principle of impartiality to the international order relates to that aspect of the principle that involves a willingness to compromise. For example, one way of applying this principle in the international setting is in terms of the willingness of states to submit disputes to peaceful arbitration rather than fight wars. Another way in which the willingness to compromise might be shown is the acceptance of a requirement for international agreement before a state is allowed to conduct a pre-emptive war. The basis of the principle of compromise is not a denial that states have interests and that these interests should be asserted in the international sphere. Rather the assumption is that there is a need to be clear within a rule-governed system what is a legitimate expression of interest, combined with an acknowledgement that even the legitimate interests of states might compete with one another at times, and therefore there will always be the need for compromise.

The argument so far has not attempted to spell out in detail what the implications might be for the international order of applying the Grotian norms. Rather the argument has been that whatever the exact detailed form the requirements take, we can fruitfully see those norms as a transposition of the account of the practical rationality of democratic citizenship to the international level. Instead of taking individuals as the units of association, we take states instead, and we ask what might be justifiable rules to govern the terms of their association in the limited realm of an international order. Although we change the scope and character of the obligations, we do not change their stringency. The duties fall on the states from the relevant understanding of impartiality, just as the duties fall on individual citizens.

The establishment of Grotian norms presupposes a global pact for the institutionalisation of the principles of fair co-operation. In that sense, the logic is one of 'ideal theory' in the Rawlsian sense that actors within the system are assumed to comply with the underlying associational logic (Rawls, 1999a: 8). What happens, however, when we move from the world of ideal theory to the world in which non-compliance often occurs and in which the motive of Hobbesian eminence operates for some states, especially those who might be tempted to think that they have greater military capacity than others? In other words, what happens when some states choose to operate on Stalin's principle that everyone imposes his own social system as far as his army can reach?

If it is not possible to establish a reliable global security regime in which all members will follow the Grotian principles of association, then the logic of military alliances is triggered. In effect, those who feel threatened by a putative assertion of Hobbesian eminence by one or more states have an incentive to join together to form a pact of mutual protection. In Rousseauian terms, the members of such a pact have a general will with respect to one another but a partial will with respect to other states in the international system outside the membership of the pact. Again in Rousseauian terms the set of such pacts exhibits a collective will that is the sum of all rather than a general will. (It was partly this logic that led Rousseau himself to his pessimistic conclusion about international relations, as I have already noted.)

Military alliances can be thought of as a specific form of political association, where the primary 'we-intention' among the members of the alliance is to participate in a form of collective security. Following the general analysis of we-intentions offered in Chapter 3, the fundamental question for any such alliance is how the members of the alliance can offer sufficient assurance that mutual support and aid will be given in times of need. One such mechanism for assurance might seem to be the existence of the alliance itself, but the difficulty is that military allies sometimes end up fighting one another (Bueno de Mesquita, 1981). It would seem that the declaration of a military alliance may amount to little more than 'cheap talk'. Obviously, too, the option of instituting a sovereign with the power to punish those who renege on associational agreements is not possible in the international order, at least as far as it is presently constituted.

Thomas Risse-Kappen (1996) has persuasively argued, however, that it is possible for military alliances to institutionalise a culture of cooperation and that empirically this is likely to be far easier for democratic societies to undertake than non-democratic ones. In particular, he argues that the democratic peace proposition means that democracies can have greater confidence in the benign intentions of those with whom there may be temporary disagreements and that the culture of compromise and consultation is adopted from domestic politics. Thus, one of the norms of impartiality that it is important to have respected in any norm-governed international order – the principle of compromise – becomes more strongly institutionalised in certain military alliances. Risse-Kappen illustrates his argument with respect to the history of NATO and in particular in respect of the two main crises – Suez and the Cuban missile crisis – that might have destabilised the alliance when they occurred.

Essential to this interpretation of military alliances is a claim that democratic societies can create a culture of cooperation spilling over from the operation of democratic norms at the domestic level. Moreover, in terms of the logic of assurance in political associations, it may be that these norms do not have to operate on very large numbers of people. Rather they have to be norms for key decision makers and officials in a collective organisation. Indeed, the logic of military association in this form is compatible with recognising that the units of association (nation-states for example) may exhibit political disagreements in themselves about the merits of the alliance, as has been true of NATO during the course of its life. The issue is not so much one of identity but of reasonable grounds for reliability.

The rationale behind this form of we-intentions stems obviously from the underlying strategic logic of security dilemmas. If the supply of Hobbesian security is a fundamental purpose of political associations, the purpose is seldom one that any political association can achieve on its own. Hence, a political association will typically find that it needs to join an association of associations in order to achieve one of its basic purposes. However, precisely because the implications of committing military resources are so serious, prudent states will want to ensure that the scope of their commitments is limited. In this respect, the logic of military alliances is the opposite of the logic of integration within the EU, for at least on one plausible interpretation of European integration, a crucial element in the success of the EU is spill-over from one policy sector to another. In other words, the principle of military alliances is that of extensive commitments, but within a limited range, whereas the logic of European integration, at least in its early stages, was that of unlimited commitments but of a modest kind. It is this logic that made, and still makes, the EU more than a regime and less than a federation. Are there reasons for thinking that this characterisation should change in respect of security and how might those reasons be evaluated in terms of the practical rationality of democratic citizenship?

EU security policy

One important aspect of any security alliance is the ability of its members to agree upon a strategic doctrine, that is to say an understanding of what threats it is confronted with and what the response should be in the event that any of these putative threats looks as though it is going to be realised. Indeed, one of the key elements of the NATO pact was the development of just such a security doctrine, or to be more precise a succession of such security doctrines. For example, NATO refused to renounce the use of 'first-strike' nuclear weapons in Europe, as part of its general strategic doctrine. Indeed, as Trachtenberg (1999) has pointed out, implicit in the logic of NATO's position from its earliest days was the view that the alliance might have to use nuclear weapons pre-emptively, in order to prevent the Soviet Union from gaining a major military advantage in west Europe by means of its large conventional forces. Agreement on such security doctrines will be easier when the members of the pact face a 'clear and present danger' to their joint and individual interests, as was the Soviet Union during at least part of the post-war period. Such agreement becomes more difficult when such a danger is passed, and it becomes more difficult for states to agree a security doctrine in the face of new types of threats, and this for a number of reasons.

In the first place, by comparison with the clear and present danger of a state armed and intent on territorial aggression, judgements about the sources of new security threats are more difficult. Consider the example of a judgement about 'rogue' states committed to the support of international terrorism. Such support is unlikely to be an explicit element of policy but instead will be covert, perhaps involving the executive of the state tolerating behaviour by subordinate agencies. Judgements about the intentions of other states in the international system can be difficult under many circumstances, but in the case of rogue states the burdens of such judgements involve conflicting intelligence assessments (the interpretation of which may not be agreed), the formulation of an appropriate response and estimates of the relative effectiveness of economic and military instruments. In short, the burdens are likely to be severe, even if the penalties for mistake are not as great as they would have been during the Cold War.

Secondly, and by extension, historic ties between countries in the international system can lead to legitimate differences of interest. Even as modest a measure as a trade boycott will affect some countries more seriously than others, and the governments of the affected states have to come to a decision as to how to balance the legitimate interests of their own citizens with the need to show international solidarity in the face of a proposed boycott. Countries are typically not symmetrically situated in respect of these choices, and hence there can be differences of judgement about what to do stemming from differences of interest. When there is a clear and overriding security threat, each country has a stronger incentive to sink its differences with other countries than it does to attend to its particular circumstances.

Thirdly, dealing with some forms of new security issues involves making a judgement about taking positive military or other action, rather than a commitment to preparedness in the face of attack. One prudential reason underlying the principle of non-intervention is that it is extremely difficult, if not impossible, for outsiders to know and understand enough about the country in question to make intervention a sensible course of action, in which there are limited goals and a planned set of events leading to eventual withdrawal. Yet, security and humanitarian issues arising from failed states often call for some limited intervention. It is not difficult to see how the burdens of judgement in these circumstances will lead to different appraisals of the situation from different actors, even when those actors share a generally similar view of the world.

These problems of dealing with new security threats arise because of the changing character of the threats, even when the character of the interest – a Hobbesian interest in freedom from fear of violent attack – remains the same. However, it is part of the logic of military alliances that they are defined by the threats that they face. A central feature of military alliances is that they constitute an extensive commitment over a limited sphere of operation, well illustrated in the famous article 5 of NATO to the effect that an attack on one is an attack on all. This principle does not commit member states to conduct harmonious economic relations or freedom of movement with respect to migration or indeed to any number of other mutually beneficial agreements with one another. However, within its sphere of application, military security, it amounts to the most extensive guarantee that any state could expect. Phrased in terms of the logic of we-intentions, a military alliance represents a very strong set of commitments but across a limited sphere of action, albeit a sphere with potentially very wide-ranging implications.

The nesting of the EU in NATO during the Cold War meant that European integration could develop without the need to consider the military dimension of security. This does not mean that military integration was unimportant to a number of actors; merely that it was not realistically a subject of political or constitutional choice. However, in the post-Cold War world, an extension of the competence of the EU into its having a major security role would amount to a considerable deepening of integration, encroaching significantly into the core of state power. Although the EU has been committed for some time to a common foreign and security policy, developments in this area have been marked by what Christopher Hill (1993) accurately characterised as a capability–expectations gap. In short, the policy was long on rhetoric and short on accomplishments. The extent of the gap was cruelly exposed by the inability of the EU to deal with the break-up of the former Yugoslavia, a gap highlighted by Jacques Poos's remark, when President of the Council, in 1992 that now was the hour of Europe.

Since the mid-1990s, however, there have been significant developments. A new phase of policy began to be crystallised in the emergence of the European Security and Defence Policy, following the St Malo Declaration agreed between Tony Blair and Jacques Chirac in December 1998 (Howorth, 2001). According to this declaration, the EU was to play its full role on the international stage and 'must have the capacity for autonomous action, backed by credible, military forces, the means to decide to use them, and a readiness to do so, in order to respond to international crises, acting in conformity with our respective obligations to Nato' (cited in Deighton, 2003: 281). In following up this declaration, the European Council in Cologne in June 1999 repeated the same language and in December of that year the Council set the headline goal that the EU was required by 2003 to be able to deploy 60,000 troops at two months notice as a rapid reaction force and it should be possible to keep these troops in the field for a year, carrying out the so-called Petersberg tasks of humanitarian aid and rescue, peace-keeping and peace-making (Smith, 2003a: 46).

Although in operational terms the goals are modest, the political significance of the ESDP is its raising of issues about autonomous military capacity that is at the heart of the policy choices facing the EU and which is at the heart of competing views of the appropriate security architecture for the EU (Sperling and Kirchner, 1997: 234–67). In fact, the declaration itself combines policy objectives that are potentially in conflict with one another. On the one hand, it says that the EU needs a capacity for autonomous action; on the other, it says that any action needs to be in conformity with obligations to NATO. The dilemma implicit in the joining together of these two ambitions was highlighted by Madeline Albright, who with her characteristic bluntness and clarity of language, stipulated that from the point of view of the Clinton administration, the ESDP should not involve the '3Ds': the decoupling of European defence from NATO; the duplication of NATO's capabilities; and any discrimination against NATO member countries that do not belong to the EU (cited in Rifkin, 2004: 313). By contrast it is possible to see the ESDP as a nascent independent security capacity for the EU, and this ambition might be associated with seeking to offer an alternative to US hegemony in a multipolar world. How might this conflict look from the viewpoint of democratic citizenship?

Consider the logic of this dilemma in simplified form. In the first instance, the EU is faced with the question of whether it continues to see its security arrangements as nested within those of NATO, perhaps with some modest independent scope for action, or whether it prefers to develop a properly autonomous, but integrated, set of security arrangements that might support the vision of a multipolar world rather than one in which the *pax Americana* rules. If the choice were made to develop an autonomous military capacity, with the intention of balancing the power of the US, then it would be necessary both to finance that development properly, otherwise it would not be credible, and to formulate a supranational and agreed security doctrine that could form the basis for European action. If the choice of autonomy were not followed by both of these developments, then the US would remain hegemonic and the best that the EU could hope for would be to band-wagon rather than to balance. In short, the logic of the situation is not one in which a multipolar world emerges simply as a consequence of developing independent supranationally controlled military capacity. The choice for serious autonomy requires resources and a significant leap forward in strategic thinking.

Conversely, if the choice is made to maintain the EU's security arrangements under the umbrella of NATO, then there is no issue in relation to the EU's security doctrine, but there is an issue of financing. In order to win a more balanced partnership with the US in NATO, the issue of burden-sharing in the alliance would need to be settled. The disproportion between the US contribution and that of its European allies has been a long-standing question in the alliance and remains relevant to the debate (Schake, 2003). During the period of the Cold War, the balance of judgement among US policy-makers was that it was better to stick with the alliance, even at the cost of carrying a disproportionate share of the economic burden it implied, than it was to leave Europeans without the support of the alliance – a paradigm instance of Olson's (1965: 29) principle of the exploitation of the great by the small. Some of the US position on burden sharing may not have been entirely sincere. There is after all some advantage in a position where you take the lead in an alliance while continuing to complain at the unwillingness of your allies to carry a fair share of the burdens. However, there is enough on the historical record to make it clear that over an extensive period US policy-makers wanted European countries more united, more willing to take a lead in NATO and more willing to bear a proportionate share of the financing of the alliance.

Thus, whether the intention is to create a multipolar system challenging the *pax Americana* or to balance the influence of the US in NATO, there would be a need to devote a higher proportion of resources to defence. Is this a feasible proposition for EU member states? It is difficult to see that it is. The Stability Pact is already leading to a situation in which there are cuts in social programmes in order to balance the public finances, and this can still leave some countries in breach of their obligations. Governments in Germany, France and Italy are running into considerable political opposition to their plans to cut social expenditure, and making even further cuts would be difficult. Moreover, there are considerable segments of the populations of all member states that are pacifist or pacifist leaning in their sentiments. Political parties would find it easy to rally opposition to substantial military investment at the cost of social programmes, even if they did at the same time want a reduction in US influence in the world; as Cornford (1908: 17) once said of academic politics, the discrepancy is happily reconciled in the voting. The dilemma here is nicely captured in the contradiction in Rifkin's (2004: 297–303 and 313–14) discussion, where Europe is both praised for offering a non-military vision of the world compared to the US and exhorted to provide more funds to make itself militarily independent of NATO. In short, it is difficult to make a plausible case for saying that finance would be forthcoming to support greater European independence. If so, the consequences would clearly be worse had Europe chosen the autonomous option, in pursuit of a multipolar world, than remaining inside the NATO framework.

It can be argued that the logic of this conclusion, which turns on the downside risk of the EU seeking to develop a genuinely autonomous capacity without adequate financing, implicitly assumes that the US remains committed to the trans-Atlantic alliance, and this cannot be guaranteed. There are reasons to think that this is a serious issue. In the wake of 9/11, NATO invoked Article 5 of the treaty, but this met with at best a lukewarm US response. The disagreements over Iraq have led some US policy makers to distinguish between old Europe and new Europe, leaving no doubt as to where their sympathies lay. Robert Keohane (2003) has advanced a more general argument that hegemonic powers are less likely to cede sovereignty to international organisations and agreements than others and in this regard Europe and the US swapped positions over the course of the last two centuries. Finally, there has always been a strand of unilateralism in US thinking about foreign and defence policy, and in the period after the Cold War with new security threats, the attractiveness of this position in public and policy debates could be expected to increase.

This is a line of argument that needs to be taken seriously, and it is difficult to predict how defence debates will be played out in the US over the next few years and what their implications will be for transatlantic security. As Lundestad (2003: 279–93) has pointed out, though the pressures pulling the two continents further apart after the Cold War are serious, disputes between the US and Europe are not new. Yet, in analysing policy alternatives, one has to assume a certain rationality to the choices of those with whom one is interacting (otherwise one might as well be playing with a random number generating machine), and from this point of view, there are considerable pressures pushing the US towards continuing multilateralism. In the first place, the difficulties of establishing a legitimate government in post-Saddam Iraq can well be read as a lesson in the dangers of trying to do too much unilaterally. Secondly, Joseph Nye (2002) has advanced a whole set of reasons why US superiority in 'hard power' terms of military might need to be supplemented with the use of 'soft power' to deal with issues like terrorism and cross-boundary pollution. If there is any substance in this argument, US policy would be pushed to looking increasingly at promoting international cooperation rather than pursuing a strategy of going it alone.

There is no point in seeking to predict the future course of international relations from the viewpoint of normative theory. In any case, the way in which I have presented the issues of choice is far too simple when compared to the complexities of the development of alliances in the real world. The point of such an exercise is not to influence events but to clarify the values that are implicit in possible choices. From this perspective, the provision of effective security is an important value of democratic citizenship; indeed, it underlies many other democratic values. Those values are not well served by supposing that the capabilities–expectations gap can be wished away or rhetorically confounded. The achievements of European integration can serve as a model of how it is possible to construct political cooperation among previous military opponents and to create new sets of we-intentions for new forms of political association. Whatever the future of security alliances holds, there is still a case for exploring that process of expanding integration, which is the topic of Chapter 7.

7

Citizenship and enlargement

Earlier chapters have argued that democratic citizenship is to be conceived in terms of its shared goods and a relation of impartiality among citizens, where the principle of impartiality is understood as having a number of components. When political association works well, it is a way by which citizens secure for themselves these goods, and arrange for the economic and social systems to allocate these goods on an impartial basis. However, a 'we' seems to imply an 'other', for, as Chris Brown (2002: 19) has noted, political life seems impossible without some kind of bordering, or distinction between insiders and outsiders and this applies even a system of multi-level governance. Indeed, it can be argued that any approach in political theory that makes the idea of we-intentions central will have to take the distinction between insiders and outsiders seriously, since it is upon that distinction that the 'we' is defined. This 'we' in turn defines the distinction between those who participate in rule-making and share the benefits and burdens that it produces and those who do not.

It is often asserted that in recent years the boundaries of the nation-state have become porous and that the rise of transnational actors means that the role of the nation-state is becoming less important. This may be so in some respects, but in others it is less obvious. Consider for example the problems faced by asylum seekers. What they wish for is the protection of the state, including protection from states of which they were formerly members. It matters to them that they should be able to find a new home, and membership of the political association to which they have fled is a desired good. For many people, often the most vulnerable, it matters whether they are on the outside looking in or on the inside looking out. It may be that countries find it increasingly difficult to police their borders effectively, but no one can deny that, insofar as countries can maintain those borders, they are doing something that has normative significance.

The history of European state-building in the Rokkan narrative is a history of drawing sharp boundaries around the territory upon which the nation is built. In particular, where there was aggressive state building, the typical sequence was a gradual 'build-up of the ethnic centre, rapid imperial expansion, consolidation within a more homogeneous territory' (Flora *et al.*, 1999: 161). Boundary maintenance was reinforced by linguistic standardisation and in some cases the nationalisation of the religion in the shift from Catholicism to Protestantism, the two trends reinforcing one another as the Protestant bible became one of the principal means for disseminating the linguistic standard. In the period of democratisation this trend is further reinforced, since the franchise, though extended, was made dependent upon citizenship. With the development of the welfare state, the boundary maintenance is even further extended as contribution conditions delimit the range of social insurance benefits to those people, principally citizens, who have participated in the national labour force over a long period of their working lives.

To say that a sharp distinction is presupposed in any political order is not to hold that insiders have no duties to outsiders either individually or collectively. The Grotian norms of the international order described in Chapter 6 provides an example of the duties that states owe to one another in that order. Within the Grotian scheme, the 'natural' duties that countries owe to one another are negative, consisting of injunctions to preserve territorial integrity and respect the equality of states in the international system. Of course, even in this form they are still duties, that is to say requirements on action to be respected by those who might have the power to violate them. Moreover, within the Grotian scheme, one way in which states can acquire positive duties to one another is through entering into international agreements. If we think of these positive obligations from the point of view of the Rokkan narrative, they are still compatible with the ideal of collective self-determination, since it may be presumed that democratically accountable governments would not enter into international agreements unless it were to the benefit of their citizens that they did so. As noted in Chapter 6, Sidgwick (1891: 230) suggested that the Grotian norms corresponded at the international level to the principles of minimal state liberalism at the individual level. Just as the principles of minimal state liberalism embody an ethic of self-determination for persons, so the Grotian norms embody an ethic of self-determination for states.

A world of national democratic states, who acknowledge only negative duties to one another together with only those positive duties into which they have freely entered into, is a world where the goods of citizenship are restricted to insiders and those with whom insiders willingly share. Of course, in practice this is a purely hypothetical world. Cross-border kinship, political values and physical interdependence are likely to produce a sense of positive norms among at least some members of the international community. However, at least as an ideal of national autonomy and self-determination, we can see how a negative set of Grotian norms among democratic states might function and be seen to express a set of political values.

By contrast with this imagined world of democratic nation-states interacting according to a minimal set of Grotian norms, we have the history of the EU. During its relatively brief history it has expanded its membership from the original six of 1957 to the nine of 1973 through the Mediterranean expansion of the 1980s, the neutrals expansion of the 1990s and the central and east European expansion of 2004. NATO more quickly expanded its membership after the end of the Cold War, but though as a military alliance NATO involves a serious commitment from its members, it does not require the degree of mutual involvement that the EU requires. The we-intentions of NATO, though involving military commitments, are nonetheless limited in scope. With the EU the commitments are more extensive, reflecting the density of the issue linkage that its system of governance involves, so that membership involves potentially a wide series of changes in policy and institutional arrangements for any one country. At any one time the membership of the EU define its boundaries of political association and maintain the distinction between insiders and outsiders. Over time, however, those boundaries have expanded considerably and rapidly. Indeed, the EU has formally held itself open to any European country that wishes to join, a commitment renewed in the proposed constitution.

Yet, this process of expansion has never been uncontroversial. The UK's application in 1961 was vetoed by de Gaulle. Norwegian citizens voted against joining in 1972. The Commission originally recommended that Greece was not ready to join in 1981, only for the Council to take a different view. The negotiations over Spain and Portugal each took over six years. Morocco's attempt at an application was quickly rebuffed. The membership of Austria, Finland and Sweden could only take place after the end of the Cold War, when it would be clear that it would involve no threat to Russia. Negotiations with the ten countries who joined in 2004 have been arduous and protracted. Moreover, the controversy is likely to continue. Although Romania and Bulgaria are scheduled to become member states in 2007, there are difficult issues surrounding the accession of the Balkan states, and there is considerable controversy about the status of Turkey, controversy that is unlikely to disappear during the ten years or so that it would take for Turkey to be ready to join.

From the point of view of democratic citizenship, what should we make of these issues? In particular, are there reasons that we can derive from the principles of democratic citizenship to evaluate the process of enlargement and its possible limits? How far, for example, does enlargement threaten or support the democratic values that the EU as a political association aims to serve? One reason why this is important is that unlike the other policy domains that we have so far considered, the policy of enlargement transforms the identity of the 'we' among whom we-intentions are to be formulated. Hence, what we have to consider is not just how to formulate a justifiable content of we-intentions, but what conditions need to be in place in order for such transformative intentions to be able to emerge in a form that makes sense from the point of view of the practical rationality of citizenship.

Reconciliation and functionality

In an interesting paper Lily Gardner Feldman (1999) points to the historic role that the original founding and development of the EU played in reconciling wartime enemies, most notably France and Germany. Gardner Feldman sees the role of the EU in consolidating and securing peace as a central value, not only in the sense that it has been an historically important motive for key actors, but also in the sense that it can characterise the process of enlargement. From this perspective, reconciliation involves more than simply a truce maintained by a suitable structure of incentives and institutional containment. It also involves a transformation of the actors, so that they come to conceive of their relationship in a different way and develop feelings of belonging so that there can be a genuinely internalised sense of we-intentions (Gardner Feldman does not use the language of 'we-intentions' herself). To be sure, the EU has used the means of market and economic integration, but it has done so with the aim of peace in Europe in mind. In any case, peace and prosperity should be thought of as complementary rather than rival.

Gardner Feldman sees these ideas as central to a long-standing thought that a number of authors have had about the EU, namely that it should aspire to be a civilian power. The idea of the EU as a civilian power is not well defined, but it means something like using instruments other than the traditional instruments of international relations in order to achieve the goals of the political association. Such a conception need not preclude the use of some military force, as with the Petersberg tasks of the ESDP, but would also include giving a high priority in foreign policy to the promotion of global development and environmental protection. Within this context of thinking of the EU as a civilian power, Gardner Feldman notes that EU policy on enlargement is controversial, but she also asserts that the value of reconciliation is central. As well as securing democracy and a market economy in central and eastern Europe, the EU wishes to create through enlargement a psychological environment of mutual trust and a feeling of belonging (Gardner Feldman, 1999: 81). In short, the impetus to enlargement follows from the very *raison d'être* of the Union.

This is an interesting thesis and it builds upon an understanding of motives and purposes that have been important among key actors in the historical development of the EU. One cannot understand the actions of Monnet and Schuman or Adenauer and Kohl (and even de Gaulle in his more positive moments of European policy) without understanding this element. Moreover, from a broader point of view, there is considerable merit in seeing a political association in terms of the reconciled conflicts that it embodies. One does not have to be a card-carrying Hegelian to see that the identity of political associations is in important ways constituted by the conflicts that they embody, and that political competition is not an end to such conflict but a way in which conflicts are reconciled with one another in a civilised way. The political culture of European nation-states for example is constituted by the legacy of previous conflicts, many of them often extremely violent, including secular versus religious in France, Spain and Italy, Catholic versus Protestant in Northern Ireland, Germany and the Low Countries, and capitalist versus worker in most places. The Lipset-Rokkan (1967) thesis that the party systems of western Europe are made up of the frozen legacy of such cleavages is a thesis of democratic reconciliation.

The value of compromise in the principle of impartiality is a more bloodless, if more general, way of putting the same point. Democratic politics is not the end of conflict, but a way of dealing with conflicts, even where disputes are deep and long-standing. A sense of reconciliation is likely to be important in assisting compromise especially where historically there have been violent or destructive episodes of conflict. Yet, despite the impeccable pedigree once can give the idea of reconciliation in the project of European integration, it cannot be the sole element in an account of enlargement from the viewpoint of the rationality of citizenship. One reason why not becomes clear if we ask the question as to why reconciliation has to take the form of countries joining together in a novel form of political association. Forgiveness for past collective wrongs and attempts at reconciliation are widespread practices (Digeser, 2001). They can range from formal apologies made by a government for past deeds through payment of financial compensation to the restoration of cultural artefacts. If reconciliation was the goal of European countries, there is no specific reason why it should have taken the form of economic integration and political union. Countries can be reconciled to one another and still remain politically distinct.

There may well be an argument to the effect that only with a commitment to political cooperation leading to union between France and Germany would it have been possible for the two countries to establish the important relationship they have managed for much of the post-war period, and certainly since 1957. However, even this argument must remain speculative, and it cannot provide a basis for other members of the EU, especially those who were neutrals in the wars of the twentieth century. No one who is familiar with the bloody history of Europe can fail to be impressed by the reconciliation of France and Germany brought about through the creation of the EU. But the danger of making this reconciliation a model for subsequent enlargement is that it depends too much on the principle of atonement and not enough on the principle of promise. In short, there is a balance to be struck between the value of political associations making amends on behalf of their citizens for previous wrongs and the need for new relationships and understandings to be forged if successive generations are to secure their own good in their own way.

Even if these difficulties can be overcome, there is another problem. Expansion as a process may be an ambivalent instrument of reconciliation. European integration may itself reopen old wounds. No doubt there are a variety of reasons why the issue of the Czech treatment of the German Sudentenland inhabitants might have been reopened, but the collapse of the Iron Curtain and the bringing together of the Czech Republic with the countries of the European Union provides a context in which what might have been thought dead grievances can be revived. Perhaps the example can be dismissed as simply a vigorous expression of what has been termed 'Alpine populism', with its emphasis upon regional identity and a general hostility to the project of European integration (Rupnik, 2003: 38). Yet, responsible policy-making requires that the reactions to initiatives are considered as well as the values of the ends sought in the initiative itself.

To say that reconciliation can be an important value served by European integration is not to say that European integration in general, or expansion in particular, is only about reconciliation. The most one can get from the principle of reconciliation is something like the following. If there is going to be a viable project of European integration, one of the aims that it may be able to serve is that of reconciliation between former enemies. However, reconciliation by itself cannot be the rationale since it will only work if a number of other conditions are met. Clearly, what goes for the rationale of the project as a whole goes for the issue of expansion.

Even if we assume that reconciliation is important, the project of European integration will not be successful as reconciliation if the project itself is not successful. What this line of reasoning suggests is that when we turn to the EU, the general form of answer about membership that we should be looking for is one that relates enlargement to the purposes that the EU is designed to serve. In other words, the logic has to be functional or consequentialist, in the sense of showing that the results of enlargement are beneficial and are consistent with the conditions that prevail and upon which integration has to be built. What might be the general form of such a line of argument? In this context consider the following form of argument. Suppose we were to compare the development of EU integration with an hypothetical alternative European history in which the conditions for Rokkanesque nation-states were maintained; would we find any deficiencies from the point of view of democratic values? The form of argument here may be called 'derivation'. That is to say, we imagine a possible world in which a process does not exist and then consider what would be missing in such a world compared to some known alternative (Weale, 1999: 42).

Suppose, then, a set of European nation-states having the form and history that Rokkan described, but without the Monnet-inspired process of European integration having occurred. Suppose, too, that the Grotian norms of international relations were operative among these states, so that there was respect for territorial integrity and there was no recourse to unjustified war. In such a state system there would still be the need for international agreements to regulate matters of trade and investment, cross-boundary pollution, the movement of people, the control and facilitation of international transport, the protection of common pool resources like shared river basins and fish stocks as well as relationships with third parties. However, instead of there being one forum of decision making in which these problems could be discussed, there would be a series of functionally specific regimes concerned with discrete areas of international policy. There is no reason why these independent states should join a 'super-regime'.

In such a world the operation of these functionally specific regimes is likely to be subject to various pathologies of decision making, of which the following are some of the most important. The first, and most obvious, is that the relevant decision rule in each regime, if the norms of international negotiation were followed, would be that of unanimity, by which decisions would be made at the pace of the most reluctant member. Moreover, by virtue of being functionally specific, the scope for 'package deals', which involve log-rolling across different issues and which have been a conspicuous feature of agreements at European Council meetings, would be correspondingly reduced, thus further inhibiting the possibility of problem solution. By the same token, it would be difficult to deal with negative spillovers from one regime to another. For example, there would be no guarantee that agreements made in the area of free trade would be consistent with the environmental aspirations of regime members. This difficulty would arise not simply because linkage mechanisms would be difficult to establish but also because membership of regimes that were interlinked in the effects and outcomes they produced need not be the same. In short, what might be functionally sensible in the specific case may easily turn out to be dysfunctional in the general case.

It may be argued that the EU has its own pathologies of decision making and that its super-majoritarian rules mean that it is difficult to move as much in the direction of positive integration as has been possible in the field of negative integration. Scharpf's (1988) account of the 'joint decision trap' in EU policy making is the clearest account of this possibility. However, the pathologies of a super-majoritarian system show up against the hypothesised advantages of a decision-making system in which it is possible for political actors to negotiate agreed solutions to common problems. By comparison with a situation in which the principle of unanimity applies to decision making in institutionally discrete areas, which would be the situation in a world of European inter-state agreements for functionally specific regimes, the pathologies of the EU are likely to be less marked.

If this argument has any weight, it shows why in functional terms the EU – more than a regime but less than a federation – might be superior to the most likely alternative course of evolution in the European state system. However, even such a functional argument on its own does not gives us a justification for the pattern of expansion that the EU has followed, at least if functionality is defined primarily in economic terms. In the case of some enlargements the application of this argument is going to be straightforward. The 1973 enlargement including Denmark, Ireland and the UK as well as the 1994 enlargement to include Austria, Finland and Sweden could both be justified on straightforward functional grounds. Their economies were already well integrated with those of member states, and to the extent that there were going to be dynamic effects arising from participation in a single market and all that followed, then this functional argument was enhanced. However, the same functional reasoning cannot be so straightforwardly applied to the Mediterranean accessions of the 1980s or to the 2004 accessions from central and eastern Europe.

One possible reply at this point, still within a broadly functional account is to highlight the substantive significance of there being public goods that are shared both by states that are members of the EU and by states that are not. In such cases, it may make sense to share political authority in relation to the rules governing those public goods. If the range of such public goods is sufficiently extensive, then there is an obvious chain of reasoning to membership of the same system of political authority, thus producing a logic of accession. For example, it has been long recognised that many environmental problems in Europe, ranging from sulphur dioxide emissions through river pollution to species protection, arise across east and west, and that solutions applied only in one part of the continent may be ineffective or inefficient in overall terms. Moreover, once the barriers to trade and investment were reduced with the collapse of communism, there were good reasons not to allow environmental quality in Europe to be damaged by creating production zones outside of the borders of the EU in which standards of control were lower than inside the EU.

By the same token, it can be argued that the overall European capacity to deal with the cumulative, unintended consequences of individual behaviour would be strengthened if political integration accompanied social and economic integration. For example, although there can be considerable advantages in labour mobility, too great a movement of people to particular places at particular times can cause problems of housing supply as well as strains on the social services. Insofar as migration is governed by push rather than pull factors, it can only be counteracted by effective regional policy and such a policy is more likely to arise among actors joined within a political association. In short, in a Europe in which interconnections of various sorts are growing rapidly, and have a clear structural basis, the public purposes of the EU, which involve a high standard of environmental protection and balanced regional development, may best be served through a policy of expansion.

Can we supplement this functional line of reasoning with a prospective argument about the contribution that the EU might make to the prevention of war? The problem with this line of argument is obvious, however. Nobody supposes that before their accession either Poland or the Czech Republic, say, was planning aggression against western Europe, quite the contrary. Indeed, the anxiety of these countries to join NATO has been a striking feature of their politics. And a similar line of argument goes for all the other accession and candidate countries. Moreover, it is difficult to show that expansion has needed to secure the goal of peace. West Europe could have remained peaceful even without the EU, if only for the reason that developed democracies do not fight one another. Perhaps, even, Nietzsche was right, and prosperous, modern societies do not do much to favour the heroic virtues.

The shortcomings of the functional rationale might be overcome if expansion could be built upon an essentialist notion of what constitutes being European. Yet, the historic religious and cultural divisions of Europe, between Protestant, Catholic and Orthodox or between secular humanism and Christianity are deep and make it impossible to identify any common core of European identity. There can certainly be no appeal to a common set of Enlightenment values, without expunging from European intellectual history those strong currents of thought that reacted against the Enlightenment including nationalism and cultural particularism. In many parts of Europe democracy is a plant of new growth, not a well-established part of the landscape. In any case cultural similarity is seldom sufficient for political association, otherwise the Nordic countries would not be separate entities, nor would Austria and Germany. So, there is no obvious common European cultural heritage that all member states and potential member states share, and even if there were that would not be sufficient to establish the case for an ever deeper political union.

One can go further than these negative points. It is a merit of the we-intentions approach that it does not require there to be a common culture that is constitutive of an associational identity. As already noted, common culture may contribute to the assurance on which the construction of we-intentions rests, but that is not the same as saying that we-intentions are an expression of some common culture, though in particular circumstances they might well be. So, if we are looking for reasons that might move democratic citizens to favouring enlargement, we cannot appeal to considerations of reconciliation, economic functionality or a mythic common European identity waiting to burst forth from its political integument. It is simply implausible to believe that western Europe faced security threats from central and eastern Europe of a type for which political expansion was a solution. There is even greater implausibility in the argument from identity and a common European culture. Even if we restrict ourselves to Europe's Christian traditions, the differences among conceptions of the political good stand out strongly whether we are referring to Protestantism, Catholicism or Orthodoxy. Moreover, the problem is made even harder once we note that citizens within the EU have to carry burdens that they would not otherwise have to incur by virtue of enlargements that are undertaken for the purposes of consolidating democracy. Policy compromises are more extensive, public expenditure is spread more thinly and competition in domestic labour markets, particularly in unskilled sectors, is likely to become more intense. Given these conditions, is there an argument of practical reason that can be advanced?

The democratic case

If we go back to the basis of political association within the theory of democratic citizenship, we see that it rests on two foundational points. The first is that the purpose of political association is to promote the good of citizens, where this good is understood in terms of powers, rights and benefits. The second is that, in their political relationships with one another, citizens are expected to act on the principle of impartiality, which itself is understood as a complex combination of the principles of inclusion, non-exploitation and reciprocity. According to this conception, citizens should advance their own good within the constraints of fairness, and public purposes are defined and decided through democratic political institutions. I have argued that in terms of international relations, the way in which this conception can be developed is to say that states stand to one another in the international order just as individuals do in the social order. To secure goods internationally, there is a need for states to find impartial terms of association.

As Tim Dunne has made clear in his discussion of the Grotian tradition of the English School of international relations, there has been a desire among writers in that tradition to go beyond the negative duties that states owe one another to some idea of international solidarity. This was particularly true of Hedley Bull, but it has also been taken up by other writers in that tradition (Dunne, 1998: 136–60). The notion of solidarity or solidarism has been variously understood by these writers, sometimes meaning little more than the international regulation of war and sometimes countenancing intervention for humanitarian purposes. However, whatever its exact meaning, the idea that duties can be taken up as responsibilities to be exercised in a spirit of solidarity is an important one and can be made relevant to the question of EU expansion. The clue here, I suggest, is to be found in the case of the Mediterranean accessions in the 1980s. In those accessions, the rationale for expansion was not functional in an economic sense, but political. Indeed, to the extent to which economic considerations were relevant, they would have indicated cautiousness about expansion on the part of existing member states. The point of the Mediterranean accessions, however, was to consolidate democracy in countries that had only recently escaped authoritarian rule (Pridham, 1991).

How might this sentiment be generalised? Consider the following points. It is something of value to be a citizen of a democracy. It is no trivial thing. Whatever the goods that a political association is able to secure for its members, the citizens of a democracy participate as equals in the association, and therefore secure for themselves greater dignity and a sense of self-respect. By contrast, the subjects of an authoritarian regime have merely the obligations of obedience. To think that the democratic way of life is a valuable way of life is to think that it is of value to everyone, or that at least, in the words of John Stuart Mill, it should 'be the inheritance of everyone born in a civilized country' (Mill, 1861b: 145). Where there is an opportunity to consolidate the enjoyment of the goods of democracy to those who were previously subject to authoritarian regimes, by an act of association, then such an act can be construed as a form of democratic solidarity.

By democratic solidarity I mean a parallel to the sentiment of civic friendship that has often be thought to be a part of citizenship in a democracy. Citizens will of course relate to one another as political rivals, but they will not secure the goods of democracy until they can also relate as political associates who can share certain purposes and points of view, which is part of what is involved in civic friendship, or at least can see that their purposes and points of view need to be negotiated with others in the formation of a public purpose. Democratic solidarity may be conceived on a par with this pattern of relationships at the collective level. By associating ourselves collectively with those who stand for democratic values in what were previously authoritarian regimes, we affirm the importance of those values to ourselves and the world at large. The accession of Greece, Spain and Portugal in the 1980s can be interpreted as an act of democratic solidarity in the sense in which I am using the term here.

Although we cannot construct the new Europe on the basis of a false sense of community, not even the false sense that constituted the imagined communities of European nation-states, we can acknowledge that aggressive nationalism and ethnic assertion have been and continue to be destructive forces in Europe, and therefore that the extension of a political association within which these forces can be tamed is of value. Although we cannot point to a strong causal argument that the EU prevented renewed war in Europe, there may be a broader, more diffuse sense in which European integration contributes to the reduction of war in diminishing the attractions of nationalism and therefore of war. When states needed to fight wars using large land-based armies, there was an incentive for state elites to foster a strong nationalist ideology using all the means of cultural formation – in particular education – at their disposal. European integration has provided a counter-weight to these tendencies. The construction of the EU acts as a demonstration that an alternative form of political association can exist, apart from the national state, and that such a form of association is capable of realising the goods of citizenship. It is a form of political association that gives each political associate a common political purpose while allowing each to develop its own distinctive political life.

This means being willing to expand the 'we' that underlies the formation of we-intentions. Relevant here is the phenomenon that I shall call 'reconstitutive rationality'. To explain this notion, let me begin with the idea of constitutive rationality at the level of the individual. Bernard Williams (1981:104) pointed out that for individuals practical reasoning sometimes took a constitutive form. For example, someone wishes for a satisfying career, but is unclear as to what choices would lead to such an outcome. When puzzled in this way, individuals have to think about the character of the choices on offer to them, and deliberate about the implications of making one choice rather than another, not so that they can weigh up their relative strength of preference but so that they can see more clearly what is involved. It may be, however, that in reasoning in this way, I come to reconstitute what I previously took to be my system of ends. It may, for example, that my characterisation of my desires focused too exclusively on my career aspirations, and that as I thought about the matter, I came to see that issues of work–life balance were also important to me. In this way my constitutive reasoning leads on to reconstitutive reasoning, in which in identifying more precisely the features of what I want, I come to realise that I have other wants and other ambitions.

I suggest that there can be a process at the collective level that is analogous to this process of reconstitutive reasoning. The public purposes that we take to define the system of ends of a political association can alter and be modified as citizens and their representatives reflect upon what is involved in those purposes. Hence, the widening of the EU is not so much a matter of implementing a pre-existing plan of what is involved in the construction of a European political order so much as a redefinition of that political order within an ongoing enterprise. It is thereby a reconstitution of the 'we' of a political association. Here we are reasoning not about the past and its legacy of traditions, but about the future.

For countries of the European Union, the accession of new member states provides an opportunity for the exercise of this reconstitutive rationality. For example, the accession of the Mediterranean states in the 1980s involved a set of issues concerned with environmental protection that were not at the top of the agenda for the northern, 'green' states of Denmark, Germany and the Netherlands (Weale *et al.*, 2000: Chapter 14). In part, this new dynamic involved a reconsideration of what was becoming the policy norm in the north, namely that there was no inherent tension between economic growth and environmental protection. In part, however, the reconsideration also reflected the fact that the character of environmental issues, and therefore the priorities for policy, varied between north and south. For example, issues of forest fire and water shortage had a much higher priority than they did in the north. In noting these examples, I am not claiming that the environmental leaders of the north were always responsive to these new demands and priorities, but the Mediterranean accession did begin the long process of putting such issues onto the agenda. Conversely, the accession of new member states reconfigures the domestic politics of those societies, providing new points of reference for the practical rationality of democratic citizenship. Membership itself embeds an accession country into a system of governance formed by countries in which democratic practices are the norm, and so lends the force of practice to existing inclinations.

Political conditionality

Solidarity is not gratuitous generosity and therefore it is not a one-sided transfer of commitment and resources. Democratic political associations show democratic solidarity when they associate themselves with those who themselves have a commitment to democracy. From the point of view of applicant countries, making oneself fit for accession is a demanding task. In the first place, accession requires countries to implement the *acquis*, which is no light task, and can be seen as a test of commitment to democratic norms and practices. This test was strengthened in the early 1990s when the EU developed in the Copenhagen criteria tests of the democratic credentials of applicant countries. These tests include the stability of institutions guaranteeing democracy, the rule of law, human rights and respect and protection of minorities. In meeting these tests, applicant countries with an authoritarian past are putting themselves in a position where the possibility of a regress to authoritarian rule is reduced.

As tokens of commitment these tests are burdensome, and there is inevitably a question about the extent to which it is fair or reasonable for the EU to make such demands. Karen Smith (2003b) has usefully summarised some of the relevant issues here. The first of these illustrates the way in which the enlargement process exemplifies the principles of democratic citizenship. I have noted that one element in the principle of impartiality is the principle of compromise as a way of dealing with conflicting opinions and interests among citizens. Transposed to the international level, the principle of compromise involves a willingness of countries not to pursue their own interests at any costs, but for example to submit disputes to some form of arbitration. As Smith (2003b: 118) points out, an approach consistent with these principles has been applied in the 'good neighbourliness' test, which has been imposed in addition to the Copenhagen criteria. In particular, the good neighbour principle has been used to encourage applicant countries to refer matters of dispute to the International Court of Justice if necessary. Under the operation of this principle, the secession of the Czech and Slovak republics was conducted peacefully and Hungary and Slovakia were pressed to refer their dispute over the Gabcikovo dam to the International Court of Justice.

Although it might be argued that the EU was using the prospect of membership in these cases – the sort of big carrot that can look like a stick – to encourage countries to do what they would otherwise not have done on their own account, it was not itself an unreasonable condition to impose. If the scheme of arbitration is functioning well, then there is no favouritism being shown to one country rather than another in imposing this condition. All that is being required is that countries subject their claims of legitimate interest to a fair international test. From the point of view of the principle of impartiality in international relations, no country could expect to do better than a fair scheme of arbitration. Moreover, there is an obvious prudential value in having applicant countries settle major points of difference before accession rather than after it. Precisely because one of the advantages of the EU over a series of functionally specific regimes in Europe is the possibility of package deals and log-rolling at European Council level, it would be giving potentially disproportionate bargaining power to some member states to allow them to import their problems into the European Union. It is better to have them solve the problem before joining than using the Union as a forum in which the arguments continue.

Less straightforward, however, is Smith's second example, namely the issue of the need to accept the entire *acquis*, particularly in cases where commitments pose considerable political difficulties. The example that Smith (2003b: 112–13) cites is that of the common foreign and security policy under the Maastricht Treaty and the problems that this posed for the traditional policy of neutrality for Austria, Finland and Sweden. The difficulty here was that the common foreign and security policy included the development of a common defence policy, and as we saw in Chapter 6, after the St Malo declaration, such a defence policy was a commitment that was more than a mere ambition. Moreover, the example shows that there are limits on the extent to which enlargement leads to reconstitutive rationality for the EU. Although in the case of environmental policy one can argue that priorities were subjected to new scrutiny in the light of the interests of the new members, the requirement to accept the *acquis* must mean that there are limits to how much can be renegotiated. When the *acquis* touches on such sensitive issues as defence policy for traditionally neutral countries, it looks as though it is being used as a bargaining counter of great weight. The impression becomes almost overwhelming when one remembers that Denmark had secured an opt-out from the common defence policy in the Maastricht Treaty. This is one case where it is better to have been on the inside early than on the outside late.

Of course, the position is not all one-sided. The Commission could argue with some plausibility, as indeed it did, that membership is attractive because the EU is effective and its effectiveness would be weakened if opt-outs were allowed for the new entrants. It could also point out that Ireland, another traditional neutral, was willing to swallow the common defence commitment. As Smith points out, there was also the let-out clause in the Maastricht Treaty to the effect that the common defence policy should not prejudice the specific character of the security and defence policies of member states. Perhaps most importantly, however, the strongest argument for insisting upon the new members accepting the whole of the *acquis* was that, insofar as their reservations involved defence policy, this was an area that was subject to unanimity in the Council. Austria, Finland and Sweden would each be in a position to veto any proposals that they found unpalatable. Given that the same issue was a problem for all three, it could not be argued that just one country was being placed in a position where it would later be subject to strong-arm tactics over particular proposals.

Setting out the pros and cons of the matter in this way makes it clear that the judgement as to the unfairness involved in this example is not an easy one to make. From the point of view of those who wished to strengthen the capacity for meaningful we-intentions in defence policy, it is important not to weaken the capacity of the EU as a political association to develop policy effectively, and it is more difficult to develop policy effectively if the practice of allowing opt-outs in enlargement negotiations were to become routine. This is the danger that is often referred to as *Europe à la carte*. Moreover, it might be urged that there inevitably is an element of reconstitutive rationality involved in defence policy with the ending of the Cold War. The circumstances of the end of the Cold War provided the occasion for rethinking the place and character of defence policy in Europe. So, what the new entrants were being asked to accept was something other than what had been of concern to them in the period when their neutrality was not simply a political option but a matter of survival. Nevertheless, with all these qualifications, it is difficult to avoid the argument that this was a case where impartiality and a concern for effectiveness came into conflict and effectiveness won – not such a good advert, one might think, for the aspiration to being a civilian power.

The third area of interest that Smith (2003b: 120) mentions is that of minority rights. Here she points out that the Copenhagen conditions require applicant countries to agree to respect for the protection of the rights of minorities. The difficulty is that some states that were already members (including France, Belgium, Greece, the Netherlands and Portugal) had not in 2001 ratified the Council of Europe's Framework Convention on National Minorities. Smith herself is inclined to think that the imposition of this condition on new members violates the principle of reciprocity, and the lack of trust that this engenders is likely to make the future integration process more difficult.

Here it is important to make a distinction – no matter how difficult it is to draw in practice – between cases where there is a genuine principled objection to a concept of group rights within a civic culture and cases where the unwillingness of countries to accept minority national rights simply reflects difficulties of political management for historic reasons. The French position traditionally on minority national rights is clear: such rights are at odds with a republican tradition in which all individuals are treated equally under the law. This position is one that stems from the Revolution with its opposition to local and status privileges under which citizens were treated unequally. Successive French governments have been entirely consistent in upholding this principle, even when they might have bought political peace by acceding to it, as in the case of Corsica. In other words, the French opposition cannot be regarded simply as a smokescreen to provide cover for a failure to deal with difficulties of the political management of a problem with minorities. Moreover, this position can be given an extended philosophical defence, as Brian Barry (2001) has shown. Hence, it cannot be the case that a concern for democracy entails by itself the conclusion that minority groups should be given some form of institutionalised protection, where there are grounds for thinking that such protection violates deeply the principle of equality under the law.

My own view is that it ought to be possible to distinguish between rights that are special in the sense that they give protection to a distinct group of persons identified by some group criterion and rights that are special in the sense that they are privileges. It is privileges that are the object of criticism in the republican tradition and if a valid distinction can be made between special rights and privileges, then there is no reason in principle why special rights should not be consistent with equality under the law. Moreover, the problem of minority group rights is a serious one in many parts of central and eastern Europe, and the opposition to dealing fairly with minority groups in terms of special protection is not articulated against the background of a democratic republican civic culture. For these reasons, it does not seem to me that the conditions imposed on the new applicants are unfair, *provided there is a commitment to continue exploring the way in which the special needs of minority groups might be met within the European Union.* In other words, rather than treat this as an issue in which through bargaining advantage onerous terms are imposed on new member states, it would be better to see it as providing the prompt for reflection on what is involved in the practical rationality of democratic citizenship in respect of minority interests and values.

Over-expansion?

It might be argued that there is an obvious problem with the positive line of argument for EU expansion developed as here, namely that it is too good. It does not deliver a stopping point. Given that there is no essential content ascribed to the identity of Europe, we might construct a European Union that ran from the Atlantic to the Pacific. Although some might be happy to endorse this prospect, for others it would simply be a *reductio ad absurdum* of the argument. I have suggested that membership involves ideas of democratic commitment and reciprocal democratic solidarity, but that hardly constitutes a ground for distinguishing cases where it is sensible to consider membership and cases where it is not. Many societies scattered throughout the world might meet that condition.

However, to draw this inference would be to mistake the character of the argument. In the first place, although we may wish to go beyond the instrumental and functional considerations involved in the construction of the EU to notions of democratic solidarity, there is no doubt that there are practical limitations of a functional kind on the type of political association that can be built. Such considerations still remain as necessary components of an overall view, even when they do not comprise the whole of such a view. Ernest Gellner (1983: 134–5) once pointed out that the cultural similarities between New Zealand and the UK were so great that the two political units would not have separated had they been contiguous geographically. In other words, the causes of separation were not cultural but functional. And by the same token the causes of failure to unite may lie not in culture or commitment to democracy but simply lack of proximity and the lack of a common space.

Secondly, although I have stressed that sharing a common culture is not a necessary condition of a political association, not least because national political cultures are complex and contradictory constructions, there are limits to the extent to which divergent cultures can share political projects. I doubt whether there is a society in which, when the idea is seriously tested, its inhabitants would want to live under a theocratic political system rather than a democratic one. But that is clearly a logical possibility, and one that has to be tested empirically rather than by a priori argument. Suppose there were such cultures. Then, in their own terms, they would be disqualified from membership of the European Union. It is not difficult to see the logic by which the Turkish government has stressed the secular, liberal and modernising elements of Turkish political culture rather than its traditionalist and Islamic elements. That logic speaks to the need to show that, whatever one's cultural background, it possesses resources that are capable of linking it to democratic aspirations.

Of course, the aim of expanding the EU in order to consolidate democracy might be at odds with the other aims associated with European integration. This possibility is acknowledged in the Copenhagen criteria, one of which states that the EU itself must have the capacity to absorb new members without endangering the momentum of European integration. There were doubts of this kind at play in the Commission's scepticism about Greece's accession in 1981 and in the attempt in the early 1990s to come up with an alternative relationship with central and eastern Europe in the form of a trade association. At one time it was common to identify two possible courses of political development in the EU, widening or deepening, with the implication that these were conflicting goals. To date, this conflict has not been as sharp as was once supposed. In the last twenty years the European Union has undergone a significant process of both deepening and widening. However, there are presumably some limits to the number of countries that can be allowed to join without the decision-making machinery grinding to a halt, even were the new constitution to be in place.

The test of any value, however, is the willingness to give up something else of value in order to secure it. Every new accession takes the EU closer to the point where decision making becomes so difficult as to be practically impossible. However, the willingness to take such risks is a way of measuring the commitment of the EU to democratic values. The risk here, seen from the perspective that I have been developing, is one that is internal to the values of democracy. There are good democratic reasons for favouring expansion, in order to consolidate democracy, and yet with every expansion the capacity of the EU to act democratically is diminished.

Some may see an irony here. It has often been said that if the EU itself applied to join the EU as a member, it would be rejected for being insufficiently democratic. If this is so, then there appears to be some hypocrisy in the EU applying the stringent criteria for membership that it does. At one level, this is an irrefutable point. As I note in Chapter 8, one problem with the EU, from the point of view of democratic citizenship, is that it does not provide the sort of popular control over the process of governance that is provided for in the parliamentary systems of the member states. However, though a good debating point, it is not clear that this problem is quite as telling as one might think. Part of the difficulty with the EU is that it is a 'compound republic' in the sense that it is a political association of political associations. We cannot assume that the forms of government that are suitable for the member states can simply be transposed onto higher levels of political authority. At the very least we should avoid premature closure on our judgements about the political legitimacy of the EU, since there is no obvious consensual solution to the problem of the EU's democratic deficit that is waiting to be implemented. Perhaps there is an irony in the EU playing a strong role in consolidating democracy among accession and candidate countries. As ironies go in politics, however, it would be a relatively benign one.

8

Political powers and rights

Within the theory of political association developed in this work, government is a device for the authoritative formation of we-intentions. Such we-intentions constitute public purposes embodied in policy. They are also embodied in institutions and practices (including systems of property rights, family law, social services and so on) by which those citizens who wish can formulate more specific and personal we-intentions. When they are constructed on a democratic basis, governments perform these tasks in ways that depend upon an electoral connection making them responsive to the opinions and interests of citizens. In this context, the goods of citizenship are the political powers and rights that citizens possess, the exercise of which contributes to the formation and choice of policy. Among these goods are the rights to vote, participate in political associations, communicate freely on political matters and enjoy protection in the exercise of these political freedoms. Political rights are therefore both goods in themselves and goods the use of which is to protect and advance one's other goods.

The role and value of these rights obviously depend upon the precise institutional framework within which they are exercised. To take just one example: in political systems in which there is a high threshold of votes needed in order for a political party to obtain the right to sit in the legislature, the value of freedom of association is obviously different from that which it would be in systems in which there was only a low threshold for representation. With a low threshold, it is easier for new or small parties to obtain legislative representation, and therefore one would expect political parties in general to exhibit a higher degree of ideological homogeneity since there is less need for members of a party to sink their differences purely in order to be successful electorally. The value of other political rights obviously also depends upon the precise institutional arrangements in which they are embedded. Yet, despite what can be significant differences such as these, it is still possible to identify some general features of representative democracy that are common or general to all its institutional variants, and to examine what values are promoted by representative government as such.

The first and most obvious of such values is the protection of interests. Although within the theory of democracy government is seen as the agent of citizens who function as the principal, in practice the powers ceded to governments to carry out their tasks risk being misused by those in authority. As Madison (1787: 322) wrote in the *Federalist Paper No. 51*, the great difficulty in designing a government is to enable the government to control the governed, and then oblige it to control itself. The utilitarian tradition, going back to James Mill (1822), has identified elections as the main institution that contributes to the resolution of this Madisonian problem, since the institution of elections gives an incentive to those in power to restrain their abuse of authority, since they will be answerable for their actions. Because voters are unlikely to vote knowingly against their own interests, the institution of representative government itself is a device by which citizens can protect their interests.

Interests, however, are not fixed or self-evident. Within political life, the exercise of the faculty of practical rationality in many respects consists in defining and refining one's conception of one's own interests. In part the need for this task derives from the complexity of cause and effect relationships in society, so that it can be difficult for individuals and social groups to know whether a particular government measure favours or harms their interests. Even something as apparently simple as a change in tax rates, for example, can be uncertain in its effects in different sectors of the economy, leaving its implications unclear for the welfare of different citizens. In addition, practical rationality is needed to determine specifically what the meaning is of an interest considered abstractly. For example, while the promotion of prosperity or improving the quality of life may be general aspirations, they do not have clear implications in terms of specific courses of action without there being a process of deliberation about what in practice they involve. If this is so when we consider the specification of interests, it will be even more so when we turn to political values like the promotion of justice and security or the protection of the environment. It is not simply that it is difficult to specify what policies would best bring about these values. Rather there is difficulty in knowing what states of the world would correspond to those values, even if those states could be brought into being. For example, as Gallie (1956: 121) pointed out many years ago, the conflict between liberal morality and socialist morality is one that can be found just as much within the hearts and minds of individuals as marking out disputes in thinking between individuals. Thus, whether justice permits the more talented to reap the rewards of their abilities, and therefore favours market arrangements or not, is a question to which few people, on reflection, can return a simple answer. The political rights of freedom of association and freedom of expression within a representative democracy in part find their rationale in the dilemmas created by this exercise of practical rationality. Freedom of expression enables different views to be put forward about what would constitute a successful resolution of dilemmas of practical reasoning. Freedom of association enables like-minded people to explore collectively their understandings about what their interests and values entail in relation to specific issues and questions.

Together, freedom of expression and association also create the conditions for criticism and opposition. Tied to the search for office there are strong incentives for actors to dispute the justifiability of the actions of those in power. Within representative democracies, it is political parties that compete in elections and seek to define collective interests and values. Parties formulate programmes that are representative of broad movements of opinion and interest; they mobilise opinion and movements; they help define alternatives; they articulate arguments in the legislative process; and they provide an alternative team of government in waiting should the present incumbents fail. Thus, they not only represent citizens but inaugurate the process of opening up public deliberation to alternative considerations. Political parties also provide a linkage mechanism between citizens and the state alongside other interest groups. Thus, Schumpeter's (1954: 269) competitive struggle for the people's vote means that the interests and ideals of political opponents receive scrutiny, so that proponents of any view are forced to expound and develop it in the light of criticism.

There is a further sense in which the system of party competition contributes to the good of deliberation. Political parties typically have to compete with one another across a whole range of policy choices. Of course, there are examples of some single-issue parties, as can happen with regionally concentrated parties or 'flash' parties that take their energy from particular grievances. Yet, considered as long-term competitors in the system, there is pressure on political parties to show how they will deal with the whole range of problems that governments face. One clear way in which parties can distinguish themselves is to show how their stances on any particular issue are related to a broader set of political principles and views. This is not to say that parties do always distinguish themselves in this way. For example, many parties in the Italian system in the post-war period scarcely sought to compete on differences of policy programme. But where differences of policy programme are relevant, the process of party competition will force an articulation of the grounds of the programme, and in articulating their views parties will be contributing to public deliberation.

In this context, scrutiny and criticism of governments serves the value of accountability and so plays a role in contributing to the political goods of citizenship. There is a case to be made for saying that accountability is not equally an important value across all representative systems, since it is more likely to be a central part of a country's political culture where the voting system is a simple plurality or first-past-the-post one. In such systems, there are seldom coalition governments, and therefore it is more difficult for governing parties to blame the responsibility for mistakes upon others who held office in government. However, even within political systems in which coalition government is common, there are clearly mechanisms of communication that identify the responsibility for mistakes upon office-holders from specific parties. Moreover, governing coalitions may themselves publish an agreed programme showing the aims of the coalition and thereby providing standards by which its performance in office can be judged by the electorate. To that extent the value of accountability is served.

Democratic government in general, and representative government in particular, is sometimes said to be government by consent. The relevant notion of consent here is not that of individual consent, on the paradigm of a bilateral contract, but that of consent by institutions representative of broad swathes of opinion and interest and involved in various ways in the decision-making process. Moreover, there is a sense of consent that is specifically related to the processes of democratic government through party competition, namely that the rules by which elections are fought are accepted by participants. This does not mean that participants do not seek to influence the results of elections through changes in electoral law, attempts to ensure that electoral regulations are administered to their own advantage or opportunistic behaviour to push back the limits of the acceptable where they can. However, it is a far cry from these normal, if somewhat dubious, practices of electoral competition to a refusal to accept a result that goes against you or to stuffing the ballot boxes with votes should you be in a position to do so.

Not all democratic values find expression in representative democracy, and the most obvious instance of this is the value of participation. Classical and modern theorists of democracy have valued participation as an important element of citizenship, most notably for the contribution that political participation makes to the human development of citizens. For authors as diverse as Aristotle, Arendt and John Stuart Mill, the exercise of the powers of citizenship is an exercise of faculties to realise distinctively human forms of excellence. Mill also pointed to the widening of sympathies that it encourages and the importance of engaging with other minds on important common problems. Proponents of participatory democracy are therefore typically critical of the representative system for limiting and attenuating the opportunities to exercise these faculties. Where the vote is merely a choice among political candidates rather than an opportunity to take part in the work of government itself, something significant of value is lost. At least, so it is argued from the point of view of the participationist.

For the purposes of assessing the European transformation, however, it is not necessary to take a view on the importance of the value of participation. One can admit that the values promoted by participation are important, and that a participatory system of democracy would promote those values more adequately than a representative system, but still hold that these questions are not important in the context of Europeanisation. After all, the scale at which EU political decisions are made means that the Europeanisation of politics is not going to produce an increase in participation, except perhaps of the kind that is involved in national referendums to ratify treaty changes. Consequently, the evaluation of the threats to representative government from Europeanisation is not going to depend upon the role we give to a strong account of participation.

A more important value in the present context, however, is impartiality and in particular those aspects of impartiality related to the values of inclusion and compromise. A system of representative government works well, according to the standards of democratic citizenship being advanced here, when it fosters the fair inclusion of individuals and social groups in the decision-making process and when it enables fair compromises to be brokered among competing interests and values. Clearly, the historic tendency of voter entitlement over the last one hundred years has been to expand inclusion in respect of property qualifications, gender and age. However, it can also be argued that other processes – including the development of public information and consultation and the rise of mass polling – have also played a role in expanding the range of voices and interests that are represented in the decision-making process. Inclusion in this sense is important, since it expresses the value to be placed on the principle of political equality, which itself is clearly central to a democratic ethos. Inclusion, however, depends upon behaviour as well as institutions. As Schattschneider (1960: 71) famously remarked, politics is the mobilisation of bias. Political actors use institutions for their own purposes. In particular, political parties form around certain views and issues, leaving other questions to one side, questions that may turn out to be significant for some citizens or perhaps for all. It is one thing, therefore, to ask in general what values are served by representative government. It is another thing to consider those values in the specific context of European politics.

European representative democracy

The historical processes by which European societies came to institutionalise party competition as a means of democratic consent are complex and vary in great detail from country to country. In some cases the rise of the mass party can be seen as a democratisation of a parliamentary competition between teams who fought one another for executive office. In other circumstances the institutionalisation of party competition seemed to all the participants a preferable alternative to the threat or continuation of a civil war. In some cases the process was imposed by the allied forces after the Second World War. In yet other cases, democratic party competition was emulated by democratising movements in previously authoritarian societies. Yet, whatever the particular historical process, the most important feature of such institutionalisation, from the point of view of a theory of democratic political legitimacy, is that it provided a practical means by which, in some sense, government by consent, at least in the extended sense in which I have characterised it, could be institutionalised.

If we ask what specific form the mobilisation and organisation of interests took, the best answer is given by Lipset and Rokkan (1967), who saw the political contest within European democracies as reflecting certain historically important forms of social cleavage present during the extension of the franchise. These cleavages were formed according to a number of dimensions of difference, including social class, religion, language and the relation between centre and periphery. The party systems that incorporated these cleavages thereby froze them into the party system, so that political competition became organised by forces that favoured the salience of certain sorts of issues and reduced or downplayed the salience of others. In one way the freezing of these social cleavages in the party system could be said to have facilitated representativeness, in the sense that, given the origin of these cleavages in the social life of citizens, their projection onto the political agenda was a form of representation. However, the freezing *in* of certain points of political difference is the freezing *out* of other points of political difference, in effect amounting to a marginalisation of certain forms of political opposition. Thus, in European politics environmental issues were excluded for some time from mainstream discussion, because dominant parties accepted the outlook of a productivist orientation to public policy, thereby giving priority to conventional economic growth. Only when minor parties began to break upon the scene did this exclusionary consensus begin to change.

However, if we allow that shifts of ideological cleavage are rare, we are forced back to the issue of how far party competition serves the value of representation in relation to dominant dimensions of difference. Recent work in comparative politics (McDonald, Mendes and Budge, 2004) has confirmed the extent to which parties in office secure representation of the opinion of the median voter. This result depends upon the assumption that most salient political differences among electors can be summarised in terms of their position on a left–right spectrum and so, in many ways, reflects a limited form of representation. To assume that important differences are adequately captured by a one-dimensional representation, and that the median position has some claim to be the will of the majority is not without problems. However, even allowing for these qualifications, a great deal of the variation in party programmes and positions can be summarised by location on a left–right scale, and the median position has some attractive normative properties. In particular, under certain conditions, the issue median provides an alternative that can beat any other alternative under majority rule when placed in pair-wise comparison against those alternatives (Ordeshook, 1986: 245–57). Thus, although in some ways an oversimplified account of how public opinion is represented, the demonstration that parties in government in European party systems do represent median voters provides some justification in normative terms of the system of party competition as a system of representation.

The value of political parties in their representative function is enhanced in Europe because of the predominance, with the partial exception of France, of parliamentary, as distinct from presidential, government. As Juan Linz (1990) has pointed out, from the point of view of the principles of representation, parliamentary systems have advantages over presidential ones. In presidential systems, the chief executive can enjoy winner-takes-all power, sometimes on a minority share of the popular vote. Indeed, chief executives in Westminster plurality systems, like Mrs Thatcher in the UK during the 1980s, can arrogate considerable power to themselves and their programmes. But, quite apart from whether this fact alone does not constitute a decisive argument against plurality electoral systems, the overwhelming majority of European political systems have required governing coalitions to form, with the dispersal of power that such coalitions bring. Moreover, as Linz also points out, parliamentary systems are free of the possibility of conflict or deadlock between a directly elected chief executive and a parliamentary assembly. By contrast in presidential systems, since both the legislature and the executive derive their powers from the results of elections, there is no obvious principle in terms of which disputes between them can be democratically arbitrated.

Moreover, within parliamentary systems, there are institutional incentives and procedures that foster a sense of a public purpose and clarify the structure of political we-intentions. The disciplines of producing a government budget and more generally a legislative programme mean that governments have to consider relative priorities. To be sure, such a forcing of priorities requires a number of conditions to be in place, including the willingness of governments to accept a hard budget constraint. And, of course, in strong two-chamber systems like that of Germany there is an attenuation of a clear public purpose since budgetary and programmatic negotiation between the *Bundestag* and the *Bundesrat* means that what emerges reflects the bargaining strength and will of the negotiators. Nonetheless, parliamentary party government has a capacity for programmatic coherence that it is difficult to find in presidential systems.

So far I have concentrated upon the process of party competition as providing the link between citizens and the political authorities. However, functional representation (the representation of citizens by social group, usually occupational, rather than as individuals) has also been important in the workings of European national democracies. Functional representation has always had a somewhat ambivalent role in democratic theory. On the one hand, there are strands of democratic thinking, going back to Rousseau and Bentham among others, that have been sceptical and sometimes hostile to functional representation, since it is seen as the means by which 'partial' or 'sinister' interests supplant the public purpose. On the other hand, within the Madisonian tradition functional representation is seen to be an expression of the pluralism of interest that characterises a free society.

Within a theory of democratic citizenship, there are likely to be two broad – not necessarily contradictory – ways of justifying functional representation. The first stresses the significance of intense preferences. Within any society, there are bound to be some groups whose legitimate interests are more closely bound up with the outcome of a political decision than other groups or the public at large. Interests can vary by locality, age, occupation or religion. If, as a result of being in a particular social group, some citizens find themselves more involved or affected by the outcome of a particular decision than others, then they have a greater stake in the matter, and it would not seem unfair that they should have the opportunity to put their point of view or be consulted about the matter. Although the requirements of impartiality within democracy may mean that no particular point of view should be given a privileged position, this is not the same as saying that no group should have an opportunity to put a point of view reflecting their special circumstances.

A second justification for functional representation is in terms of the information and intelligence needs of policy making. It is common to find in matters of economic or environmental regulation, for example, that there is an asymmetry of information, such that the sector of the economy or social group whose affairs are to be publicly regulated has more knowledge of relevant details than the public authorities proposing the regulation. In these circumstances, governments need to be able to enter into discussion and consultation with the interests concerned in order that adequate regulations are crafted. Indeed, this practice is so widespread that it has even spawned a specialist sub-discipline of political science to study 'policy networks', the central proposition of which is that networks involved in the formulation of policy arise in situations where government and interest groups stand in a relation of mutual dependence (Marsh and Rhodes, 1992; Smith, 1993).

One way of reconciling functional representation with the principles of democratic citizenship is to say that such representation should always be subordinate to the decisions of elected representatives. One of the democratic concerns about corporatist systems of economic policy-making has always been that the agreements negotiated between labour and capital, in the orbit of government coordination, lack the accountability that is associated with the parliamentary process. It is of course implausible to say that parliament should be involved in all decisions that are negotiated by means of functional representation, since there is simply not enough time for this to be practicable. However, the point is not so much one of practice as one of principle, namely that a concern with the values of democracy would require constraints on what can be legitimately negotiated though a closed system of consultation and coordination.

It can be argued that the period between 1945 and 1975 saw a remarkable nationalisation of public policy responsibilities in the welfare state across Europe. When we observe the development of social security, health, education and environmental policy in the post-war period, we are typically not observing the transition from private market arrangements to public state arrangements, but rather the transition from public or semi-public sub-national arrangements to greater nationalised responsibilities. For example, in the field of health policy, there were often municipal or industry based arrangements that secured protection to individuals and their families against the financial consequences of ill health. The welfare state transferred the financial responsibility to the national level, or provided other forms of national subsidy or regulation. Similarly, environmental policy was quite heavily developed in all liberal democracies before its fuller development at the end of the 1960s and beginning of the 1970s. It is just that the powers and responsibilities were typically exercised at a sub-national, rather than national, level (Weale, 1992: 186–7).

From the point of view of the theory of democratic legitimacy, there is a clear sense in which political parties competing with one another in a programmatic way and with the majority of important policies being the responsibility of the national government, enjoy the institutional conditions within which they can deal with the supply of public goods. When in office, they have at their disposal the full range of policy instruments – including public finance, administrative rule-making and voluntary exhortation – and they are in a position to balance competing demands against one another. Of course, it is always possible for governments under such conditions to strike the wrong balance. This after all was the critique that successful demand management has produced private affluence and public squalor. Yet, to say this is quite different from saying that the system was constructed in such a way that the job could not be done at all. In short, European representative government, to varying degrees and with varying success, could be measured normatively against a theory of democratic citizenship in which the will of citizens was the basis of state action.

Because there are always significant minorities in any representative democracy, we have to be careful about the extent to which we can ever say that in such a system the people rule. There is no collective entity called 'the people' whose will is not the manufactured will of political procedures. Nonetheless, where parliamentary governments with broad political support develop policy programmes with a rationale that can be articulated in terms of public values, there is a sense in which, contra Schumpeter, even in a representative democracy, the people can be said to rule. This sense of popular government is likely to be stronger where there is some identity of language and political culture. In such a situation there are common media and channels of communication both across social groups and between government and citizens. There is less contest about the identity of the 'we' of we-intentions and the public space of discussion – the means of opinion exchange, the role of different actors and the understanding of where public discussions have reached hitherto – is more well defined. So, although there is a gap between government and citizens in a representative democracy, there is a sense in which the political authorities will be seen as embodying a justifiable public purpose. Perhaps the circumstances and practices of the Nordic democracies have exemplified these possibilities most clearly since 1945. But there are grounds for saying that virtually all western European democracies enjoyed the high levels of legitimacy that a justifiable public role requires. Thus, despite the claims of some theorists that western welfare states have suffered a legitimacy crisis since the 1970s, there is no systematic survey evidence to support this view. As Kaase and Newton (1995: 74–5) note, European public opinion is just too subtle and hard-headed to create the conditions for a legitimacy crisis. European representative governments have been legitimate governments.

The effects of European governance

By contrast with the political systems of the member states, the European Union is characterised as a system of multi-level and horizontally complex governance (Marks *et al.*, 1996; Weale *et al.*, 2000). To say that there is a system of governance is to say that member states have ceded some of their sovereignty in important fields of public policy to a distinct, if non-monopolistic system of political authority. To say that this system is a multi-level one is to say that important decisions are made at different levels of political authority and that this is not a phase through which the EU will pass but a permanent feature of its mode of operation. And to say that it is horizontally complex is to say that at the European level, there is a multiplicity of actors dividing shared powers among themselves. What might the rise of the system of EU governance mean for the goods of democratic citizenship?

We can contrast political authority in a governance system with one based on the idea of government as in representative democracies. In the representative democracies of the member states, laws and policies are formulated by governments and agreed by parliaments. Whether the governments emerge directly from the process of election themselves or whether they are formed through processes of coalition bargaining, it is always possible in principle to know which set of individuals has responsibility for making the relevant decisions. Governance, by contrast, is rule-making without governments. Although there are procedures and identifiable committees, like the Council of Ministers, the system of rule-making in the EU is one in which no one group of people can be said to be responsible for the decision in the way that a government accepts responsibility within a parliamentary system. Rather the separation of powers and the dispersal of authority make it impossible to find a point at which one set of people can be regarded as accountable for the decisions that are made.

Thus, to the extent to which the democratic systems of member states provided a collective resolution of the differences of opinion and interest in the political community, the rise of EU governance may well cut across this achievement, and detach political decision-making from the expressed preferences of citizens. One has to be careful at this point. I have argued that one cannot see the national political systems as providing the good of consent, when consent is understood in an individualist way on the model of contractual consent. Consent instead has to be understood as an acceptance of the political process that reconciles conflicting views about public policy. However, even in this attenuated sense, it may still be said that the national representative democracies provide government by consent.

With the EU system of multi-level governance, the principal way by which consent is lost is through the absence of a system of party competition at the European level to provide the link between citizen and political authority that can be an instrument of consent. Since governance means rule-making without government, the process of party competition through elections cannot result in a representative legislature on which the existence of the government depends. In turn, this means that the EU governance system could never lead to anything that could be regarded as an institutionalised embodiment of the general will of citizens. Moreover, the tools of governance are limited (for good reason) at the European level. It does not make much sense to have an intellectual discussion about the appropriate choice of policy instruments for any problem, if there are political and treaty constraints on the instruments that are available. For example, environmental policy analysts can make a good case for saying that economic instruments are required to play a central role in successful environmental policy strategies, but they waste their sweetness on the desert air, if the EU lacks the powers to impose such taxes.

Of course, the construction of we-intentions through EU-wide public policies need not follow any particular lines of pre-established political difference. Perhaps, for example, transnational interests and actors would find that on certain issues at least they shared more with citizens in other member states than they shared with the citizens of their own state. The pure logic of we-intentions does not require that the set of actors constituting the 'we' remains constant across the full range of political action, any more than it requires that individuals participate in one and only one social group. Nevertheless, in empirical terms, it can be important to a political association that its members feel that they share a specific fate with other citizens. For one thing it facilitates reciprocal action across a range of issue areas and it may well make some groups cautious about advocating some measures for fear of retaliation from other groups. As Weiler (1999: 72–3) has stressed, the implication of majority voting being the norm is that member states (and by extension their citizens) face binding norms that may be wholly against their will, a situation that is not attenuated if there is no shared political experience and culture to mitigate resentments.

There is a political culture at the EU level of course. Among key decision makers there has to be a commitment to the 'European idea' in some sense, in order for the inevitable short-term concessions to be made and for constructive bargains to be struck. However, there is no evidence that this has the same degree of grip on peoples' thinking at the mass level as the ideas associated with national political cultures, and in any case the notion of the European idea is phrased at such a high level of abstraction that it can be interpreted to mean many different things by policy makers, often in a contradictory sense. Moreover, at the national level, the key agents of political bargaining and negotiation over social interests and values are the political parties and so the democratic culture is reinforced by institutional role.

There is one important argument that has sometimes been put here, which may be thought to act as a counter-weight to the drift of the analysis so far. This argument says that political party behaviour in the EU replicates in the legislative process exactly the same set of ideological conflicts that are found in party competition in the nation-state. If we examine voting behaviour in the European Parliament, we find that the party families largely vote along lines of ideological, rather than national, difference. In this respect, so it is argued, their behaviour is no different from that of national parties. Moreover, as the powers of the European Parliament have grown, so the rule-making process has come to resemble much more the pattern that we find at the national level. Indeed, it may be even argued that it is more democratic, since the Parliament more regularly votes on proposed rules than is true in national parliaments, where equivalent measures are undertaken through administrative rule-making procedures (Hix, 2001).

However, the problem here is that, whatever the behaviour in the European Parliament, the linkage between citizens and political parties at the European level is weak, since elections are second-order events and there is no common public forum within which discussion of policy alternatives takes place. From the point of view of citizens, strengthening parliament is not the same as strengthening democratic input, when the line of connection between voters and legislators is a long one. However much parties in the European Parliament vote along ideological rather than national lines, they do not perform the governance–populace linkage function that parties at the national level perform.

Such problems are compounded by the multi-level and horizontally complex features of EU decision-making. For example, in the economic sphere, where the rules for monetary policy operate at a different level of governance from those of fiscal policy, it is difficult to see how there can be any identification of an assignable authority responsible for economic management. In this sense, the EU cannot replicate the conditions for economic management of the member states and cannot to that degree be an agent of collective decision-making. The horizontally complex nature of the decision-making process brings about a dispersal of authority that also makes it difficult to see who is accountable for the policies that are adopted. Insofar as the EU functions as a separation of powers system, it suffers from the problems that have been identified with presidentialism compared to parliamentary government – in a continent where there is little tradition or experience of presidential government.

It can be argued that, although there are these effects that attenuate the scope and reach of democratic powers within the EU, this matters less than one might think. There is a decline in democracy considered as an 'input' value, but this is the price we have to pay for an improvement in 'output' capacity (Scharpf, 1999). Policy-making capacity is needed at the European level because nation-states now lack the capacity to secure the rights of citizenship that it was previously assumed they could advance. It was this chain of reasoning, as we saw in Chapter 4, that has been taken to explain, for example, the commitment of the Mitterrand government to monetary union in the wake of the failure of redistributive Keynesianism in one country. The argument is one of principle. Provided, we can find some areas of policy where international coordination is needed to provide for the substantive goods of citizenship, then it becomes reasonable to ask whether democratic inputs should be attenuated as the price for securing outputs that could receive some form of democratic endorsement.

Yet, this argument for dropping the input criterion moves rather too quickly. There are input pressures in the European Union. Functional representation plays an important role in European Union policy making, with interest groups, lobbying organisations and non-governmental organisations advocating particular lines of policy. Indeed, given the relatively small size of the Commission, there are good reasons for thinking that as a policy-making body it is peculiarly dependent upon the informational resources that interest groups and the like can bring to the process. The situation then is not one in which we have a set of disinterested Platonic guardians with privileged access to a vision of the good for the community. Rather, we should think of the Commission and other policy makers in the European

Union as being particularly prone to outside influence, with no guarantee that the interests in question are impartial. The choice, therefore, is not one between policy making with no inputs from civil society and policy making with inputs, but between policy making with partial inputs and policy making with the fuller range of inputs that in national systems are provided through the processes of party competition.

Some might argue that the problem is less serious in practice than this theoretical prediction would imply, because the Commission goes to a great deal of trouble, particularly in the policy areas that are of particular concern to citizens, like the environment, to institutionalise methods by which they can respond to the demands of a broader civil society. For example, the Commission has funded to a considerable extent the work of organisations like the European Environment Bureau, the role of which is to act as an umbrella organisation for a range of environmental groups and to act in such a way as to rebalance political representation. Whatever may be the advantages of this approach as a practical way of broadening the range of actors who contribute to policy discussion, it cannot be the entire solution to the problem. The representation achieved by non-governmental organisations is issue-specific and cannot perform the balancing of values and interests that is an essential part of any democratic procedure. Moreover, there are voices at present raising serious concerns about the accountability of groups that purport to speak on behalf of the public interest, but without the electoral mandate or chain of accountability that would provide them with legitimation.

One might challenge this argument by saying that the system of interest group pluralism, which is fostered by current policy making, is as effective a form of citizen participation as elections for political parties at the nation-state level, at least for the sort of policy issues on which the EU has major competence. Competitive elections at the national level take place primarily along a left–right continuum, in which the underlying dimension is economic. Many of the rule-making domains in which the EU is involved are unrelated to this underlying dimension of conflict, being restricted to relatively technical issues of market harmonisation or mutual recognition. Although the main spending area of the EU, agriculture, is one that is associated with some political cleavages in some member states, usually along the lines of centre–periphery differences, it can hardly be said to define political differences more generally. Hence, it can be argued that the scope of EU responsibility simply does not call forth the type of political competition that is necessary to give citizens a meaningful choice.

Despite the appeal of this argument, it is difficult to see its carrying quite the degree of force that is needed to deliver the conclusion. Although much EU policy making is technical, there are areas, most notably in the fields of worker health and safety and consumer and environmental protection, in which the technicalities are what is important. Although these technical issues will not figure in party manifestos, voters will select candidates with the possibility of being aware which candidates are likely to take a tough regulatory stand and which are likely to take a more liberal one. Moreover, the claim that EU policy domains were largely of a purely technical kind may have been true up to the implementation of economic and monetary union with the single currency, but it is more difficult to maintain that view thereafter. With the advent of the single currency and the associated Stability Pact, decision making at the level of the EU is now impinging on the central functions of the member states in terms of their ability to raise and spend revenue. If any set of issues were likely subjects for democratic competition, it is surely these.

It should be noted that, if the above line of argument is correct, the proposed European Constitution does not offer a remedy. Undoubtedly it strengthens the power of the European Parliament in legislative matters and the confirmation of the Commission. It also explicitly includes a procedure for member states to leave the Union for the first time, which insofar as the possibility of 'exit' is an important political resource could be said to add to the power of those who feel threatened by the growth of unaccountable authority. However, it maintains the horizontally complex and multi-level structures of decision making that depart so much from the norm of member states. Moreover, the problems would not be solved by a constitution that was established on more explicitly federal principles, for the social and political conditions that would make for a successful federation, not least an overarching sense of political identity and communality of discourse and culture are absent in Europe. By whatever means the 'we' of European we-intentions are to be extended and developed, there are not existing models to follow.

The practical rationality of constitutional choice

Is there a way out of this dilemma of political legitimacy? To assess this question, let us return to the core idea of a democratic society, namely that political authority should be the agent of the citizens as principal. This idea goes beyond the thought that the task of the political authorities is to act in the interests of citizens, since such a conception would be satisfied by a benevolent and paternalistic, but non-democratic, system of government. Whatever difficulty there is in finding plausible specimens of benevolent, paternalistic and non-democratic forms of government, the possibility is sufficient to show that democratic representation is not the same as politically effective action. What then is it to be represented politically?

To answer this question we need to return to the basic concepts of the will and political association. The will is not an event in the mind, but a state of mind constituted by reasons for action that dispose the agent to a course of action. A political association is a body of citizens who are prepared to act on a range of we-intentions. Putting these two ideas together, we can see that a political association can be created if a sufficiently large number of citizens are prepared to act on reasons that would give them sufficient grounds for entering into common courses of action across a wide enough range of social life supported by a system of authority. A political association represents the will of its members when it acts for reasons that an authoritative fraction of its members favour. The constitutional

problem is whether there are forms of political association that citizens have reason for thinking will provide them with political representation in this sense. What
might this mean for the EU?

In the first place, the EU is an extension of the political authority of the collective agency of its member states, which by the argument of this chapter are
legitimate. From this point of view, inter-governmentalism is not an alternative
to democratic legitimation, but a development of it. If our wills can be embodied
in the we-intentions of the political association of the member states, then they
can be embodied in the association of associations that is the EU.

The EU can also be seen as an extension of the political authority of the
national collective for just those problems that the national collectives cannot
solve. I have argued that one of the goods of democratic citizenship is the power
that citizens have to authorise the actions of their governments. However, within
an individualistic theory of the good, such authorisation is only valuable insofar as it enables the collective to create the conditions under which individuals
can, in the words of John Stuart Mill, pursue their own good in their own way. It
may turn out, for obvious reasons to do with a mismatch of the scale at which
governments operate and the policy issues with which they are confronted, that
the authorisation of national governments is insufficient to enable governments
to create the conditions within which individuals can pursue their own good in
their own way. The instrumental value of collective organisation is therefore reduced, unless some appropriate level of collective organisation can be found. Hence,
international cooperation, including extensive international cooperation embedded in continuing and deepening institutions, may be viewed as implementing an
original mandate to create the conditions for a good and valuable life for citizens.
It would take a lot of research to show that this development of policy responsibility was causally related to the functioning of mass democratic competitive politics
operating in a relatively secure international environment (at least as compared to
the pre-war situation) and underpinned by unprecedented sustained economic
growth, but for the purposes of normative theory a coincidence is as good as a causal
relation.

It can also be argued in this connection that the increase in duties and responsibilities for citizens as a result of the operation of the EU are relatively light
and unproblematic. The tax burden of the EU is light, although there are problems about the efficacy and probity with which the revenues are spent. There is no
obligation of military or civilian service as there is in many member states. Even if
citizens do not themselves carry the obligation of military service, since it is still
member states that have the power to declare war, the citizens of those states are
the ones who incur the burdens of being in combatant status with other countries. And the EU does not demand that citizens serve its needs in the form of jury
or other types of service. Certainly, there are obligations implied by EU rules and
policies, for example obligations to accept greater economic competition across
boundaries or obligations to extend to migrant citizens from other member states
rights that they would not otherwise have. Yet, whatever the scale of the particular

obligations, they cannot be compared in extent and seriousness with the potential obligations that citizenship in the nation state normally connotes.

In one obvious sense, EU governance enhances the value of freedom of political association, since it provides an institutional context in which groups of political actors can join together, with possible profit, to pursue a common cause. Perhaps the most obvious example of this trend at work is to be found in the field of environmental politics. Since many environmental and pollution issues have a trans-boundary character, there are citizen interests that are affected not simply within the borders of member states but across them as well. It may be difficult for these interests to find adequate articulation and representation within national political systems, but a European body, like the EU, may be a more hospitable set of institutions, and indeed the EU has played a role in facilitating and supporting the development of trans-national environmental groups in Brussels. In this sense, at least, the EU system of governance can be seen as a way of enhancing representation.

John Stuart Mill (1861a: 430) suggested that it was in general 'a necessary condition of free institutions, that the boundaries of the governments should co-incide in the main with those of nationalities'. Having concluded this, he then went on to demonstrate how few political societies in Europe satisfied this condition. Moreover, the relationship among many European societies means that few satisfy Mill's conditions for successful federation. From this perspective the constitutional choice facing the democratic development of the EU is unpromising. But the choices facing those who originally constructed the EU looked unpromising in the light of history. If human will means anything, it means that people can make more of their future than circumstances suggest. If political will means anything, it means that this can be done collectively as well as individually. The task is not to build upon Europe, but to build it.

BIBLIOGRAPHY

Baldwin, D.A. (ed.) (2003) *Neorealism and Neoliberalism: The Contemporary Debate* (New York: Columbia University Press).

Bardsley, N. (2001) 'Collective Reasoning: A Critique of Martin Hollis's Position', *Critical Review of International Social and Political Philosophy* 4:4, pp. 171–92.

Barry, B. (1965) *Political Argument* (London: Routledge and Kegan Paul).

Barry, B. (1968) 'Warrender and His Critics', *Philosophy* 48, pp. 117–37.

Barry, B. (1989) *Theories of Justice* (London: Harvester-Wheatsheaf).

Barry, B. (1995) *Justice as Impartiality* (Oxford: Oxford University Press).

Barry, B. (2001) *Culture and Equality: An Egalitarian Critique of Multiculturalism* (Cambridge: Polity Press).

Bellamy, R. (1996) 'The Political Form of the Constitution: The Separation of Powers, Rights and Representative Democracy', *Political Studies* 44:3, pp. 436–56.

Bellamy, R. (1999) *Liberalism and Pluralism: Towards a Politics of Compromise* (London and New York: Routledge).

Bellamy, R. and Castiglione, D. (1997) 'Constitutionalism and Democracy – Political Theory and the American Constitution', *British Journal of Political Science* 27:4, pp. 595–618.

Bellamy, R. and Warleigh, A. (1998) 'From An Ethics of Integration to An Ethics of Participation: Citizenship and the Future of the European Union', *Millenium* 27:3, pp. 447–68.

Berger, S. (ed.) (1981) *Organizing Interests in Western Europe: Pluralism, Corporatism and the Transformation of Politics* (Cambridge: Cambridge University Press).

Bonoli, G., George, V. and Taylor-Gooby, P. (2000) *European Welfare Futures: Towards A Theory of Retrenchment* (Cambridge: Polity Press).

Brack, D. (1995) 'Balancing Trade and the Environment', *International Affairs* 71:3, pp. 497–514.

Brittan, S. (1983) *The Role and Limits of Government: Essays in Political Economy* (London: Temple Smith).

Brittan, S. (1995) *Capitalism with a Human Face* (Aldershot: Edward Elgar).

Brown, C. (2002) *Sovereignty, Rights and Justice: International Political Theory Today* (Cambridge: Polity Press).

Bueno de Mesquita, B. (1981) *The War Trap* (New Haven, CT: Yale University Press).

Carson, R. (1962) *Silent Spring* (Harmondsworth: Penguin, 1983 edition).

Castles, F.G. (1985) *The Working Class and Welfare* (London: Allen and Unwin).

Castles, F.G. (2002) 'The European Social Policy Model: Progress since the Early 1980s', *European Journal of Social Security*, 3:4, pp. 299–313.

Chryssochoou, D.N. (2001) *Theorizing European Integration* (London, Thousand Oaks, CA and New Delhi: Sage Publications).

Clasen, J. and van Oorschot, W. (2002) 'Changing Principles in European Social Security', *European Journal of Social Security* 4:2, pp. 89–115.

Coase, R.H. (1960) 'The Problem of Social Cost', *The Journal of Law and Economics*, 3, pp. 1–44, reprinted in R.H. Coase, *The Firm, The Market and the Law* (Chicago and London: University of Chicago Press), Chapter 5.

Cohen, J. (1989) 'Deliberation and Democratic Legitimacy' in A. Hamlin and P. Pettit (eds), *The Good Polity: Normative Analysis of the State* (Oxford: Basil Blackwell), pp. 17–34.

Cornford, F.M. (1908) *Microcosmographia Academica* (London: Bowes and Bowes).

Crosland, C.A.R. (1956) *The Future of Socialism* (London: Jonathan Cape, revised 1964).

Deighton, A. (2003) 'The European Security and Defence Policy' in J.H.H. Weiler, I. Begg and J. Peterson (eds), *Integration in an Expanding European Union: Reassessing the Fundamentals* (Oxford: Blackwell), pp. 275–96.

de Swaan, A. (1988) *In Care of the State* (Cambridge: Polity Press).

Digeser, P.E. (2001) *Political Forgiveness* (Ithaca, NY and London: Cornell University Press).

Dobson, L. (2003) 'Towards Political Agency in the Community of Rights? Citizenship of the European Union and the Philosophy of Alan Gewirth' (PhD thesis, University of Essex).

Duke, S. (1996) 'The Second Death (or the Second Coming?) of the WEU', *Journal of Common Market Studies* 34: 2, pp. 167–90.

Dunne, T. (1998) *Inventing International Society: A History of the English School* (Houndmills: Macmillan).

Dyson, K. and Featherstone, K. (1999) *The Road to Maastricht: Negotiating Economic and Monetary Union* (Oxford: Oxford University Press).

Emmet, D. (1966) *Rules, Roles and Relations* (London: Macmillan).

Esping-Andersen, G. (1990) *The Three Worlds of Welfare Capitalism* (Cambridge: Polity Press).

Esping-Andersen, G. (1996) 'After the Golden Age? Welfare State Dilemmas in a Global Economy' in G. Esping-Andersen (ed.) *Welfare States in Transition* (London: Sage), pp. 1–31.

Evans, R.G. (1982) 'Health Care in Canada: Patterns of Funding and Regulation' in G. McLachlan and A. Maynard (eds), *The Public/Private Mix for Health* (London: The Nuffield Provincial Hospitals Trust), pp. 371–424.

Feinberg, J. (1970) 'The Nature and Value of Rights', *The Journal of Value Enquiry*, 4, pp. 243–57, reprinted in J. Feinberg, *Rights, Justice and the Bounds of Liberty* (Princeton, NJ: Princeton University Press), pp. 143–55.

Flora, P. and Alber, J. (1981) 'Modernization, Democratization, and the Development of Welfare States in Western Europe' in P. Flora and A.J. Heidenheimer (eds), *The Development of Welfare States in Europe and America* (New Brunswick and London: Transaction Books), pp. 37–80.

Flora, P., Kuhnle, S. and Urwin, D. (eds) (1999) *State Formation, Nation-Building, and Mass Politics in Europe: The Theory of Stein Rokkan* (Oxford: Oxford University Press).

Franck, T. (1992) 'The Emerging Right to Democratic Governance', *American Journal of International Law*, 86:1, pp. 46–91.

Galbraith, J.K. (1970) *The Affluent Society* (Harmondsworth: Penguin, second edition).

Gallie, W.B. (1956) 'Liberal Morality and Socialist Morality' in P. Laslett (ed.), *Philosophy, Politics and Society* (Oxford: Basil Blackwell), pp. 116–33.

Gardner Feldman, L. (1999) 'Reconciliation and Legitimacy: Foreign Relations and Enlargement of the European Union' in T. Banchoff and M.P. Smith (eds), *Legitimacy and the European Union: The Contested Polity* (London and New York: Routledge), pp. 66–90.

Garrett, G. (1992) 'International Co-operation and Institutional Choice: The European Community's Internal Market', *International Organization* 46:2, pp. 533–60.

Garrett, G. (1995) 'The Politics of Legal Integration in the European Union', *International Organization* 49:1, pp. 171–81.

Garrett, G. and Weingast, B. (1993) 'Ideas, Interests and Institutions: Constructing the European Community's Internal Market' in J. Goldstein and R. Keohane (eds), *Ideas and Foreign Policy: Beliefs, Institutions and Political Change* (London: Cornell University Press), pp. 173–206.

Gellner, E. (1983) *Nations and Nationalism* (Oxford: Blackwell).

Gewirth, A. (1978) *Reason and Morality* (Chicago, IL: University of Chicago Press).

Gewirth, A. (1996) *The Community of Rights* (Chicago, IL and London: University of Chicago Press).

Golding, P. and van Snippenburg, L. (1995) 'Government, Communications, and the Media' in O. Borre and E. Scarbrough (eds), *The Scope of Government* (Oxford: Oxford University Press), pp. 283–312.

Goodin, R.E. (1988) 'What Is So Special about Our Fellow Countrymen?', *Ethics* 98:4, pp. 663–86.

Goodin, R.E. (1992) *Motivating Political Morality* (Cambridge, MA. and Oxford: Blackwell).

Goodin, R.E. (2001) 'Work and Welfare: Towards A Post-Productivist Welfare Regime', *British Journal of Political Science* 31:1, pp. 13–39.

Gough, I. (1979) *The Political Economy of the Welfare State* (London: Macmillan).

Greenleaf, W.H. (1983) *The British Political Tradition. Volume One: The Rise of Collectivism* (London: Routledge).

Griffiths, R.T. (1995) 'The European Integration Experience' in K. Middlemas, *Orchestrating Europe: The Informal Politics of the European Union 1973–95* (London: Fontana Press), pp. 1–70.

Grofman, B. and Feld, S.L. (1988) 'Rousseau's General Will: A Condorcetian Perspective', *American Political Science Review* 82:2, pp. 567–76.

Haas, E. (1960) 'International Integration: The European and Universal Process', *International Organization* 15, pp. 366–92.

Haas, E.B. (1968) *The Uniting of Europe: Political, Social and Economic Forces, 1950–1957* (Stanford, CA: Stanford University Press, second edition).

Hacker, J.S. (2002) *The Divided Welfare State: The Battle over Public and Private Social Benefits in the United States* (Cambridge: Cambridge University Press).

Hacker, J.S. (2004) 'Dismantling the Health Care State? Political Institutions, Public Policies and the Comparative Politics of Health Reform', *British Journal of Political Science* 34:4, pp. 693–724.

Hall, P.A. (1986) *Governing the Economy* (Cambridge: Polity Press).

Hardin, R. (1982) *Collective Action* (Baltimore, PA and London: The Johns Hopkins Press).

Hart, H.L.A. (1955) 'Are There Any Natural Rights?', *Philosophical Review*, 64, pp. 175–91.

Hart, H.L.A. (1961) *The Concept of Law* (Oxford: Clarendon Press).

Hegel, G.W.F. (1807) *The Phenomenology of Mind*, translated with an Introduction and Notes by J.B. Baillie (London: George Allen and Unwin Ltd., 1949).

Heidenheimer, A.J., Heclo, H. and Adams, C.T. (1990) *Comparative Public Policy* (New York: St. Martin's Press).

Hill, C. (1993) 'The Capability–Expectations Gap, or Conceptualizing Europe's International Role', *Journal of Common Market Studies*, 31:3, pp. 305–28.

Hix, S. (2001) 'Legislative Behaviour and Party Competition in the European Parliament: An Application of Nominate to the EU', *Journal of Common Market Studies* 39, pp. 663–88.

Hobbes, T. (1651) *Leviathan*, edited with an Introduction by M. Oakeshott (Oxford: Basil Blackwell, n.d.).

Hoffmann, S. (1965) *The State of War: Essays in the Theory of International Politics* (London: Pall Mall Press).

Hoffmann, S. (1966) 'Obstinate or Obsolete? The Fate of the Nation-State and the Case of Western Europe', *Daedalus* 95:3, pp. 862–916.

Hohfeld, W.N. (1923) *Fundamental Legal Conceptions* (New Haven, CT: Yale University Press).

Hollis, M. and Smith, S. (1990) *Explaining and Understanding in International Relations* (Oxford: Clarendon Press).

Howorth, J. (2001) 'European Defence and the Changing Politics of the European Union: Hanging Together or Hanging Separately', *Journal of Common Market Studies* 39: 4, pp. 765–89.

Hume, D. (1742) 'Of the First Principles of Government' in *Essays, Moral, Political, and Literary*, edited T.H. Green and T.H. Grose (London: Longmans, Green and Co., 1889 edition), pp. 109–13.

Inglehart, R. (1977) *The Silent Revolution: Changing Values and Political Styles Among Western Publics* (Princeton, NJ: Princeton University Press).

James, S. (1992) 'The Good-Enough Citizen: Female Citizenship and Independence' in G. Bock and S. James (eds), *Beyond Equality and Difference: Citizenship, Feminist Politics and Female Subjectivity* (London and New York: Routledge), pp. 48–65.

Jordan, A. (2002) *The Europeanization of British Environmental Policy: A Departmental Perspective* (Houndmills: Palgrave Macmillan).

Kaase, M. and Newton, K. (1995) *Beliefs in Government* (Oxford: Oxford University Press).

Katzenstein, P.J. (1985) *Small States in World Markets: Industrial Policy in Europe* (Ithaca, NY: Cornell University Press).

Keesbergen, van K. (2000) 'The Declining Resistance of Welfare States to Change?' in S. Kuhnle (ed.), *Survival of the European Welfare State* (London: Routledge), pp. 19–31.

Kenny, A. (1975) *Will, Freedom and Power* (Oxford: Basil Blackwell).

Keohane, R.O. (2003) 'Ironies of Sovereignty: The European Union and the United States' in J.H.H. Weiler, I. Begg and J. Peterson (eds), *Integration in an Expanding European Union: Reassessing the Fundamentals* (Oxford: Blackwell), pp. 307–29.

Klein, R. (1996) *Only Dissect: Rudolf Klein on Politics and Society*, edited by P. Day (Oxford: Basil Blackwell).

Kleinman, M. (2002) *A European Welfare State? European Social Policy in Context* (Basingstoke: Palgrave).

Knill, C. (2001) *The Europeanisation of National Administrations: Patterns of Institutional Change and Persistence* (Cambridge: Cambridge University Press).

Kostakopoulou, T. (2001) *Citizenship, Identity and Immigration in the European Union: Between Past and Future* (Manchester and New York: Manchester University Press).

Kronsell, A. (1997) 'Sweden: Setting A Good Example' in M.S. Andersen and D. Liefferink (eds), *European Environmental Policy: The Pioneers* (Manchester and New York: Manchester University Press), pp. 40–80.

Kuhnle, S. (1981) 'The Growth of Social Insurance Programs in Scandinavia: Outside Influences and Internal Forces' in P. Flora and A.J. Heidenheimer (eds), *The Development of Welfare States in Europe and America* (New Brunswick and London: Transaction Books), pp. 125–50.

Kuhnle, S. (2000) 'The Scandinavian Welfare State in the 1990s: Challenged but Viable', *West European Politics*, 23:2, pp. 209–28.

Lakoff, S. (1996) *Democracy: History, Theory, Practice* (Boulder, CO: Westview Press).

Lauber, V. (1997) 'Austria: A Latecomer which Became A Pioneer' in M.S. Andersen and D. Liefferink (eds), *European Environmental Policy: The Pioneers* (Manchester and New York: Manchester University Press), pp. 81–118.

Lehmbruch, G. and Schmitter, P.C. (eds) (1982) *Patterns of Corporatist Policy-Making* (London: Sage).

Lijphart, A. (1984) *Democracies* (New Haven, CT and London: Yale University Press).

Lindberg, L. and Scheingold, S. (1970) *Europe's Would-Be Polity* (Eaglewood Cliffs, NF: Prentice Hall)

Lindberg, L.N. (1963) *The Political Dynamics of European Economic Integration* (London: Oxford University Press).

Linz, J.J. (1990) 'The Perils of Presidentialism', *Journal of Democracy* 1:1, pp. 51–69, reprinted in A. Lijphart (ed.), *Parliamentary versus Presidential Government* (Oxford: Oxford University Press).

Lipset, S.M. (1963), *Political Man* (London: Mercury Books).

Lipset, S.M. and Rokkan, S. (1967) 'Cleavage Structures, Party Systems, and Voter Alignments' in S.M. Lipset and S. Rokkan (eds), *Party Systems and Voter Alignments* (New York: Free Press), pp. 1–64.

Lundestad, G. (2003) *The United States and Western Europe since 1945: From 'Empire' by Invitation to Transatlantic Drift* (Oxford: Oxford University Press).

Madison, J. (1787) 'Federalist Paper No. 51' in *The Federalist Papers*, edited with an introduction by C. Rossiter (New York: The New American Library Inc., 1961 edition).

Majone, G. (1996) *Regulating Europe* (London and New York: Routledge).

Marks, G., Scharpf, F.W., Schmitter, P.C. and Streeck, W. (1996) *Governance in the European Union* (London: Sage).

Marmor, T.R. and Klein, R. (1986) 'Cost vs Care: American's Health Care Dilemma Wrongly Considered', *Quarterly Journal of Health Services Management* 4:1, pp. 19–24, reprinted in part as Chapter 6 of T.R. Marmor, *Understanding Health Care Reform* (New Haven, CT and London: Yale University Press, 1994).

Marmor, T.R., Mashaw, J.L. and Harvey, P.L. (1990) *America's Misunderstood Welfare State: Persistent Myths, Enduring Realities* (New York: Basic Books).

Marsh, D. and Rhodes, R.A.W. (1992) *Policy Networks in British Government* (Oxford: Oxford University Press).

Marshall, T.H. (1950) *Citizenship and Social Class and Other Essays* (Cambridge: Cambridge University Press).

Marshall, T.H. (1972) 'Value Problems of Welfare Capitalism', *Journal of Social Policy* 1:1, pp. 15–32.

McDonald, M.D., Mendes, S.M. and Budge, I. (2004) 'What Are Elections For? Conferring the Median Mandate', *British Journal of Political Science* 34:1, pp. 1–26.

Meade, J.E. (1948) *Planning and the Price Mechanism* (London: Allen and Unwin).

Mellor, D.H. (1982) 'The Reduction of Society', *Philosophy* 57, pp. 51–75.

Mendus, S. (2002) *Impartiality in Moral and Political Philosophy* (Oxford: Oxford University Press).

Mill, J. (1822) 'Government' reprinted in T. Ball (ed.), *James Mill: Political Writings* (Cambridge: Cambridge University Press, 1992).

Mill, J.S. (1859) *On Liberty*, reprinted in J. Gray (ed.), *John Stuart Mill On Liberty and Other Essays* (Oxford: Oxford University Press, 1991).

Mill, J.S. (1861a) *Considerations on Representative Government*, reprinted in J. Gray (ed.), *John Stuart Mill On Liberty and Other Essays* (Oxford: Oxford University Press, 1991).

Mill, J.S. (1861b) *Utilitarianism*, reprinted in J. Gray (ed.), *John Stuart Mill On Liberty and Other Essays* (Oxford: Oxford University Press, 1991).

Miller, D. (1995) *On Nationality* (Oxford: Clarendon Press).

Miller, M. (1985) 'We-Intentions and Process-Oriented Problems of Social Action' in G. Seebass and R. Tuomela (eds), *Social Action* (Dordrecht: Reidel), pp. 139–47.

Mitrany, D. (1975) *The Functional Theory of Politics* (London: Martin Robertson).

Moravcsik, A. (1991) 'Negotiating the Single European Act' in R.O. Keohane and S. Hoffmann (eds), *The New European Community* (Boulder, CO, San Francisco, CA and Oxford: Westview Press), pp. 41–84.

Moravcsik, A. (1993) 'Preferences and Power in the European Community: A Liberal Intergovernmentalist Approach', *Journal of Common Market Studies* 31:4, pp. 473–524.

Moravcsik, A. (1998) *The Choice for Europe: Social Purpose and State Power from Messina to Maastricht* (London and New York: Routledge).

Moravcsik, A. (2003) 'In Defence of the "Democratic Deficit": Reassessing Legitimacy in the European Union' in J.H.H. Weiler, I. Begg and J. Peterson (eds), *Integration in an Expanding European Union: Reassessing the Fundamentals* (Oxford: Blackwell), pp. 77–97.

Mundell, R. (1963) 'Capital Mobility and Stabilization Policy under Fixed and Flexible Exchange Rates', *Canadian Journal of Economics and Political Science* 29, pp. 475–85.

Nida-Rümelin, J. (1997) 'Structural Rationality, Democratic Citizenship and the New Europe' in P.B. Lehning and A. Weale (eds), *Citizenship, Democracy and Justice in the New Europe* (London and New York: Routledge), pp. 34–49.

Nye, J.S. (2002) *The Paradox of American Power* (Oxford: Oxford University Press).

Oakeshott, M. (1975) *On Human Conduct* (Oxford: Clarendon Press).

O'Connor, J. (1973) *The Fiscal Crisis of the State* (New York: St Martin's Press).

Offe, C. (1984) *Contradictions of the Welfare State* (London: Hutchinson).

Olson, M. (1965) *The Logic of Collective Action: Public Goods and the Theory of Groups* (Cambridge, MA: Harvard University Press).

O'Neill, O. (1989) *Constructions of Reason* (Cambridge: Cambridge University Press).

Ordeshook, P.C. (1986) *Game Theory and Political Theory* (Cambridge: Cambridge University Press).

Perelman, C. (1963) *The Idea of Justice and the Problem of Argument* (London: Routledge).

Peterson, J. (1995a) 'Decision-Making in the European Union: Towards a Framework for Analysis', *Journal of European Public Policy* 2:1, pp. 69–93.

Peterson, J. (1995b) 'Playing the Transparency Game: Consultation and Policy-Making in the European Commission', *Public Administration* 73:3, pp. 473–92.

Pettersen, P.A. (1995) 'The Welfare State: The Security Dimension' in O. Borre and E. Scarbrough (eds), *The Scope of Government* (Oxford: Oxford University Press), pp. 198–233.

Pierson, P. (1994) *Dismantling the Welfare State?* (Cambridge: Cambridge University Press).

Pierson, P. (1996) 'The Path to European Integration: An Historical Institutionalist Account', *Comparative Political Studies* 29:2, pp. 123–63.

Pierson. P. (ed.) (2001) *The New Politics of the Welfare State* (Oxford: Oxford University Press).

Pierson, P. and Leibfried, S. (1995) 'Multitiered Institutions and the Making of Social Policy' in S. Leibfried and P. Pierson (eds), *European Social Policy: Between Fragmentation and Integration* (Washington DC: The Brooking Institution), pp. 1–40.

Plamenatz, J. (1963) *Man and Society, Volume 1*, (London: Longman).

Pridham, G. (1991) 'The Politics of the European Community, Transnational Networks and Democratic Transition in Southern Europe' in G. Pridham (ed.), *Encouraging Democracy: The International Context of Regime Transition in Southern Europe* (Leicester: Leicester University Press), pp. 212–45.

Quiggin, J. (2001) 'Globalization and Economic Sovereignty', *Journal of Political Philosophy* 9:1, pp. 56–80.

Rawls, J. (1996) *Political Liberalism* (New York: Columbia University Press, paperback edition).

Rawls, J. (1999a) *A Theory of Justice* (Oxford: Oxford University Press, revised edition).

Rawls, J. (1999b) *The Law of Peoples* (Cambridge, MA: Harvard University Press).

Rifkin, J. (2004) *The European Dream: How Europe's Vision is Quietly Eclipsing the American Dream* (Cambridge: Polity Press).

Risse-Kappen, T. (1996) 'Collective Identity in a Democratic Community: The Case of NATO' in P.J. Katzenstein (ed.), *The Culture of National Security: Norms and Identity in World Politics* (New York: Columbia University Press), pp. 357–99.

Roller, E. (1995) 'Political Agendas and Beliefs about the Scope of Government' in O. Borre and E. Scarbrough (eds), *The Scope of Government* (Oxford: Oxford University Press), pp. 55–86.

Roosevelt, G.C. (1990) *Reading Rousseau in the Nuclear Age* (Philadelphia, PA: Temple University Press).

Ross, F. (2000) 'Interests and Choice in the "Not Quite so New" Politics of Welfare', *West European Politics* 23:2, pp. 11–34.

Rousseau, J.-J. (1762) *The Social Contract*, translated by G.D.H. Cole (London: J.M. Dent and Sons, 1973).

Royal Commission on Environmental Pollution (1998) *Twenty-First Report. Setting Environmental Standards* (London: The Stationery Office), Cm 4053.

Rupnik, J. (2003) 'Joining Europe Together or Separately? The Implications of the Czecho-Slovak Divorce for EU Enlargement' in J. Rupnik and J. Zielonka (eds), *The Road to European Union. Volume 1: The Czech and Slovak Republics* (Manchester and New York: Manchester University Press), pp. 16–50.

Ryle, G. (1949) *The Concept of Mind* (Harmondsworth: Penguin Books, 1963).

Sabatier, P.A. (1987) 'Knowledge, Policy-Oriented Learning and Policy Change: An Advocacy Coalition Framework', *Knowledge: Creation, Diffusion, Utilization* 8:4, pp. 64–92.

Samuelson, P.A. (1954) 'The Pure Theory of Public Expenditure', *Review of Economics and Statistics* 36, pp. 387–89.

Samuelson, P.A. (1958) 'An Exact Consumption-Loan Model of Interest With or Without the Social Contrivance of Money', *Journal of Political Economy* 66:6, pp. 467–82.

Sbragia, A.M. and Damro, C. (1999) 'The Changing Role of the European Union in International Environmental Politics: Institution Building and the Politics of Climate Change',

Environment and Planning C 17:1, pp. 53–68.

Schake, K. (2003) 'Rhetoric and Reality: A Comment on Deighton' in J.H.H. Weiler, I. Begg and J. Peterson (eds), *Integration in an Expanding European Union: Reassessing the Fundamentals* (Oxford: Blackwell), pp. 301–5.

Scharpf, F. W. (1988) 'The Joint-Decision Trap: Lessons from German Federalism and European Union', *Public Administration* 66:3, pp. 229–78.

Scharpf, F.W. (1999) *Governing in Europe: Effective and Democratic?* (Oxford: Oxford University Press).

Scharpf, F.W. (2003) 'The European Social Model: Coping with the Challenges of Diversity' in J.H.H. Weiler, I. Begg and J. Peterson (eds), *Integration in an Expanding European Union: Reassessing the Fundamentals* (Oxford: Blackwell), pp. 109–34.

Schattschneider, E.E. (1960) *The Semi-Sovereign People: A Realistic View of Democracy in America* (New York: Holt, Rinehart and Winston).

Schmitter, P.C. (1996) 'Examining the Present Euro-Polity with the Help of Past Theories' in G. Marks, F.W. Scharpf, P.C. Schmitter and W. Streeck, *Governance in the European Union* (London: Sage Publications), pp. 1–14.

Schumpeter, J.A. (1954) *Capitalism, Socialism and Democracy* (London: Allen and Unwin, first edition 1943).

Sen, A.K. (1982) *Choice, Welfare and Measurement* (Oxford: Basil Blackwell).

Shklar, J.N. (1976) *Freedom and Independence: A Study of the Political Ideas of Hegel's Phenomenology of Mind* (Cambridge: Cambridge University Press).

Sidgwick, H. (1891) *The Elements of Politics* (London: Macmillan).

Sinnott, R. (1995) 'Policy, Subsidiarity, and Legitimacy' in O. Niedermayer and R. Sinnott (eds), *Public Opinion and Internationalized Governance* (Oxford: Oxford University Press), pp. 246–76.

Smith, K.E. (2003a) *European Union Foreign Policy in a Changing World* (Cambridge: Polity).

Smith, K.E. (2003b) 'The Evolution and Application of EU Membership Conditionality' in M. Cremona (ed.), *The Enlargement of the European Union* (Oxford: Oxford University Press), pp. 107–39.

Smith, M.J. (1993) *Pressure, Power and Policy* (Hemel Hempstead: Harvester Wheatsheaf).

Spelsberg, G. (1984) *Rauchplage* (Aachen: Alano Verlag).

Sperling, J. and Kirchner, E. (1997) *Recasting the European Order: Security Architectures and Economic Cooperation* (Manchester and New York: Manchester University Press).

Ståhlberg, A.C. (1997) 'Sweden: On the Way from Standard to Basic Security?' in J. Clasen (ed.), *Social Insurance in Europe* (Bristol: The Policy Press), pp. 40–59.

Strachey, J. (1952) 'Tasks and Achievement of British Labour' in R.H.S. Crossman (ed.), *New Fabian Essays* (London: Turnstile Press, 1970 edition), pp. 181–215.

Taylor, C. (1993) *Reconciling the Solitudes*, edited by G. LaForest (Montreal and Kingston: McGill-Queen's University Press).

Taylor, M. (1976) *Anarchy and Cooperation* (London: John Wiley and Sons).

Taylor, P. (1983) *The Limits to European Integration* (London and Canberra: Croom Helm).

Titmuss, R.M. (1950) *Problems of Social Policy* (London: His Majesty's Stationery Office and Longman, Green).

Tobin, J. (1970) 'On Limiting the Domain of Inequality', *Journal of Law and Economics* 13:2, pp. 263–77.

Trachtenberg, M. (1999) *A Constructed Peace: The Making of the European Settlement, 1945–1963* (Princeton, NJ: Princeton University Press).

Tuomela, R. (1984) *A Theory of Social Action* (Dordrecht: Reidel).

Tuomela, R. (1985) 'Reply to Seebass and Miller' in G. Seebass and R. Tuomela (eds), *Social Action* (Dordrecht: Reidel), pp. 149–50.

Tuomela, R. (1995) *The Importance of Us: A Philosophical Study of Basic Social Notions* (Stanford, CA: Stanford University Press).

Tuomela, R. (2000) *Cooperation* (Dordrecht: Kluwer).

Underdal, A. (1980) 'Integrated Marine Policy. What? Why? How?', *Marine Policy* 4:3, pp. 159–69.

Van Parijs, P. (1997) 'Basic Income and the Political Economy of the New Europe' in P.B. Lehning and A. Weale (eds), *Citizenship, Democracy and Justice in the New Europe* (London and New York: Routledge), pp. 161–74.

Vogel, U. (1991) 'Is Citizenship Gender-Specific?' in U. Vogel and M. Moran (eds), *The Frontiers of Citizenship* (Houndmills: Macmillan), pp. 58–85.

Wæver, O. (1996) 'European Security Identities', *Journal of Common Market Studies*, 34: 1, pp. 103–32.

Weale, A. (1983) *Political Theory and Social Policy* (London and Basingstoke: Macmillan).

Weale, A. (1991) 'Citizenship Beyond Borders' in M. Moran and U. Vogel (eds), *Frontiers of Citizenship* (Basingstoke: Macmillan), pp. 155–65.

Weale, A. (1992) *The New Politics of Pollution* (Manchester: Manchester University Press).

Weale, A. (1994) 'Environmental Protection, The Four Freedoms and Competition among Rules' in M. Faure, J. Vervaele and A. Weale (eds), *Environmental Standards in the European Union in An Interdisciplinary Framework* (Antwerp-Apeldoorn: MAKLU), pp. 73–89.

Weale, A. (1999) *Democracy* (London: Macmillan).

Weale, A., O'Riordan, T. and Kramme, L. (1991) *Controlling Pollution in the Round: Change and Choice in Environmental Regulation in Britain and West Germany* (London: Anglo-German Foundation).

Weale, A., Pridham, G., Cini, C., Konstadakopoulos, D., Porter, M. and Flynn, B. (2000) *Environmental Governance in Europe: An Ever Closer Ecological Union?* (Oxford: Oxford University Press).

Weber, E. (1979) *Peasants into Frenchmen* (Stanford, CA: Stanford University Press).

Weber, M. (1947) *The Theory of Social and Economic Organization*, translated by A. M. Henderson and T. Parsons (New York: Oxford University Press).

Weiler, J.H.H. (1999) *The Constitution of Europe* (Cambridge: Cambridge University Press).

White, J. (1995) *Competing Solutions: American Health Care Proposals and International Experience* (Washington, D.C.: The Brookings Institution).

White, S. (2000) 'Social Rights and the Social Contract – Political Theory and the New Welfare Politics', *British Journal of Political Science* 30:3, pp. 507–32.

Williams, B. (1981) *Moral Luck* (Cambridge: Cambridge University Press).

Williamson, O.E. (1985) *The Economic Institutions of Capitalism: Firms, Markets, Relational Contracting* (New York: The Free Press).

Wils, W.P.J (1994) 'Subsidiarity and EC Environmental Policy: Taking People's Concerns Seriously', *Journal of Environmental Law* 6:1, pp. 85–91.

Wokler, R. (2001) *Rousseau: A Very Short Introduction* (Oxford: Oxford University Press).

Wurzel, R.K.W. (2002) *Environmental Policy-Making in Britain, Germany and the European Union* (Manchester and New York: Manchester University Press).

Zito, A.R. (2000) *Creating Environmental Policy in the European Union* (Houndmills: Macmillan).